WITHDRAWN

STUDIES IN ENGLISH LITERATURE

Volume XII

SHELLEYAN IDEAS
IN
VICTORIAN
LITERATURE

by

ROLAND A. DUERKSEN

Purdue University

1966

MOUTON & CO.

LONDON · THE HAGUE · PARIS

Printed in The Netherlands by Mouton & Co., Printers, The Hague.

To Susan, Bill and Ken

ACKNOWLEDGMENTS

Portions of Chapter III of this book appeared in *The Victorian Newsletter,* No. 26 (Fall 1964). The "George Henry Lewes and George Eliot" section of Chapter V appeared in the *Keats-Shelley Journal,* XIV (Winter 1965). Chapter VII is reprinted by permission of the Modern Language Association from *PMLA,* LXXVIII (March 1963).

I wish to express my appreciation to the Purdue Research Foundation, Lafayette, Indiana, for a summer grant which enabled me to finish the manuscript and for assistance in its publication.

For his helpful criticism and counsel, I wish to thank Professor Russell Noyes. With gratitude I acknowledge the assistance of my wife Mary who, in addition to typing and proofreading, has given patient encouragement and advice throughout the preparation of this book.

West Lafayette, Indiana   R. A. D.

December 1965

TABLE OF CONTENTS

I

SHELLEY'S IDEAS

HIS POETIC PURPOSE

On 24 January 1819, Percy Bysshe Shelley wrote from Naples to his friend Thomas Love Peacock as follows:

O, if I had health, and strength, and equal spirits, what boundless intellectual improvement might I not gather in this wonderful country! At present I write little else but poetry, and little of that .... I consider Poetry very subordinate to moral and political science, and if I were well, certainly I should aspire to the latter; for I can conceive a great work, embodying the discoveries of all ages, and harmonising the contending creeds by which mankind have been ruled.[1]

The two essential facts contained in this passage are: first, poetry was of secondary importance to Shelley and served him as a means to an end; secondly, Shelley had lofty aspirations for mankind – not otherworldly and apocalyptical, but very much oriented to the history as well as the attainable future of society. Considering that the one all-encompassing work of which he speaks is out of his reach, Shelley tells Peacock that he is making every effort to add the weight of his poetry to the side of the right in the scales of social justice.

Keats, in his letter of 16 August 1820, warned Shelley that as a poet he must cultivate "self concentration" or "selfishness per-

---

[1] See Percy Bysshe Shelley, *The Complete Works* (Julian Edition), eds. Roger Ingpen and Walter E. Peck, 10 vols. (London and New York, 1926-30), X, 21. This edition is used for references to Shelley's writings throughout this study and is hereafter referred to as *Works*.

haps", that he must be "more of an artist".[2] Shelley, in direct contrast to advice of this kind, strove to abolish the self-centered approach to poetry and emphasized the importance of fellow-feeling – of identification with all men. He asserts in his *Defence of Poetry:*

> The great secret of morals is love; or a going out of our own nature, and an identification of ourselves with the beautiful which exists in thought, action, or person, not our own. A man, to be greatly good, must imagine intensely and comprehensively; he must put himself in the place of another and of many others; the pains and pleasures of his species must become his own. The great instrument of moral good is the imagination; and poetry administers to the effect by acting upon the cause.[3]

In addition to defining poetry in a more social sense than had either Sidney or Wordsworth, Shelley devotes two-thirds of his essay to an examination of its effects upon society. Finding this examination to support his argument that the imagination speaks through poetry, he reaffirms his conviction that didactic reasoning has no place in poetic expression.

Earlier, in the Preface to *Prometheus Unbound,* he writes, "Didactic poetry is my abhorrence", and explains that his purpose has always been to impart to his readers the "idealisms of moral excellence; aware that until the mind can love, and admire, and trust, and hope, and endure, reasoned principles of moral conduct are seeds cast upon the highway of life which the unconscious passenger tramples into dust, although they would bear the harvest of his happiness".[4] The more specifically the poet seeks to prescribe for his generation, says Shelley, the more liable he is to error. He must, therefore, rely upon the imagination which teaches men, not specifically *what* they should think and feel, but *how* to think and feel justly.[5] Thus clarifying his stress upon purpose in poetry, Shelly indicates that he does not equate

[2] See John Keats, *The Poetical Works and Other Writings* (Hampstead Edition), ed. H. Buxton Forman and Maurice Buxton Forman (New York, 1939), VIII, 234.
[3] *Works,* VII, 118.
[4] *Works,* II, 174-175.
[5] Newman Ivey White, *Shelley* (New York, 1940), II, 432.

poetry with the prose essay but, rather, designates it as a guide to philosophy.

Shelley's emphasis on the creative imagination indicates that he was abreast of his time and could see that an aggressively individualistic and primarily commercial society was gradually relegating man to the status of a mere part in the production machine. Anticipating the multiplication of this problem in the immediately succeeding years, he urged the growth of love and sympathetic relationship among individuals and groups. He warned against the continuing and growing trend to put economic gain above human considerations.

Whilst the mechanist abridges, and the political economist combines, labour, let them beware that their speculations, for want of correspondence with those first principles which belong to the imagination, do not tend, as they have in modern England, to exasperate at once the extremes of luxury and want. . . . The rich have become richer, and the poor have become poorer; and the vessel of the state is driven between the Scylla and Charybdis of anarchy and depotism. Such are the effects which must ever flow from the unmitigated exercise of the calculating faculty.[6]

Shelley maintains that although men know what is right morally, governmentally, and economically – or at least what is wiser and better than that which they practice or endure – they need the creative faculty to imagine that which they know. They lack the generous impulse to translate imagination into action. They do not have the poetry of life. "Poetry, and the principle of Self, of which Money is the visible incarnation, are the God and Mammom of the world." [7] The Victorian Age proved that his analysis of society, his prediction, and his warning were all correct and to the point.

HIS PHILOSOPHY AND SOCIALISM

Before we can adequately judge the extent to which Shelley influenced Victorian writers, we must examine carefully the actions

---

[6] *A Defence of Poetry*, in *Works*, VII, 132.
[7] *Ibid.*, p. 134.

which his own imaginative thinking about nineteenth-century social and economical problems led him to propose.

Edward and Eleanor Marx Aveling, in a lecture read to the Shelley Society, claimed Shelley as a fellow Socialist and supported their contention by asserting that Karl Marx used to say of the real difference between Byron and Shelley: "Those who understand them and love them rejoice that Byron died at thirty-six, because if he had lived he would have become a reactionary *bourgeois*; they grieve that Shelley died at twenty-nine, because he was essentially a revolutionist and he would always have been one of the advanced guard of socialism." [8] Whether or not Shelley's proposals for the betterment of society place him among the Socialists is, of course, difficult to establish; the term came into use some years after his death and has had a great variety of definitions.

This difficulty of positively identifying Shelley's position has, nevertheless, not prevented the expression of various opinions about his socialism. Crane Brinton cites several reasons why the adoption of Shelley by the leaders of the Socialist movement is justified. These reasons are: his frequently-expressed sympathy with the poor, his antagonism toward the commercial classes, and his conviction that man's labor constitutes the only real wealth.[9] Carlos Baker, however, maintains that, having found that both "mad Shelley" and "angelic Shelley" are worthless labels, neither will we profit by attempting "to button the poet into a denim shirt and make of him an accomplice before the fact of Marxism".[10] Professor Baker presents him as, above all, a sane and serious poet who combined with his remarkable lyrical powers a number of strong convictions about eradicating evil

---

[8] Read to the Society on 14 December 1887; see Shelley Society, *Publications*, ser. 1, no. 1, vol. 1, pt. 2. Henry S. Salt, an ardent Shelleyite of the late nineteenth century, considers Marx's statement to be true of Shelley but unjust to Byron. See his *Percy Bysshe Shelley: Poet and Pioneer* (London, 1896), p. 169.

[9] *The Political Ideas of the English Romanticists* (Oxford, 1926), pp. 171-172.

[10] "The Permanent Shelley", *Sewanee Review*, XLVIII (October-December 1940), 518.

from man's environment. Whatever one concludes about Shelley's stand in relation to the later Socialism, it is obvious that he was not a Marxist. In poetry as well as in prose he sought to point out that the way to a better life for all mankind, especially for the unfortunate masses, is to change man's thinking rather than to enforce revolutions by political and military means.

The "Peterloo" massacre near Manchester on 16 August 1819 roused Shelley (then in Italy) to high fury and inspired him to write a series of political poems which were, however, not published until years afterwards. Chief among these is the vehement *Masque of Anarchy*; others are *Song to the Men of England* and the sonnet *England in 1819*. At about the same time he wrote the prose essay *A Philosophical View of Reform*, which was known only by excerpts and paraphrases until it was published by T. W. Rolleston in 1920. That this essay came to nothing in Shelley's lifetime, or even during the entire nineteenth century, was most unfortunate for Shelley's reputation as well as for his influence on Victorian literature. Treating the reform movement in relationship to world history and emphasising that it stemmed from the economic evils in English society, Shelley points to the central fact of the situation: that social reform, and not only political reform, is necessary if a violent revolution is to be averted. The two causes of misery and discord, in his view, are wealth on the one hand and want on the other; and he insists that society must learn to think in terms of a future in which these extremes will have been abolished. These same assertions are the basis of the "Peterloo" poems; but in the essay the approach to the problem is made without the intense passion and emotion of the poems, and the solution is rationally and systematically set forth. Together, the poems and the essay present Shelley as an artist of intense social feeling who, though perhaps momentarily carried away by an emotional reaction to flagrant injustice, could compose himself and think most rationally and sanely about practical solutions to social evils. What the nineteenth century read of his political works included only the intensely emotional poetic reaction to tyranny and injustice and his prophesies of a perfected future. His real capacity for practical political analysis not being readily apparent in these works, the Victorians found it easy to regard him as a fanatic or a visionary.

Helping to establish this view was the fact that Shelley was not in his lifetime an active member of the reform movement itself. He did not, like Cobbett, Cartwright, Bentham, and others, make organized reform the center of his life. He was, rather, a talented, eager, and sympathetic observer who depended upon his art as a primary means of supporting the active reformers. Unlike them, he saw the accomplishment of social revolution not only as an immediate goal, but also as a part of the vast sweep of historical forces bringing society progressively out of the past into the future of a democratic republic, and eventually into an equalitarian state.[11] Thus the poems of 1819 and the *Philosophical View of Reform* are a part of the great poetic vision which culminated in *Prometheus Unbound*. Without an awareness of all aspects of this vision it is most difficult to be fair with Shelley; and the Victorians knew very little of one important part of it.

Specifically, what the Victorians, because the *Philosophical View* was unpublished, could not realize was that Shelley had outlined two primary practical reforms: (1) former liberties to be restored to the people and (2) government to be improved to preserve these rights. Among his direct proposals, of which the Victorians were unaware, were the abolition of the national debt as well as of sinecures, tithes, and religious inequalities; the disbanding of the standing army; the extension of the jury system; and the acceleration of legal processes. Newman Ivey White points out that virtually everything which Shelley proposed in the essay may be regarded as a restoration rather than an innovation.[12] But this does not mean that Shelley was limited by history in his view of the future possibilities. The restorations and innovations he proposes are but means to an end:

We derive tranquillity and courage and grandeur of soul from contemplating an object which is, because we will it, and may be, because we hope and desire it, and must be if succeeding generations of the

[11] See Kenneth Neill Cameron, "Shelley and the Reformers", *ELH,* XII (March 1945), 85.
[12] White, II, 147.

enlightened sincerely and earnestly seek it.... But our present business is with the difficult and unbending realities of actual life, and when we have drawn inspiration from the great object of our hopes it becomes us with patience and resolution to apply ourselves to accommodating our theories to immediate practice.... It is no prejudice to the ultimate establishment of the boldest political innovations that we temporize so as, when they shall be accomplished they may be rendered permanent.[13]

What often confuses readers of Shelley is the superficial paradox of his extremely violent denunciation of iniquity among the ruling classes, and his impassioned declaration that resistance to it must be non-violent. But the latter is a logical consequence of Shelley's political attitude; he insisted that people must be worthy of the perfection of which he considered them capable. To achieve a peaceful society, people must be able effectively to adopt peaceful means. Consistent with this attitude is his insistence that a majority of people in a democratic society must *believe* in equality of possessions as a moral and religious truth before such equality can be realized. Social reform, and not the mere political rule of the working-class, is the answer.[14] This reform involves the defeat of the competitive or baser element of human nature and the establishment of love, the element which is more noble and ultimately more powerful. This conception of mankind's essential equality and brotherhood constitutes the ideal anarchism which Shelley proclaims.

If Shelley cannot be classed with the Socialists of later years, it is because of his insistence on reforming men before society can be reformed. He believed that human nature can change and that it *must* change in some important respects if society is to be revolutionized. He strongly opposed the imposition of a new regime by the very methods which had made the old order unbearable to him.

Not that Shelley absolutely ruled out violent revolution. In both the *Philosophical View* and *Men of England* there is the

---

[13]   *A Philosophical View of Reform,* in *Works,* VII, 43-44.
[14]   See John Middleton Murry, "Percy Bysshe Shelley, 1792-1822: Means and Ends", *Heaven − and Earth* (London, 1938), pp. 318-321.

indication that he considered violence a final resort.[15] But it was to be employed only after all peaceful methods had been tried and as the result of the most unbearable provocation. Shelley's creed does not allow for the coexistence of true freedom with hatred and revenge. The fair prospects of the French Revolution had been ruined by these passions. And it is the recalling of the formerly-pronounced curse on Jupiter which gives Prometheus the victory. Gandhi's efforts on behalf of India and other non-violent reforms have proven that Shelley's proposed method can achieve practical success. And the hope which Shelley saw for an avoidance of violent revolution in England lay in the fact that "the will of the People to change their government is an acknowledged right in the Constitution of England".[16] Subsequent history has proven him to be essentially correct.

HIS RELIGION OF LOVE

From 1818 onwards the theory of cosmic love informs Shelley's religion as well as his philosophy. Love is the One which remains while the Many change and pass, and Shelley makes this concept the core of all his major poems. Although, as Professor Baker points out, this emphasis on love links Shelley to the greatest figure of the Christian tradition,[17] the poet referred to himself as an atheist. When Trelawny said to him, "Why do you call yourself an atheist? It annihilates you in this world", Shelley replied, "It is a word of abuse to stop discussion, a painted devil to frighten the foolish, a threat to intimidate the wise and good. I used it to express my abhorrence of superstition; I took up the word, as a knight took up a gauntlet, in defiance of injustice. The delusions of Christianity are fatal to genius and originality: they

[15] In *A Philosophical View of Reform*, p. 53, Shelley states, "The last resort of resistance is undoubtedly insurrection." *Men of England* contains the line, "Forge arms in your defence to bear." That Shelley is here somewhat inconsistent seems an unavoidable conclusion.

[16] *A Philosophical View of Reform*, p. 8. This statement is italicized in Shelley's essay.

[17] Baker, "The Permanent Shelley", p. 517.

limit thought." [18] His public expressions on the subject were not any more guarded than this remark which was made in conversation with a friend. He did not care about expediency, and Trelawny's concern about "annihilation" meant little to him. He appears to have realized that his own principles were becoming increasingly like those of Christ and, consequently, to have intensified his vituperation against any perversion of Christ's teachings.

Being deeply religious, Shelley recognized that in religion, as in politics, a revolution was necessary. Touring Pisa with Hunt on 7 July 1822, he paused with his friend to listen to the cathedral organ and enthusiastically agreed with him "that a truly divine religion might yet be established, if charity were really made the principle of it, instead of faith".[19] Thus, in religion as in sociological concern, Shelley's motivating principle is his belief in the force and revivifying power of cosmic love. His early "atheism" and later "pantheism" appear to be the negative and the affirmative sides of a life-creed which progressed but did not essentially change. As a youth he was disposed to deny vehemently a theology which he never ceased to detest; in later years he more frequently referred to the great World Spirit in whom he had always believed. Although, as he grew older, he exercised his religious faith more wisely, that faith did not change.[20] It was a faith in the spirit of love and it was later to hold a tremendous appeal for certain young Victorian writers, challenging their fundamental assumptions and affecting the whole of their lives and works. How strongly some of them fought against the power of the new creed will be shown in the succeeding chapters.

THE GREAT MISUNDERSTANDING

Perhaps the one factor which has done more than any other to

[18] E. J. Trelawny, *Recollections of the Last Days of Shelley and Byron* (London, 1858), p. 60.
[19] Leigh Hunt, *Autobiography* (London, 1885), p. 294.
[20] See Henry S. Salt, *Shelley's Principles; Has Time Refuted or Confirmed Them? A Retrospect and Forecast* (London, 1892), p. 35, n.

make the Victorians as well as their successors misunderstand and depreciate Shelley is the faulty assumption that the poet believed in the achievement of an ideal society by a sudden act of the will on the part of mankind. Mary Shelley's remark in her Note on *Prometheus Unbound* is an oversimplification which may well have been primarily responsible for this widespread misconception. She asserts, "Shelley believed that mankind had only to will that there should be no evil, and there would be none." [21] Ever since Mrs. Shelley published her Note, scholars and critics have made remarks which take her comment at face value. Typical is Lionel Stevenson's authoritarian pronouncement about Shelley's social philosophy: "All the world's problems were to be solved in one vast millenial transformation-scene, as soon as certain existing institutions such as kings and priests should be overthrown and a few simple axioms of liberty accepted by all mankind." [22] Mr. Stevenson's comment refers to the conclusion of *Prometheus Unbound*, and it indicates that he did not take into consideration all of Shelley's writings on the subject of social amelioration.

It is true that the Prometheus fable provided Shelley with little opportunity to make his point that the liberation of mankind will demand a gradual, toilsome progression such as has been responsible for all partial and transient attainments throughout history. The letters Shelley wrote during the time when he was composing *Prometheus Unbound* indicate that he considered the toleration of individual abuses for an indefinite period to be a practical necessity. And in the *Philosophical View of Reform*, written about the same time, he says, "Nothing is more idle than to reject a limited benefit because we cannot without great sacrifices obtain an unlimited one. . . . Let us be content with a limited *beginning*, with any whatsoever opening . . . it is no matter how slow and cautions be the change; we shall demand more and more with firmness and moderation, never anticipating but never de-

---

[21] *Works*, II, 269.
[22] Lionel Stevenson, "Tennyson, Browning, and a Romantic Fallacy", *TQ*, XIII (January 1944), 176.

ferring the moment of successful opposition." [23] His one insistence was that the principle of reform be kept alive and advanced.[24] In November 1819, he wrote to Leigh Hunt:

The great thing to do is to hold the balance between popular impatience and tyrannical obstinacy; to inculcate with fervour both the
right of resistance and the duty of forbearance. You know my principles incite me to take all the good I can get in politics, for ever
aspiring to something more. I am one of those whom nothing will
fully satisfy, but who [are] ready to be partially satisfied [by] all
that is practicable.[25]

How could Shelley have made more explicit his conviction that
the liberation of humanity from its long-standing superstitions
and oppressions was not to be easily or quickly won? Earlier, in
the preface to *The Revolt of Islam*, he had said specifically that
it was to be a "slow, gradual, silent, change". And underlying all
his warnings against excessive expectations was the already-
emphasized certainty that men's ways of thinking must be
changed before social evils can be eradicated. Indeed, he stresses
patience and endurance rather than idealistic expectation of an
imminent social paradise.

Crane Briton has ably described that aspect of Shelley which
enabled him, by means of an earth-born aspiration, to bring
heaven down to earth:

He possessed . . . more of that nameless quality that makes a civilized
man – wisdom, sanity, common sense, all just fail to describe it –
than his admirers will allow us to remember. And at all times he
was willing to admit the necessity of making contingent reforms. The
day of complete political regeneration may be far off and it is well
to prepare the way for it by useful changes in political detail.[26]

Perhaps nowhere did Shelley more clearly state his belief about
man's ability to solve his social problems than in the following
lines from *Julian and Maddalo*:

It is our will
Which thus enchains us to permitted ill –

[23] *A Philosophical View of Reform*, p. 46.
[24] White, II, 112.
[25] *Works*, X, 130-131.
[26] Brinton, p. 169.

We might be otherwise – we might be all
We dream of happy, high, majestical.
Where is the love, beauty and truth we seek,
But in our mind? And if we were not weak,
Should we be less in deed than in desire?

(lines 170-176)

THE INTERIM: 1822 TO THE 1830'S

During the first ten to fifteen years after Shelley's death, it appeared that his works were likely not to become popular. To the great majority of Englishmen the views he held were repugnant, and the sincere eulogists of his poetry were careful to dissociate themselves from any support of his social, economic, and religious beliefs. There was, however, a subsiding of the vehement antagonism which had been expressed against Shelley during his lifetime. While many reviewers acknowledged the cruelty of the treatment he had received, the periodicals which had been most vigorous in opposing him either kept silence or incidentally mixed comments on his great genius with their condemnations of his principles.[27] Mrs. Shelley, following the lead of Thomas Love Peacock, who in his 1817 novel *Nightmare Abbey*, had patterned the character of Scythrop after Shelley, presented her husband as a character in two novels – *The Last Man* (1826) and *Lodore* (1834). And numerous editions of Shelley's works, both selections and "complete" collections, as well as biographical writings, appeared during the period of 1822 to 1841. Yet Shelley remained virtually unknown and his contribution to English literature unacknowledged for the greater part of that period.

When, late in 1829, a Cambridge debating team, of which Arthur Henry Hallam was a member, visited Oxford to defend Shelley's merits against those of Byron, so little was known of Shelley that the Oxford team could venture a pretense of confusing him with Shenstone. That same year Hallam and other young admirers of Shelley had *Adonais* reprinted, thus helping

[27]   White, II, 396.

the growth of Shelley's fame by associating it with that of Keats.[28] Prominent men had, of course, known of Shelley before this time and had commented on his works. Their opinions were generally unfavorable. In 1824 Hazlitt had written, "Instead of giving a language to thought, or lending the heart a tongue, he utters dark sayings, and deals in allegories and riddles." [29] In the *Atlas* of 8 March 1829, his denunciation of the poet was even sharper: "Mr. Shelley, who felt the want of originality without the power to supply it, distorted everything from what it was, and his pen produced only abortions." [30]

This was still the general view when the young Thackeray wrote in May 1829 that Shelley's "strong and perhaps good feelings" had been perverted by an "absurd creed", and that conceit and false religion had misguided his "high powers".[31] But Thackeray was not vindictive toward Shelley because of this "false religion". Writing to his mother about a proposed periodical, "The Chimaera", he declared:

An Essay on Shelley is in progress for the Chimaera – There is an excellent motto (tho' a long one) in Devereux ... about Bezoni the Atheist. [I shall] write it very small; "I know that the intention of Bezoni was benevolence, & that the [practice] of his life was virtue, & while my reason tells me that my God will not punish the reluctant & invol[untary] errors of one to whom all God's creatures were so dear, my religion bids me hope that I shall meet him in that world where no error is, & where the great Spirit to whom all passions are unknown avenges the momentary doubt of his justice, by a proof of the infinity of his mercy" – There – it has not taken up much room and I think will express the character & I hope the fate of Shelley.[32]

Thackeray's reaction to Shelley's social and political ideas is revealed in yet another excerpt from a letter to his mother: "The

[28] See Samuel C. Chew, *Byron in England* (New York, 1924), p. 261.
[29] William Hazlitt, *The Complete Works*, ed. P. P. Howe, Centenary Ed. (London and Toronto, 1934), XVI, 265.
[30] *Ibid.*, XX, 211.
[31] Letter of 11-17 May 1829, to his mother, Mrs. Carmichael-Smyth. See *William Makepeace Thackeray, The Letters and Private Papers*, ed. Gordon N. Ray (Cambridge, Harvard Univ. Press, 1945-46), I, 74.
[32] Letter of 2-4 September 1829. See *Ibid.*, pp. 98-99. Neither the essay nor "The Chimaera" ever appeared.

Revolt of Islam ... is in my opinion a most beautiful poem – Tho' the story is absurd, & the republican sentiments in it conveyed if possible more absurd." [33]

Macaulay, in his 1830 essay on Bunyan, disgresses unexpectedly to take a favorable view of Shelley's poetry. He contends that Shelley turned atheism itself into a rich mythology by giving to the abstract the interest of the concrete. "The spirit of Beauty, the Principle of Good, the Principle of Evil ... were no longer mere words, but 'intelligible forms'; 'fair humanities'; objects of love, of adoration, or of fear." [34] But, although Macaulay goes on to term Shelley's poetry "not ... an art, but an inspiration", he also concurs with the popular opinion and declares some of the poet's ethical views "most absurd and pernicious". A similar opinion of Shelley's social ideas is the basis of Sir Henry Taylor's declaration in 1834 that Shelley was merely a man of feeling whose purpose it was to lead his followers to "regions where reason ... is all unknown ... to seats of anarchy and abstraction, where imagination exercises the shadow of an authority, over a people of phantoms, in a land of dreams".[35]

At a time when such was the prevailing attitude among writers, the youthful Robert Browning, as we shall see in the following chapter, made his discovery of Shelley and pledged himself to Shelley's principles. Private though Browning's devotion was, it was not unique in the England of the 1820's and 30's. Relatively minor poets were writing verses in praise of Shelley. Their tributes range from the 1822 elegies by Bernard Barton, Arthur Brooke, and Thomas L. Beddoes, to a highly appreciative sonnet written by Thomas Wade in 1835. Wade is drawn to Shelley not only by the aesthetic quality of his works but also by the rational insights which he, unlike most Englishmen, detects in them:

> Holy and mighty Poet of the Spirit
> That broods and breathes along the Universe!
> In the least portion of whose starry verse

[33] Letter of 29 March-8 April, 1829. See *Ibid.*, p. 51.
[34] Thomas Babington, Lord Macaulay, *Miscellaneous Works,* ed. by his sister, Lady Hannah Trevelyan (New York, Harper, n.d.), I, 527.
[35] From Taylor's 1834 preface to his *Philip van Artvelde* (London, 1883), p. xv.

Is the great breath the spheréd heavens inherit,
No human song is eloquent as thine;
For, by a reasoning instinct all divine,
 Thou feel'st the soul of things; and thereof singing,
With all the madness of a skylark, springing
From earth to heaven, the intenseness of thy strain,
Like the lark's music all around us ringing,
Laps us in God's own heart, and we regain
Our primal life ethereal! Men profane
Blaspheme thee; I have heard thee *Dreamer* styled –
I've mused upon their wakefulness – and smiled.[36]

A GENERAL VIEW OF SHELLEY AND VICTORIANISM

In view of Wade's insights about Shelley, it seems incredible, as
H. S. Salt points out, that so many distinguished Victorians, from
Carlyle and Ruskin to Kingsley and Matthew Arnold have failed
so grotesquely in their attempts to enlighten the world concerning
Shelley. Salt concludes that these Victorians are out of sympathy
with the objects which Shelley envisioned, and that an ability to
see as Shelley saw is absolutely essential for a right understanding
of his life's meaning. Thus they have found chaos in a life which
was outstanding for its directness of aim, have heard only what
Carlyle called an "inarticulate wail" when Shelley's clear trum-
pet-call sounded, and have created a mythical personage out of
the dust of their own minds.[37]

It is important, on the other hand, to recognize that Shelley
never limited his own sympathies or his own impulses in order
to conform to the romantic inclinations of the average citizen.
He could not assent to the control of his emotions by the demands of a corporate loyalty, but wrote and acted as he felt.
Victorians read him because, bound by conventions, they could
not act in accordance with their feelings. In so far as he did not
prod their feelings into unrest and discontent, Shelley provided
an impetus toward moral stability. "The vital truth Shelley everywhere enforced", wrote G. H. Lewes in 1841, "although treated

---

[36] Quoted by Salt, *Shelley's Principles*, p. 20.
[37] Salt, *Shelley's Principles*, pp. 16-17.

as a chimaera by most of his contemporaries, and indulged as a
dream by some others, has become the dominant Idea – the
philosophy and faith of this age, throughout Europe – it is
progression, humanity, perfectibility, civilization, democracy –
call it what you will – this is the truth uttered unceasingly by
Shelley, and universally received by us." [38] It is true that Lewes's
series of synonyms describes clearly a common basis of Shelley's
thought and Victorian ideals: a belief that the better human instincts will assert themselves continuously to struggle for a higher
level of life. But Lewes does not point out the discrepancy
between the means proposed by Shelley and the means employed
by the Victorians. Shelley consistently urged the freedom and
the supremacy of the individual; the Victorians instinctively
thought in terms of traditional institutions.

Early Victorian liberal criticism, which showed an apologetic
appreciation of Shelley, fostered the later critical view that Shelley was among the great poets of England but that he was "dead
wrong" in virtually all the beliefs that really matered to *him*.
These later Victorians seldom bothered even to study those areas
of thought to which Shelley had devoted himself most seriously.[39]

There was an adoption of Shelley by respectable people, and
it is worth considering. For many his poetry undoubtedly provided a pure aesthetic pleasure, expressing to them no more
moral or sociological ideas than did the music they listened to. But
the cant of modern art greatly exaggerates the number of those
who read poetry for the sake of sensations utterly detached from
their relationship to society. And that many Victorian readers
of Shelley found his poetry to fall into their scheme of things
seems a fair assumption. His restless striving, his extension of
emotional concern, his seeking to unite himself with all things
are dreams common to all who ceaselessly push onward to en-
large the boundaries of experience.[40] But most of those Victorians
for whom Shelley was an inspiring source of dynamic political

[38] G. H. L[ewes], in a review of several editions of works by Shelley,
Westminster Review, XXXV (April 1841), 163. This essay places Lewes
among the first critics to speak out with enthusiasm for Shelley's ideas.
[39] See White, II, 415-416.
[40] See Brinton, pp. 188-189.

and social ideas found that they could not go all the way with him. They were not willing to abandon, as he had done, the ties of family, tradition, wealth, and institutions when their vision of the truth demanded such abandonment.

The Shelley Society, which flourished from 1886 to 1888 and did a great deal to promote Shelley's literary status, is in one respect representative of the situation in which Victorian followers of Shelley found themselves. The famous explorer H. M. Stanley evidenced keen insight when he said to one of the Society's officers, "You are a funny people, you Shelleyites; you are playing – at a safe distance yourselves, maybe – with fire. In spreading Shelley you are indirectly helping to stir up the great socialist question which bids fair to swamp you all for a bit." [41] And it is true that, despite all attempts at a liberal view of Shelley, the Victorian mind found his fierce spirit too impatient of earthly disciplines and his revolutionary program shocking to even its most liberal political elements. "If [Shelley's] concerns were undeniably moral", writes Jerome Buckley, "his morality at best seemed dubious, fashioned from his own unchristian visions, ill-adapted to the practical demands of an industrial society." [42] It becomes obvious, then, that to be a consistent proponent of Shelley's social views in Victorian England was to break decisively with established society.

Shelley's influence on individual writers of the early Victorian era seems to fall into a rather definite pattern. There is an enthusiastic response in youth; a period of faltering in loyalty to the new-found idol, as the young writer looks back at the traditional securities which Shelley challenges; and finally a strong antagonism to Shelley's ideas about society, if not to every aspect of his being. In the following chapters Robert Browning, Benjamin Disraeli, and Charles Kingsley are presented as outstanding examples of early Victorians who, for various reasons, chose to return to a more conservative ground rather than to take the risks which became evident once they had started on the road pointed out by Shelley. It is my contention that they and others, who

---

[41] Quoted by Salt, *Shelley's Principles*, p. 25.
[42] *The Victorian Temper* (Cambridge, Harvard Univ. Press, 1951), p. 21.

evidence various lesser degrees of concern with Shelley's ideas, are responsible for establishing among the mid-Victorian writers an attitude toward Shelley which tended to disregard or depreciate his social and political thought. Thus there is but little Shelleyan influence (in the realm of sociological ideas) to be found in Victorian literature from about 1855 to 1880, and this period I deal with in one short chapter of my study.

There follows a chapter which acknowledges some figures of the late Victorian era who took a new look at Shelleyan ideas and found them worthy of serious treatment. The one Victorian, however, who virtually without reservation or retreat accepted Shelley's view was George Bernard Shaw, and the final chapter of my study is devoted to him. Not that Shaw, appropriated Shelley's social philosophy without disagreement or was always consistent in his use of Shelleyan ideas; but he took the poet seriously and adopted his views as the basis for his own attitudes toward society. What might have been the course of Victorian literature if Browning, the earliest great Shelleyite, had been as consistent as was Shaw, must remain a matter of conjecture.

We turn now to a consideration of Browning's response to Shelley, which, though it has been frequently and extensively commented upon, needs to be given a more unified and comprehensive treatment than it has thus far received.

II

SHELLEY AND BROWNING

The young Robert Browning of the *Pauline-Paracelsus-Sordello*
period was emerging from his two years of extreme enthusiasm
for Shelley. If we had the poetry he wrote during those two years
(about 1826-1828), we should doubtlessly find it very similar to
that of Shelley. And if we could compile a detailed biography
of Browning as a young atheist and vegetarian, we should find
in it a striking number of similarities to Shelley's life during the
Queen Mab period.[1] We know enough, however, of Browning's
early devotion to Shelley to recognize that the experience was
crucial in the molding of his poetic career.

It is an established fact that Browning (1812-1889) had never
heard of Shelley before he discovered him in 1826, when his
cousin and close companion James Silverthorn gave him a copy
of William Benbow's new, pirated edition of *Miscellaneous Poems*.
Immediately he read all the Shelley poetry he could lay his hands
on.[2] He obtained from somewhere a copy of *Queen Mab* and was
so impressed that for two years he professed atheism and prac-

[1] Frederick A. Pottle, *Shelley and Browning: A Myth and Some Facts*
(Chicago, Univ. of Chicago Press, 1923), p. 8.
[2] Newman Ivey White, *Shelley* (New York, 1940), II, 403, tells of the
supply of first printings of Shelley's poetry which the printer Ollier still
had on hand – indicating that Shelley was not popular. On 3 March
1886, in a letter to Thomas J. Wise, Browning recalled: "As for the early
editions of Shelley. They were obtained for me some time before 1830
(or even earlier) in the *regular way*, from Hunt and Clarke, in consequence
of a direction I obtained from the *Literary Gazette*. I still possess *Posthumous Poems*, but have long since parted with *Prometheus Unbound*,
Rosalind and Helen, Six Weeks' Tour, Cenci, and the *Adonais*." See
Robert Browning, *Letters*, coll. Thomas J. Wise, ed. Thurman L. Hood
(New Haven, Yale Univ. Press, 1933), p. 246.

ticed vegetarianism. He lived on bread and potatoes and returned to a regular diet only when his eyesight appeared to be weakening. "The atheism", says Mrs. Orr, "cured itself; we do not exactly know when or how." [3] But in her declaration that it was not a matter of rational doubt but only a passing state of rebellion and of boyish folly, with which Browning's more mature self had no concern, Mrs. Orr treats too lightly a most important phase of Browning's life. Her assertion that the return to religious belief did not shake the young poet's faith in his new prophet, but only convinced him that he had misread Shelley, is an oversimplification.

Browning left Shelley's faith in the regenerative power within humanity, a faith which was most congenial to his own nature, and attempted a return to his former religious position. Finding that he could no longer wholeheartedly accept the premises of his earlier youth – essentially those of his evangelically-minded mother – he yet professed traditional Christian views. His ideological struggle resulted in life-long concern and uncertainty about Shelley, whose poetry he never ceased to admire.[4]

The present chapter is an attempt to review chronologically and concisely the scope of Browning's reaction to Shelley's strong ideational influence. First to be discussed is the background and effect of Browning's youthful response to, and subsequent abnegation of, his Shelleyan ideals. Perhaps most important to an understanding of Browning's gradual emergence from Shelley's dominence is the section dealing with the three first-published poems. The concluding part traces the continuing effect of Browning's attraction to Shelley.

---

[3]   Mrs. Sutherland Orr, *Life and Letters of Robert Browning,* (Boston and New York, 1896), I, 60.
[4]   In support of this viewpoint, I am bringing together material from various parts of Betty Miller's biography *Robert Browning: A Portrait* (London, 1952). Mrs. Miller's comments on Browning's reaction to Shelley are interspersed throughout her book, and the most pertinent of them are here collected in one chapter and supported by additional quotations from Browning's works.

SHELLEYAN ARDOR:
ITS BACKGROUND, ABANDONMENT, AND EFFECT

Browning's mother, the former Sarah Anna Wiedemann, was Scotch on the maternal side, and Mrs. Orr ascribes to this source her "kindly, gentle, but distinctly evangelical Christianity". Browning's strong religious instincts, though derived from both parents, were "most anxiously fostered by his mother".[5] As a child Browning, in his own words, was "passionately religious", but during his early years, as well as later, his mother filled his heart. Even as a grown man, he could not sit by her without his arm about her waist. Mrs. Orr correctly observes, "It is difficult to measure the influence which this feeling may have exercised on his later life." [6]

Religion seems to have been the main inspiration of Sarah Anna Browning's life. As a girl she joined the Congregational Church in Walworth and later served there as Sunday school teacher; her husband became a member nine years after their marriage. No doubt, it was Mrs. Browning who convinced him, though he appreciated Voltaire's wit and Bernard de Mandeville's subversiveness, to worship with her at this dissenting York Street chapel. Robert later told Elizabeth that his mother quoted the Bible to reprimand her son for calling people "fools". As a gift she gave him Cruden's *Complete Concordance to the Holy Scriptures*, and, among the six thousand volumes on the Brownings' bookshelves, the one which bore her signature was Elisha Cole's *Practical Discourse of Effectual Calling and of Perserverance*. The outstanding trait of Browning's mother appears to have been her simple but forceful piety.

His early tendency to call people "fools" for disagreeing with him was but one aspect of Browning's boyhood temperament. The record indicates that he was publicly reproved in church "for restlessness and inattention", and from babyhood, he evidenced a destructive nature which was a source of harassment to the adults about him. As he grew intellectually, he became

---

[5] Orr, I, 26, 27.
[6] *Ibid.*, p. 37.

a self-confident youth, who readily and openly derided the opinions of others.[7] This characteristic, combined with his passionate
instinct for religious contemplation made it natural for Browning
to ally himself with the imagination of Shelley.[8] The Romantic
poet's ardour for divine truth and beauty, motivated by an
aspiring imagination, and his simultaneous indignant repudiation
of revealed religion must have seemed highly paradoxical to the
youthful, inexperienced Browning. He had probably not realized
before that an aspiring religious feeling could exist without a
belief in revealed religion, a fact which Shelley compelled him to
recognize. Many unorthodox poets, Byron for example, would
not have raised the question in his mind. And had he not been a
poet himself, Browning might have recoiled from Shelley's explicit doctrine to deny his poetry. Holding fast by the poetry,
however, he temporarily surrendered his Christian faith. But
upon recovering it, he found it to be no longer the "glad, confident" faith of a human fellowship. It had dwindled and had
become only a personal feeling which he was determined to
maintain in spite of the world.[9] A later poem, *Fears and Scruples*,
perhaps best describes the thinned creed to which he returned –
faith diminished to hope, certainty to courage, and belief to "a
dream":

> Never mind! Though foolishness may flout me,
>   One thing's sure enough: 'tis neither frost,
> No, nor fire, shall freeze or burn from out me
>   Thanks for truth – though falsehood, gained – though lost.
>
> All my days, I'll go the softlier, sadlier,
>   For that dream's sake!   (29-34)[10]

As already pointed out, the Shelley of Browning's early enthusiasm was the Shelley of *Queen Mab*, the poet "who would have

[7] Miller, pp. 7-8.
[8] Mrs. Orr (I, 59) says: "The extra-human note in Shelley's genius irresistibly suggested to the Browning of fourteen, as it still did to the
Browning of forty, the presence of a lofty spirit, one dwelling in the
communion of higher things."
[9] Osbert Burdett, *The Brownings* (London, 1929), pp. 90-91.
[10] See *Works*, Centenary Ed., 10 vols. (London, 1912). This edition is
used for all references in this chapter to Browning's poems. Line references are parenthetically included in the text.

remodled the whole system of religious belief, as of human duty and rights".[11] But the young enthusiast also studied *Prometheus Unbound*, which most clearly, and in exalted symbolism, sets forth the remodeled system envisioned by Shelley – demonstrating that he does not consider evil and suffering to be inherent in the nature of things. In Shelley's masterpiece the persistence of outworn ideals, such as the Force and Power symbolized by Jupiter, has made possible the tyranny of evil. Prometheus, man's revolting mind, is determined to endure all the tyrant can inflict upon him rather than to admit the justice of Jupiter's reign. In his enslaved state, he hates the tyrant; and not until pity replaces that hatred, is he freed or Jupiter overthrown. Learning to love his enemies as he loves his friends is the key to freedom for Prometheus. The remainder of the poem shows the effect upon humanity of a universal awakening of this love.

When the Spirit of the Hour sounds his trumpet in a great city, the Spirit of the Earth sees the passing of all those ugly human shapes and visages which have been the cause of its pain. They float through the air, fading

> Into the winds that scattered them; and those
> From whom they past seemed mild and lovely forms
> After some foul disguise had fallen, and all
> Were somewhat changed, and after brief surprise
> And greetings of delighted wonder, all
> Went to their sleep again.   (III, iv, 68-73)

And the Spirit of the Hour tells of other effects brought about by the adoption of Love to replace Power:

> Soon as the sound had ceased whose thunder filled
> The abysses of the sky and the wide earth,
> There was a change: the impalpable thin air
> And the all-circling sunlight were transformed,
> As if the sense of love dissolved in them
> Had folded itself around the sphered world.   (98-103)

The simultaneous reunion of Prometheus with Asia symbolizes the restoration of man's thought or knowledge to its natural re-

---

[11]   Orr, I, 59.

lationship with emotion – with all that is ultimately true and beautiful. The achievement of this reunion represents to Shelley man's highest goal.

That this proposed rejuvenation of human nature should appeal to a young man of Browning's background and temperament is not surprising. Nor, perhaps, is it surprising that his mother's religion had became so deeply ingrained in him that he could not devote his life to the new-found Shelleyan ideal. The break with this ideal constituted a major crisis in his life, for all his subsequent experience was qualified by it. Browning found it impossible completely to abandon the traditional religious assurances of his childhood and to follow Shelley's thinking to its ultimate conclusions. "It was Browning's tragedy, perhaps, that, unlike Shelley, it had been his fate to revolt, not against the authority of the 'grey tyrant father', but against the standards of an all-too-tenderly loved mother. Unable to relinquish love, he had relinquished freedom." [12]

Professor Pottle believes that Browning destroyed his first copy of *Queen Mab*; his copy of *Miscellaneous Poems*, which has survived, gives evidence of Browning's concerted effort to obliterate from it all the "foolish scribblings" with which he had earlier been exultantly profuse.[13] The elements of the struggle and the agony of the break with Shelley are reflected in *Paracelsus:* First comes the cry,

[12]   Miller, p. 140. That the religious convictions of his mother were a (or perhaps *the*) primary factor in Browning's desertion of Shelley's philosophy seems clear enough. But Mrs. Miller insists too strongly (p. 10) that for Browning this was a deliberate "Herculean effort" of re-grafting and reversal. This view is not clearly supported by *Pauline*, his first-published, autobiographical poem, which traces the first steps of Browning's alienation from Shelley and indicates that it may well have been honest doubts (very likely occasioned by considerations for his beloved mother) which led to a distrust of Shelley's principles and thence to a renunciation of his belief in the supremacy of reason. Browning's statement that he "flung All honour from [his] soul" (*Pauline*, 209-210) need not mean that, against his sense of honesty, he purposefully abandoned Shelleyan views. It may imply that, despite the fame (honour) which could have been his as an early exponent of Shelley's lasting qualities, the youthful Browning had turned from the great poet when "wandering thought" had led to disillusionment.
[13]   Pottle, pp. 26-27, 78.

> God! Thou art Mind! Unto the Master-Mind
> Mind should be precious. Spare my mind alone!
> All else I will endure . . . . (II, 229-231)

Then follows its contrary:

> Mind is nothing but disease
> And natural health is ignorance. (IV, 279-280)

Browning came to appreciate Shelley primarily for his rare individuality and his note of passion and human charity, but not for his radical prophesies.[14] He seems never to have been able to free himself entirely, however, from a feeling that he had not been true to his first and essential self. The evidences of Shelley's influence in his life and writing are often accompanied by an unmistakable twinge of remorseful awe at the memory of the unreservedly radical poet to whose ideals he had once dedicated himself.

During the period of his great enthusiasm for Shelley, Browning had adopted numerous attitudes which he later considered absurd. Of these, the two years of adolescent atheism and vegetarianism may perhaps be termed the least significant and least durable. Shelley's way of thinking, especially in regard to man's potentiality, could not be so readily or so completely discarded. The influence of Shelley was, naturally, strongest in Browning's three early poems, but it may be traced throughout his life and works. Betty Miller comments on its effect:

As Shelley himself had desired, four years after his death his words, sparks from an "unextinguished hearth", had ignited a kindred conflagration in the soul of another poet. This conflagration was to die down; it was to be smothered; it was to be forcibly quenched: but one thing remained: Browning had recognised in the fearless spiritual independence of Shelley a principle of conduct whereby to measure, in the years to come, not only the sum of his own poetic achievement, but the very nature of human integrity itself.[15]

It may be maintained that Browning, from his standpoint of dual consciousness, was able to comprehend and diagnose the perils of romanticism, despite the responsive chords it struck in his

---

[14] White, II, 403-404.
[15] Miller, p. 9.

own nature. In his three early poems he relentlessly probes and examines romantic egoism and exposes its limitless self-assertion, its vague abstractness, and its disregard of all relative progress. Romanticism, in the opinion of W. O. Raymond, disdains the finite, refuses to stoop to life's necessary conditions and negates the actual rather than the ideal aspect of man's nature. It constitues the fallacy and accounts for "the imperfect insight of these gifted though tempest-tossed men of genius, – children of the heaven-storming Titans –, whom Browning has so vividly depicted in his earlier poetry".[16]

There were Romantic poets who conformed to this description; but Shelley, as evidenced by his *Philosophical View of Reform* and other sociological essays and poems, definitely took into account actuality and finite conditions. He did not, however, allow the present to dim his vision of what might some day be. His consistent faith in humanity was willing to acknowledge all forward steps in the condition of mankind. Browning contends that an ordinary youth, having Shelley's dreams, would have concluded that all must be changed or nothing and would soon have seen the futility of what little he could do.[17] That Browning himself, in his youth, had these dreams and abandoned them for more immediate concerns, indicates a certain abnegation of qualities which he basically valued in Shelley. And he appears to have been unaware that Shelley's idealism, instead of being contradicted by the poet's attention to specific and minute social problems was accompanied by an eagerness to accept limited and partial betterment of social conditions wherever possible.

The effect of an early belief that Shelley had the best answer to the question of mankind's future was not to be easily – nor ever entirely – overcome. While residing in Pisa shortly after his marriage, Browning often walked the streets, recalling Shelley who had composed there, some years previously, poetry which

[16]   William O. Raymond, "Browning's Conception of Love", *Papers of the Michigan Academy of Science, Arts and Letters* (1925) IV, 1, 451.
[17]   Robert Browning, *An Essay on Percy Bysshe Shelley, Being a Reprint of the Introductory Essay prefixed to the Volume of [25 spurious] Letters of Shelley published by Edward Moxon in 1852*, ed. W. Tyas Harden for the Shelley Society (London, 1888), p. 22.

had revolutionized the life of the youthful Browning. The air seemed "bright with thy past presence yet", inevitably exciting the memory of the old conflict and the old betrayal of his pledge to the freedom for which Shelley stood.[18] Such a remembrance has much in common with the experience which prompted Browning's poem, *Memorabilia* (1855). This well-known poem, because of its centrality to the theme of the present chapter, deserves quotation in full:

> AH, did you once see Shelley plain,
>   And did he stop and speak to you
> And did you speak to him again?
>   How strange it seems and new!
>
> But you were living before that,
>   And also you are living after
> And the memory I started at –
>   My starting moves your laughter.
>
> I crossed a moor, with a name of its own
>   And a certain use in the world no doubt,
> Yet a hand's breadth of it shines alone
>   'Mid the blank miles round about:
>
> For there I picked up on the heather
>   And there I put inside my breast
> A moulted feather, an eagle-feather!
>   Well, I forget the rest.

William G. Kingsland has recorded for us Browning's reminiscence about the experience which occasioned the poem:

I recollect once, when the talk had ranged round the great name of Shelley, [Browning's] referring to the little poem "Memorabilia" . . . . He said he well recollected the circumstance that gave rise to the stanzas. He was in the shop of a well-known bookseller, when a stranger to himself came in, and, entering into conversation with the bookseller, began to talk about Shelley, stating, among other things, that he had both seen and spoken to him. Suddenly the stranger turned round, and burst into a laugh on observing how Browning was "staring at him", with blanched face: "and", said the poet, "I have not yet forgotten how strangely the sight of one who had spoken with Shelley had affected me." [19]

[18]   See Miller, p. 140.
[19]   William G. Kingsland, "Personal Recollections of Browning", *Poet-Lore*, II (1890), 131.

The poet's starting at the mention of Shelley, his blanched face, and his use of the term "strange" indicate something more unsettling than a deep, enduring love and admiration for the poet whom he had formerly idolized. And his comment on the stranger's having lived before and continuing to live after the meeting with Shelley betokens Browning's recollection of the difference this very poet had once made in the direction his own life was to take. The stranger, apparently so little affected by an actual meeting with Shelley, impressed Browning, no doubt, as a commentary on the distance which had developed between himself and his former inspirer. Crossing the moor of life, he had grasped a feather of the eagle, and the "hand's breadth" of time in which Shelley's vision had possessed his imagination appeared in retrospect the one illuminated portion of his life. But *Memorabilia* is not the only poem which supports the view that Browning came to recognize what he had lost by relinquishing Shelley's ideals. Already in his first three published poems there is a trace of the regret, mixed with awe, which he seems never to have overcome.

SHELLEY IN THE THREE EARLY POEMS

In *Pauline* (1833), *Paracelsus* (1835), and *Sordello* (1840) there are indications of a gradually widening chasm between Browning and his recent idol, Shelley. The famous *Pauline* apostrophe to the "Sun-treader" shows that Browning, emerging from his two years of total absorption in Shelley's ideals, retained a jealously retrospective sense of having discovered unknowingly, at its sequestered and deeply inpiring source, a mighty poetic torrent:

> Sun-treader, life and light be thine for ever!
> Thou art gone from us; years go by and spring
> Gladdens and the young earth is beautiful,
> Yet thy songs come not, other bards arise,
> But none like thee: they stand, thy majesties,
> Like mighty works which tell some spirit there
> Hath sat regardless of neglect and scorn,
> Till, its long task completed, it hath risen
> And left us, never to return, and all

Rush in to peer and praise when all in vain.
The air seems bright with thy past presence yet,
But thou art still for me as thou hast been
When I have stood with thee as on a throne
With all thy dim creations gathered round
Like mountains, and I felt of mould like them,
And with them creatures of my own were mixed,
Like things half-lived, catching and giving life.
But thou art still for me who have adored
Tho' single, panting but to hear thy name
Which I believed a spell to me alone,
Scarce deeming thou wast as a star to men!
As one should worship long a scared spring
Scarce worth a moth's flitting, which long grasses cross,
And one small tree embowers droopingly –
Joying to see some wandering insect won
To live in its few rushes, or some locust
To pasture on its boughs, or some wild bird
Stoop for its freshness from the trackless air:
And then should find it but the fountain-head,
Long lost, of some great river washing towns
And towers, and seeing old woods which will live
But by its banks untrod of human foot,
Which, when the great sun sinks, lie quivering
In light as some thing lieth half of life
Before God's foot, waiting a wondrous change;
Then girt with rocks which seek to turn or stay
Its course in vain, for it does ever spread
Like a sea's arm as it goes rolling on,
Being the pulse of some great country – so
Wast thou to me, and art thou to the world!
And I, perchance, half feel a strange regret
That I am not what I have been to thee:
Like a girl one has silently loved long
In her first loneliness in some retreat,
When, late emerged, all gaze and glow to view
Her fresh eyes and soft hair and lips which bloom
Like a mountain berry: doubtless it is sweet
To see her thus adored, but there have been
Moments when all the world was in our praise,
Sweeter than any pride of after hours.
Yet, sun-treader, all hail! From my heart's heart
I bid thee hail! E'en in my wildest dreams,
I proudly feel I would have thrown to dust

The wreaths of fame which seemed o'erhanging me,
To see thee for a moment as thou art.

And if thou livest, if thou lovest, spirit!
Remember me who set this final seal
To wandering thought – that one so pure as thou
Could never die. Remember me who flung
All honour from my soul, yet paused and said
"There is one spark of love remaining yet,
"For I have nought in common with him, shapes
"Which followed him avoid me, and foul forms
"Seek me, which ne'er could fasten on his mind;
"And though I feel how low I am to him,
"Yet I aim not even to catch a tone
"Of harmonies he called profusely up;
"So, one gleam still remains, although the last."
Remember me who praise thee e'en with tears,
For never more shall I walk calm with thee;
Thy sweet imaginings are as an air,
A melody some wondrous singer sings,
Which, though it haunt men oft in the still eve,
They dream not to essay; yet it no less
But more is honoured. I was thine in shame,
And now when all thy proud renown is out,
I am a watcher whose eyes have grown dim
With looking for some star which breaks on him
Altered and worn and weak and full of tears.   (151-229)

Browning, the narrator in this largely autobiographical poem,
can no longer "walk calm" with the "sun-treader", and he feels
a compulsion to reveal to the beloved Pauline his previous history
of frantic groping for life's meaning, which had been temporarily
arrested by his discovery of Shelley:

                              And my choice fell
Not so much on a system as a man –
On one, whom praise of mine shall not offend,
Who was as calm as beauty, being such
Unto mankind as thou to me, Pauline, –
Believing in them and devoting all
His soul's strength to their winning back to peace;
Who sent forth hopes and longings for their sake,
Clothed in all passion's melodies: such first
Caught me and set me, slave of a sweet task,

To disentangle, gather sense from song:
Since, song-inwoven, lurked there words which seemed
A key to a new world, the muttering
Of angels, something yet unguessed by man.
How my heart leaped as still I sought and found
Much there, I felt my own soul had conceived,
But there living and burning! Soon the orb
Of his conceptions dawned on me; its praise
Lives in the tongues of men, men's brows are high
When his name means a triumph and a pride,
So, my weak voice may well forbear to shame
What seemed decreed my fate: I threw myself
To meet it, I was vowed to liberty,
Men were to be as gods and earth as heaven,
And I – ah, what a life was mine to prove!
My whole soul rose to meet it. Now, Pauline,
I shall go mad, if I recall that time!   (403-429)

But immediately the poet emphasizes his disillusionment in
Shelley:

Oh let me look back ere I leave for ever
The time which was an hour one fondly waits
For a fair girl that comes a withered hag!   (430-432)

Having firmed his theories, he had planned to "look on real life",
seeking how best to attain life's end – an end "comprising every
joy" – but his pondering was fruitless:

And suddenly without heart-wreck I awoke
As from a dream: I said "'Twas beautiful,
"Yet but a dream, and so adieu to it!"   (448-450)

Thus he had lost all hope of reconciling his theories with actuality,
all belief in the possibility of mankind's immediate reform. Shelley had gone through a very similar experience; but as evidenced
by *Adonais*, *Prometheus Unbound*, and *Epipsychidion*, had kept
his ideals though realizing that their becoming actuality must be
postponed almost indefinitely. Browning, however, presents his
own experience thus:

First went my hopes of perfecting mankind,
Next – faith in them, and then in freedom's self
And virtue's self, then my own motives, ends

And aims and loves, and human love went last.
I felt this no decay, because new powers
Rose as old feelings left – wit, mockery,
Light-heartedness; for I had oft been sad,
Mistrusting my resolves, but now I cast
Hope joyously away: I laughed and said
"No more of this!" I must not think.   (458-468)

In Professor Pottle's words, "As his ideal narrowed, so increased his ability to gratify it, to 'be happy'." [20] The narrator now wants "to live this life",

To chain my spirit down which erst I freed
For flights to fame.   (505-506)

But he finds that his selfishness cannot be satiated and that his "craving after knowledge" cannot be subdued by "restlessness of passion". Finally he concludes that his soul's hunger is not for what he thinks should be, but for God. He renounces all earthly concerns and begs for God's love – in return for which he will dedicate himself to religious faith rather than human reason and aspiration:

Is it not in my nature to adore,
And e'en for all my reason do I not
Feel him, and thank him, and pray to him – now?
Can I forego the trust that he loves me? . . .

A mortal, sin's familiar friend, doth here
Avow that he will give all earth's reward,
But to believe and humbly teach the faith,
In suffering and poverty and shame,
Only believing he is not unloved.   (833-836, 855-859)

With declarations such as,

. . . only leaving all,
That tells of the past doubt. . . .
Feeling God loves us, and that all which errs
Is but a dream which death will dissipate,
(970-971, 978-979)

he attempts to appropriate for himself the old religious assurances.

20   Pottle, p. 50.

Nevertheless, the poem closes with another apostrophe to the "sun-treader"; Browning, even as he asserts his faith, gives evidence of a basic dependence upon Shelley's philosophy, a sense of being lost and out of his element when not in contact with the "sun-treader". Having broken with Shelley's religious views and with his approach to reform, Browning yet retains an undiminished love for him.[21] It seems that he has a hope of finally attaining an acceptable relationship with Shelleyan thought:

> Sun-treader, I believe in God and truth
> And love; and as one just escaped from death
> Would bind himself in bands of friends to feel
> He lives indeed, so, I would lean on thee!
> Thou must be ever with me, most in gloom
> If such must come, but chiefly when I die,
> For I seem, dying, as one going in the dark
> To fight a giant: but live thou for ever,
> And be to all what thou hast been to me!
> All in whom this wakes pleasant thoughts of me
> Know my last state is happy, free from doubt
> Or touch of fear. Love me and wish me well.

Pauline, the story of a soul's development and the "confession" of the difficulties besetting a mind in search of the light, has resemblances to Shelley's *Alastor.*

The influence of Shelley is apparent in the very subject matter of *Pauline.* In *Alastor,* Shelley had done something very similar to what Browning attempted in *Pauline.* The theme of *Alastor* is usually misunderstood. It really depicts, just as *Pauline* does, the ruin of a self-centered nature; here through solitude, as in *Pauline* through introspection. . . . "The Poet's self-centered seclusion", says Shelley, "was avenged by the furies of an irresistible passion pursuing him to speedy ruin." The only way in which he gives his approval to such blasted careers is by adding that the fate of those who feel no human sympathy is worse.[22]

The mingling of real and imaginary personality in the poem results in some confusions. The poet turns to Shelley for guidance, praises him, and laments his own failure as poet. Affirming Shelley's qualities of vision, he immediately comes to the dis-

[21] *Ibid.,* p. 51.
[22] *Ibid.,* p. 36. The Shelley quotation is from the preface to *Alastor.*

quieting realization that he does not trust his intuitions, and no personal reality asserts itself in his dreams. *Pauline* becomes vague in theme and direction.

Pauline is important in Browning's development; it marks his decision to turn from the subjective method and the style of un-restrained confession. "The introspection breeds only a deep despair; increasing disillusion overcasts an early hope, until at last the poet is driven to renounce his visions for a selfless view of the outside world": [23]

> No more of the past! I'll look within no more.
> I have too trusted my own lawless wants,
> Too trusted my vain self, vague intuition –
> Draining soul's wine alone in the still night.   (937-940)

Browning was henceforth to employ a rigid objectivity of manner and matter as his central aesthetic standard. Shelley had not found such an objectivity necessary; his adherence to the principle of liberty, whatever vagueness and other faults it may have occasioned in his poetry, had given him range in subject matter and imagination.

The influence of *Alastor,* evident in the case of *Pauline,* is not absent from *Paracelsus*[24] (begun only eighteen months after the publication of *Pauline*). Shelley, in his preface to *Alastor* writes of "one who drinks deep of the fountain of knowledge and is still insatiate", of one who suddenly awakens to the necessity of Love, the ideal of which he seeks in vain before descending "into an untimely grave". Closing his preface, he very plainly points the moral that those "who keep aloof from sympathies with their kind, rejoicing neither in human joy nor mourning with human grief; these and such as they have their appointed curse. . . .

---

[23] Jerome Buckley, *The Victorian Temper* (Cambridge, Harvard Univ. Press, 1951), p. 22.
[24] W. Hall Griffin and Harry Christopher Minchin, *The Life of Robert Browning*, 2nd. ed. (London, 1911), pp. 66-69. Griffin and Minchin, point out borrowings of words and images from both *Alastor* and *Prometheus Unbound* which helped to alter the poetical Paracelsus considerably from his historical model. See also Douglas Bush, *Mythology and the Romantic Tradition in English Poetry* (Cambridge, Harvard Univ. Press, 1937), p. 363.

Those who love not their fellow-beings live unfruitful lives".
Festus, in Browning's poem employs very similar language:

> How can that course be safe which from the first
> Produces carelessness to human love?   (I, 619-620)

Paracelsus, the hero, a pursuer of knowledge, evidences Browning's inability to bypass the Shelleyan idea of mankind's continual straining for liberty and progress. But the poet has by this time accepted certain limitations as necessary. Paracelsus says:

> 'Tis in the advance of individual minds
> That the slow crowd should ground their expectation
> Eventually to follow . . . .
>   But, alas!
> My followers . . .
> So clumsily wield the weapons I supply
> And they extol, that I begin to doubt . . .
>   If error will not fall
> Sooner before the old awkward batterings
> Than my more subtle warfare, not half learned.
>   (III, 871-899)

At the end of this poem there is the expressed hope that at some future time Paracelsus's advanced ideals, which, together with those of the poet Aprile, represent Shelleyan idealism as Browning saw it, will become perceptible to men – the implication being that a Browning could then be promulgator of these ideals.

> As yet men cannot do without contempt;
> 'T is for their good, and therefore fit awhile
> That they reject the weak, and scorn the false,
> Rather than praise the strong and true, in me:
> But after, they will know me.   (V, 895-899)

Browning's Paracelsus, an ambitious scientist who has begun with the ideal of discovering some universal principle which will serve as the key to all problems, gives up human contacts and devotes himself to communion with nature. Scorning common aims and limited intellectual processes, he expects a sudden revelation of life's ultimate secret. His friend Festus vainly argues with him, and Paracelsus, through persistence, gains outward success and fame. He, however, realizes his great deficiencies and becomes contemptuous of the public which lauds him. The Shelleyan, idealistic poet Aprile now appears.

Aprile, who lives for love as Paracelsus for knowledge, is not to be identified with Shelley, but he has unmistakable Shelleyan traits, and the dreamy pageant of his imaginary creations might stand for a summary review of Shelley's work. Had Shelley lived, he might have come nearer than any one else to fulfilling the rounded and complete ideal of which Paracelsus and Aprile were dissevered halves: the greater part of his actual achievement belonged, Browning evidently thought, to the category of those dazzling but imperfectly objective visions which he ascribes to his Aprile. But Shelley – the poet of *Alastor*, the passionate 'lover of Love', was yet the fittest embodiment of that other finer spiritual energy which Paracelsus in his Faustian passion for knowledge had ruthlessly put from him. . . . This divining and glorifying power it is that Browning ascribes to Love; the lack of it is in his conception the tragic flaw which brings to the ground the superbly gifted genius of Paracelsus.[25]

Aprile is driven by a sincere but diffuse love for mankind and has an oppressing sense of guilt for having failed in a great opportunity for leadership. An accusing voice haunts him:

> Must one more recreant to his race
> Die with unexerted powers,
> And join us, leaving as he found
> The world, he was to loosen, bound?   (II, 319-322)

Professor Raymond discusses the Shelleyan influence on Browning's creation of Aprile:

The very creation of Aprile is undoubtedly to be traced to the influence of the personality and writings of Shelley upon Browning. Just to what extent the latter was indebted to certain elements in *Prometheus Unbound, Alastor,* and *Adonais,* for the suggestion of the character of Aprile, must be a matter of conjecture. But it seems unmistakable that he had Shelley vividly in mind in his portraiture of the spiritually impassioned seeker after absolute beauty, "who would love infinitely and be loved". The limitless aim, the eager craving after emotional experience, the exquisite sensitiveness, the single-hearted impulsiveness of Shelley, are reflected in Aprile. . . . The genesis of Aprile is . . . . one form of that ideal of romantic love,

[25]   C. H. Herford, *Robert Browning* (New York, 1905), pp. 21-22.

for the notion of which Browning is primarily indebted to Shelley and to Shelley's spiritual master, Plato.[26]

Aprile, who dominates the second canto, is, nevertheless, the first of Browning's "lost leaders". He represents the over-sensitive natures that abandon productive effort to content themselves with a visionary, sensual lethargy – aesthetes who deny others "one ray" of their "so hoarded luxury of light". Although Aprile has been ambitious to interpret for his fellow-men all that is lovely in the universe, he has rejected the necessary methods.[27] Not having Festus's humble regard for humanity, he does not love realistically. He has grown

mad to grasp
At once the prize long patient toil should claim.

(II, 493-494)

This unwillingness to submit himself to the conditions life imposes, or to use the necessarily imperfect circumstances of his temporal station to work out his destiny, Aprile comes to recognize, is responsible for his downfall:

> Knowing ourselves, our world, our task so great,
> Our time so brief, 't is clear if we refuse
> The means so limited, the tools so rude
> To execute our purpose, life will fleet,
> And we shall fade, and leave our task undone.
>
> (II, 497-501)

It is evident that, like Paracelsus, Aprile fails, not because he lacks knowledge, but because he has disdained the finite conditions of life.[28]

Impatience was Aprile's flaw; because of the vastness of his vision, he was unable to single out an isolated, temporal theme and give it adequate expression. Aprile's death in bitter disap-

---

[26] Raymond, p. 452. See also p. 453 and note for a comparison of Browning's concept of love, as expressed in Aprile, with a portion of Shelley's translation of Plato's *Symposium*. Herford (p. 303) discusses the passing on of "Plato's torch" from Dante to Shelley to Browning.

[27] Frederick S. Boas, "Robert Browning's 'Paracelsus', 1835-1935", *Quarterly Review*, CCLXV (October 1935), 291.

[28] Raymond, pp. 456-457.

pointment gives Paracelsus a first insight into his own error; but it takes many years of disillusionment to subdue his egotism. On his death-bed, Paracelsus finally "attains" when he recognizes that his basic errors were the exclusion of human sympathy from his philosophy and his refusal to accept limited progress and limited human goals.

Browning's intention was to point out that Aprile's error is grounded in his failure to grasp the Christian concept of love proclaimed in the final sections of *Pauline*. This intention he made explicit by the lines he added, in one edition of *Paracelsus,* at the close of Aprile's dying speech:

> Man's weakness is his glory – for the strength
> Which raises him to heaven and near God's self
> Came spite of it. God's strength his glory is,
> For thence came with our weakness sympathy,
> Which brought God down to earth, a man like us!
>
> (Part II – omitted in later editions)

Browning later expresses the same view in *A Death in the Desert, Saul,* and *An Epistle of Karshish.* Instead of a romantic passion for an ideal of absolute beauty and perfection, love is here a "divine condescension to human imperfection, and a tender compassion for mortal frailty".[29]

Browning's frustration because of the elusiveness of his youthful ideals, in respect to both realization and expression, is evident not only in *Paracelsus* but also in *Sordello.* Paracelsus is the exalted hero of Browning's "quest of the Humanitarian Grail"; Sordello serves as a "scapegoat who exhibits for his disillusioned creator the folly of any such grandiose hopes. And not alone the folly, but the reasons why the hopes were vain".[30] There appears, then, to be a kind of progression in Browning's three early poems. *Pauline* deals with a self-examination after a major spiritual crisis, *Paracelsus* is a seeking for new stability, and *Sordello* affirms a casting off of recently held beliefs and a determination to make their replacements function in the poet's life and works.

---

[29]   *Ibid.,* pp. 458-459.
[30]   Stewart Walker Holmes, "Browning: Semantic Stutterer", *PMLA,* LX (March 1945), 252-253.

In the opening lines of *Sordello,* Browning returns once more to direct apostrophe to Shelley, this time frankly declaring his uneasiness in the presence of the Shelleyan spirit and his sense of his own poetry's unworthiness in Shelley's eyes:

> Stay – thou, spirit, come not near
> Now – not this time desert thy cloudy place
> To scare me, thus employed, with that pure face!
> I need not fear this audience, I make free
> With them, but then this is no place for thee!
>
> (I, 60-64)

Betty Miller calls this Browning's valedictory address to "his youthful god Shelley", in which he "acknowledged his own descent from grace".[31] The terms "scare", "pure face", and "fear" seem to indicate that Browning does not merely wish to avoid a comparison of poetic craftsmanship; he realizes that in basic philosophy he has departed from Shelley's precepts.

Yet the apostrophe to Shelley is evidence of Browning's continuing high regard for the Romantic poet. Later in the poem there is a description of Browning's final rejection of the humanistic idealism Shelley once had inspired in him and of a decisive turning toward the finite and immediate in human circumstances. The incident[32] is that of young Browning's idly daydreaming as he sits on a ruined palace-step in Venice, wondering which of the winsome Italian maids in the courtyard he should wish to designate the model for Palma, the queen of his poem. A pitiful beggar-maid interrupts his reverie and typifies to him the pressing needs of mankind whose condition appears immeasurably and hopelessly below the ideal which he has sought to bring within man's grasp.

Browning decides; the beggar girl will *replace* Palma as his queen. He finally gives up Palma, who represents for him the Shelleyan ideal, and narrows his loyalties to only the immediate, represented by the beggar-maid. But once having made the transition, he comes to comfortable terms with his constricted range of concern:

---

31 Miller, p. 22.
32 *Sordello,* III, 681-721.

> I love you more, far more
> Than her I looked should foot Life's temple-floor.
> Years ago, leagues at distance, when and where
> A whisper came, "Let others seek! – thy care
> "Is found, thy life's provision; if thy race
> "Should be thy mistress, and into one face
> "The many faces crowd?"   (II, 749-755)

To abandon the lofty ideal of Shelley's "Intellectual Beauty" was a torturous ordeal for Browning; and it is unjust to label him a superficial and callously "professional" optimist.[33] Having chosen a faith to live by, he found that, whatever security it might afford,

> yet God spoke
> Of right-hand, foot and eye – selects our yoke,
> Sordello, as your poetship may find!   (III, 781-783)

However, Browning immediately took a defensive attitude concerning the derelict beggar maid's condition. The humanitarianism which Shelley had imparted to him "years ago and leagues at a distance" had previously become in him a desire

> that the whole race
> Might add the spirit's to the body's grace,
> And all be dizened out as chiefs and bards.   (III, 719-721)

Pauline had recorded his disillusionment in that dream. Now his request was simply that all might have youth, strength, and health. "But the beggar maid? Forget her. Acknowledge that such as she exist, but shrug the shoulders and say, 'C'est la vie!' Don't dream of impossibilities – do something!" [34]

> As good you sought
> To spare me the Piazza's slippery stone
> Or keep me to the unchoked canals alone,
> As hinder Life the evil with the good
> Which make up Living, rightly understood.
> Only, do finish something!   (III, 726-731)

Here is the stamp of Dr. Arnold and of Carlyle, and it clearly

---

[33] Stewart Walker Holmes, "Browning's *Sordello* and Jung: Browning's *Sordello* in the Light of Jung's Theory of Types", *PMLA*, LVI (September 1941), 783.
[34] *Ibid.*, p. 782.

puts Browning in the ranks of "Victorian" thinkers. The adoption of such temporally-oriented social views, corollaries of his return to an other-wordly religious position, constitutes the essence of Browning's defection from Shelley's cause.

Turning now to the character of Sordello, we find another of Browning's self-centered, dreamy intellectuals, the product of a lonely childhood in which the romances he has read have been substituted for reality. Having, *Alastor*-like, rejected all human considerations, he endeavors to create poetry by sheer imagination, or "Will", rather than from experience or sympathy. His poems, consequently, abound in personified abstractions:

> Virtue took form, nor vice refused a shape;
> Here heaven opened, there was hell agape,
> As Saint this simpered past in sanctity,
> Sinner the other flared portentous by
> A greedy people.   (II, 527-531)

Sordello, failing as a poet, attempts public affairs and involves himself in the struggle between the Guelphs and Ghibellines. Though by blood a Ghibelline, he finds the Guelph cause to be that of the people and becomes a regenerator of the proletariate. But as he sees more and more of the degradation and poverty of the masses, he is again disillusioned, and his utopia fades. He concludes that, in the face of the overwhelming odds, he is powerless to rescue these miserable beings. Then comes the revelation:

> God has conceded two sights to a man –
> One, of men's whole work, time's completed plan,
> The other, of the minute's work, man's first
> Step to the plan's completeness: what's dispersed
> Save hope of that supreme step which, descried
> Earliest, was meant still to remain untried
> Only to give you heart to take your own
> Step, and there stay, leaving the rest alone?   (V, 85-92)

Shelley does not make the distinction of the "two sights" or double vision; he insists that man's efforts contribute toward his ultimate potential and that its attainment is man's responsibility, not a gift of God.

Sordello, however, with fresh vigor, based on his new concept of man's finite duty, goes forth to bring about a preliminary union between the two factions. He, as poet, is "earth's essential king", merging himself with the masses and intending to ameliorate their temporal condition. Unexpectedly, the badge of supreme authority is conferred upon him; but in accepting it he would need to compromise with existing atrocities. The conflict between his innate egotism and his inspiring ideal of sympathetic abnegation is too great for him and he dies. He makes a final gesture, spurning the symbol of power, thus indicating that he remains committed to human sympathy.

An inner voice has expressed to Sordello the basis for his final choice:

> All is changed the moment you descry
> Mankind as half yourself, – then, fancy's trade
> Ends once and always: how may half evade
> The other half? men are found half of you.
> Out of a thousand helps, just one or two
> Can be accomplished presently: but flinch
> From these . . .
>   and make proof
> Of fancy . . .
> See if, for that, your other half will stop
> A tear, begin a smile!   (V, 250-258, 260-261)

Browning now thinks of universal humantarian considerations as nothing but "fancy". For him a life's philosophy has become a matter of focus; look at mankind's deplorable state, and you despair of human idealism. He can not muster Shelley's persistent determination to see the actual as eventually approaching and even achieving the ideal. Browning's ultimate mainstay is a belief in divine intervention on behalf of man's frailty–in other words, a depreciation of temporal life in view of the life to come. Yet, often though he reiterates this concept, he can not rid himself of a certain realization that Shelley's daring views hold for his own poetic bent a challenge which he has not accepted. In frequently emphasizing that man must aspire, Browning follows Shelley; in placing a limit on man's aspiration, he deviates from him.

The contest between the two habitual attitudes prominent in

Browning is especially at a pivotal stage in the early poems – in *Pauline, Paracelsus*, and *Sordello*. In all three poems the heroes, characterized by a restless and self-conscious hunger for perfection, are typically romantic. They are impelled by their indomitable aspiration to press on beyond finite limits. As incarnations of romanticism – motivated by lofty idealism and clear vision of absolute spiritual values – they illustrate an elemental aspect of Browning's own genius.[35] And Shelley, as Browning understood him, had most clearly represented the romantic ideal. But the heroes in the three poems must all abandon humanitarian idealism before they can make any achievement or contribution.

Browning participated in the common error of reading into Shelley's idealism an insistence upon bringing humanity to the heights at one mighty bound. Had Shelley's *Philosophical View of Reform* been printed for Browning to read, it might have affected the emphasis and outcome of *Sordello* and numerous subsequent poems of Browning.

AFTER SORDELLO

Professor Pottle has judged that, "after *Sordello,* Browning apparently passed completely out of the Shelleyan manner. No two poets could be more distinct in their style, their thought, their philosophy. Shelley was the most subjective of the English poets; Browning became one of the most objective".[36] The correctness of this view, insofar as it relates to subjectivity and objectivity, is scarcely to be questioned. Browning's transition, however, was not sudden, nor did his increasing deviation from Shelley's style, thought, and philosophy ever fully negate the Shelleyan appeal.

Their respective masterpieces, while illustrating the differences between the two poets, also give evidence that Shelley's works continued to set a standard for Browning. Despite his *Cenci* disclaimer of any attempt to press "into the company of his betters" (meaning Shelley), Browning appears to have seen in *The*

[35] Raymond, pp. 450-451.
[36] Pottle, p. 32.

Ring and the Book his own *Cenci*.[37] But had the Franceschini murder story fallen into Shelley's hands, it would certainly have received a treatment varying in important respects from Browning's version. It is not difficult to imagine how Shelley would have dealt with the Aretine Archbishop, the Convent of Convertities, and Guido's two contemptible brothers – all corrupt functionaries of the Church. They give evidence of the Church as a destructive rather than a light-giving agency, and Browning's Pope views them with "terror". Shelley's "old Godwinian virus" woud have found in them ready material for the case against institutions and for urging emancipated souls to rise up and assert their freedom from restraint.[38] It is apparent that Browning's retained affinity for Shelley is overshadowed by his deviation from Shelleyan ideas.

In 1849, shortly after Sarah Anna Browning's death, Elizabeth persuaded Robert to accompany her on a search for new lodgings for the summer. Unwise though it may now seem, the course of their search led them to Lerici, where on the coast stood Casa Magni, the "white house, with arches", which had been Shelley's last home. In this very location Shelley had written, a week before his death: "Let us see the truth, whatever that may be. The destiny of man can scarcely be so degraded, that he was born only to die – and if such should be the case, delusions, especially the gross and preposterous ones of the existing religions, can scarcely be supposed to exalt it." [39] An entire summer spent amid

[37] Miller, p. 233. Mrs. Miller, on pages 231-232, has presented an impressive array of similarities between Shelley's *Cenci* and Browning's *The Ring and the Book*. And E. D. H. Johnson, in the *Alien Vision of Victorian Poetry* (Princeton, Princeton Univ. Press, 1952), pp. 92-95, points out how Browning's "innocent" characters foster an individualistic reaction against social convention – a reaction not unlike that of Shelley.

[38] Herford, pp. 180-181. Evidences of Browning's continuing interest in Shelley are the various corrections he made in the latter's minor poetry. The corrections relate to Shelley's *Indian Serenade* and *Similes* and to a note on *The Tower of Famine*. See Browning, *Letters*, pp. 49, 181-182, and Miller, pp. 139-140.

[39] To Horace Smith, 29 June 1822. See Shelley, *Works*, X, 410. The letter was published in 1840. Betty Miller, p. 150, n. 1, emphasizes the strong impression which this declaration must have made upon Browning: "Every word that Shelley wrote impressed itself clearly upon Browning's

Lerici's unavoidable reminders of a man who had held and expressed such views, would have been unbearable for Browning
in the disconsolate condition in which his mother's death had
left him. Elizabeth, too, found disagreeable associations there,
and the Brownings were readily agreed to look elsewhere for the
summer's lodging.[40]

Browning sought to make reparation after his mother's death
by upholding the very ideas he had once, on rational grounds,
rejected. He made belated amends in *Christmas Eve and Easter
Day* (1850) for the antagonistic spirit which had drawn him away
from the Independent chapel of his boyhood. By frequenting a
little French Independent church, he dutifully put into practice
the conclusion reached in the poem's *Christmas Eve* portion. And
in his essay on Shelley written in 1851 he went so far as to draw
that poet into an affinity with the religion which he himself now
professed.[41] That Shelley never, to the day of his death, changed
his views of "the existing religion", and that he died not as an
adolescent but as a man of nearly thirty, must have been consciously
ignored by Browning when he maintained that Shelley's ideas
were evidence of "passionate, impatient struggles of a boy towards distant truth and love . . . . Crude convictions of boyhood,
conveyed in imperfect and inapt forms of speech, – for such
things all boys have been pardoned." [42]

Nor is Browning content with glossing over Shelley's past
offences. In a passage whose tenet is that, "in religion, one
earnest and unextorted assertion of belief should outweigh, as a
matter of testimony, many assertions of unbelief", he boldly
states, "I shall say what I think, – had Shelley lived he would
have finally ranged himself with the Christians." [43] This effort to
mold Shelley to fit the concepts of Sarah Anna Browning is an

---

mind. When Buxton Forman's Library edition appeared, he was able to
detect, at a glance, a minute error in the poem *Similes*, printed over forty
years previously, 'in the 'Athenaeum' where I read it – to remember it
all my life'."

[40]   Miller, pp. 150-151.
[41]   *Ibid.*, pp. 162-163.
[42]   *An Essay on Percy Bysshe Shelley*, p. 20.
[43]   *Ibid.*, pp. 25, 23.

incongruous and disconcerting element in Browning's otherwise impressive poetic career. Thomas Hardy wrote to Edmund Gosse, "The longer I live, the more does B[rowning]'s character seem the literary puzzle of the 19th century. How could smug Christian optimism worthy of a dissenting grocer find a place inside a man who was so vast a seer and feeler when on neutral ground?" [44] Yet Browning indicates in his essay that he somehow continued to find in Shelley the unifier, insofar as was possible, of the contending extremes in his philosophy.

I pass at once . . . from Shelley's minor excellencies to his noblest and predominating characteristic.

This I call his simultaneous perception of Power and Love in the absolute, and of Beauty and Good in the concrete, while he throws, from his poet's station between both, swifter, subtler, and more numerous films for the connexion of each with each, than have been thrown by any modern artificer of whom I have knowledge; proving how, as he says,

"The spirit of the worm within the sod,
In love and worship blends itself with God." [45]

In this attitude on Browning's part, his biographer C. H. Herford sees the basis for concluding that Browning achieved a synthesis with Shelley's doctrine.

"The revelation of God in Christ" was for him [Browning] the consummate example of that union of divine love with the world – "through all the web of Being blindly wove" – which Shelley had contemplated in the radiant glow of his poetry; accepted by the reason, as he wrote a few years later, it solved "all problems in the earth and out of it". . . . It is clear that for Browning himself the essence of Christianity lay at this time in something not very remote from what he revered as the essence of Shelleyism – a corollary, as it were, ultimately implicit in his thought.[46]

Herford's view gains support from Browning's statement in the essay:

---

[44] 3 March 1899, Brit. Mus. Ashley 282. Extract quoted by Wilfred George Partington, *Thomas J. Wise in the Original Cloth* (London, 1947), p. 216.
[45] *An Essay on Percy Bysshe Shelley*, pp. 26-27.
[46] Herford, pp. 110-111.

As I call Shelley a moral man, because what he acted corresponded to what he knew, so I call him a man of religious mind, because every audacious negative cast up by him against the Divine, was interpenetrated with a mood of reverence and adoration, – and because I find him everywhere taking for granted some of the capital dogmas of Christianity, while most vehemently denying their historical basement.[47]

Yet, the biographer's evaluation seems to over-simplify Browning's concept of what Shelley stood for. The Victorian poet's orthodox pronouncements invariably get in the way of what might otherwise have been a religio-social philosophy much more closely related to Shelley's. Browning himself became too deeply concerned with Christianity's "historical basement" to continue grounding his philosophy solely on what he termed the "capital dogmas" which Shelley took for granted.

At the time he wrote the essay, as well as four years later when he composed *Memorabilia,* Browning yet retained an homage for his early idol. He must, therefore, have experienced real grief when in 1858 he was informed, by means of letters shown him by the bookseller Thomas Hookham, of Shelley's conduct toward Harriet.[48] Griffin and Minchin, early biographers of Browning, say of the letters:

These, in particular the one which she [Harriet] wrote in a state of bewilderment, inquiring where her husband might be, satisfied him that the version of the affair hitherto accepted was no longer tenable. It was apparent that husband and wife had not parted by mutual consent, but that he had deserted her. This discovery caused Browning deep regret. He considered Shelley to have been, at that period of his life, "half crazy and wholly inexcusable". He could not regard him or, by consequence, his poetry, in the same light as formerly.

[47]   Browning, *An Essay on Percy Bysshe Shelley,* p. 24.
[48]   Griffin and Minchin, p. 185. Mrs. Miller, p. 158, contends, on the basis of a comment in William Rossetti's Diary, that Browning saw the letters as early as 1851, when he was preparing the essay on Shelley. The tone and content of the essay, however, in view of Browning's belief that poet and man must be considered together, make it appear that Rossetti was mistaken. See especially Browning, *An Essay on Percy Bysshe Shelley,* p. 21. See also W. C. DeVane, *A Browning Handbook,* 2nd ed. (New York, 1955), p. 244, n. 74, for a recent conclusion that Browning probably did not see Hookham's material before 1858.

Yet Lucifer, Son of the Morning, lost not all his brightness in his fall. For Browning, Shelley's proud pre-eminence was gone; but he loved his poetry, and loved to read it aloud, to the end of his days.[49]

And William G. Kingsland, himself apparently rather incensed over Shelley's conduct in the case, commented shortly after Browning's death:

Robert Browning, – influenced as he undoubtedly was by the writings of this poet, – would have no white-washing of Shelley at the expense of Harriet. Some three years since I was writing him in a similar strain to the above [that Shelley's behavior toward Harriet was indefensible], and he replied: "I quite agree with you in your estimate of Shelley's life and character." [50]

It appears that the Harriet Shelley letters deprived Browning of the second of three props supporting his devotion to Shelley. Already having given up his faith in Shelley's social and religious convictions, Browning now could no longer maintain a belief that the Romantic poet's life, at least, was consistent with what he professed. Considering this situation, we must admire Robert Browning for retaining some devotion to Shelley, slight and dwindling though it was, on the basis of the one prop left to him – the latter's poetic genius. Even this support, however, eventually became very unstable.

In January 1870, Browning, who had aided William Rossetti in his research, wrote: "I have just been reading Shelley's life, as Rossetti tells it – and when I think how utterly different was the fancy I had of him forty years ago from the facts as they front

---

[49]   Griffin and Minchin, pp. 185-186. For evidence of Browning's attitude toward Shelley, as expressed in his letters after 1855, see Browning, *Letters*, pp. 48-49, 177-178, 181-182, 200, 222-223, 224, 242-243, 255. It is in his 29 September 1883 letter to F. J. Furnivall (p. 223) that Browning declares Shelley to have been "half crazy". See also Swinburne's 24 June 1896 letter to Rossetti (p. 371, note). Browning's strong opinion against Shelley's treatment of Harriet is clearly outlined here. Note Swinburne's comment: "Now of course Browning loves Shelley even as much as you and I do (he said so in concluding) but these, he is certain, are the facts of the case. I asked him to communicate them to you directly, but in case he does not I write this."

[50]   William G. Kingsland, "London Literaria", *Poet-Lore*, III (1891), 154-155.

one to-day, I can only avoid despising myself by remembering that I judged in pure ignorance and according to the testimony of untruthful friends." [51] Being asked in his seventy-fourth year, long after his introduction to the Harriet letters, to become President of the Shelley Society, he firmly declined. "For myself", he wrote to Dr. Furnivall, "I painfully contrast my notions of Shelley the *man* and Shelley, well, even the *poet,* with what they were sixty years ago, when I only had his works, for a certainty, and took his character on trust." [52] There is an incongruity in Browning's denunciation of Shelley on the plea of the latter's inhumanity as evidenced in the one act of deserting Harriet. The sympathetic Shelley, who all his life was "as a nerve o'er which do creep the else unfelt oppressions of this earth", contrasts sharply with the later Browning who a year before declining the presidency of the Shelley Society had published *Ferishtah's Francies,* a group of extremely complacent poems which evade the problem of evil and are cheerfully indifferent to human suffering. Mrs. Miller conjectures that this work "must have carried dismay into the ranks of the Browning Society itself".[53] The following are its most startling lines:

> I know my own appointed patch i' the world,
> What pleasures me or pains there: all outside –
> How he, she, or it, and even thou, Son, live,
> Are pleased or pained, is past conjecture . . .
>   There's the first and last
> Of my philosophy! Black blurs thy white?
> Not mine!
>   ("A Bean-Stripe: Also, Apple-Eating", 165-173)

"No heart, this", declares Mrs. Miller, "that the 'stranger's tear

[51] To Miss Isabella Blagden. See Browning, *Letters,* p. 134.
[52] 8 December 1885. See *Letters,* pp. 242-243. Kingsland commented, "Browning had been very warmly requested to become president of the Shelley Society at the time of its formation. There can be little doubt he would have accepted this office, but the 'Harriet question' stood in the way. Browning was honest to the core, and he considered that by becoming president of such a society he would be endorsing all Shelley's actions; therefore he at once refused the request on the ground that 'he could not uphold Shelley with regard to his treatment of his first wife'. Surely a 'last word' this." See *Poet-Lore,* III (1891), 155.
[53] Miller, p. 270.

might wear': much less, the utterance of one who, like the 'wholly inexcusable' Shelley,

> loved and pitied all things and could moan
> For woes which others hear not." [54]

Browning had written in 1855: "But in this respect was the experience of Shelley peculiarly unfortunate – that the disbelief in him as a man, even preceded the disbelief in him as a writer; the misconstruction of his moral nature preparing the way for the misappreciation of his intellectual labours." [55] His own experience with Shelley, as we have seen, had been the reverse of this. Knowing him only as a writer, he had believed implicitly in him as a man. Departing from a faith in Shelley's writings, he had yet loved the man. When, eventually, his faith in the man was shaken by what to him was clear evidence of Shelley's departure from avowed principles, Browning, indeed, had cause to reëvaluate his past loyalties. Perhaps, in the effect which he was able to exert upon Browning, Shelley was unfortunate in that the young Victorian poet did not have a "disbelief in him as a man" to overcome *before* he came to know him as a writer. Browning, with his basically romantic temperament, might then gradually have drawn insights from and gained a rational appreciation of Shelley – in place of going by distinct stages from near idolatry to comparative disillusionment.

Before completing this portion of our study, we need to turn back to trace another important factor in Browning's changing attitude toward Shelley – the influence of Elizabeth Barrett Browning. Elizabeth's marginal comments in her volumes of Shelley's *Essays, Letters from Abroad, Translations and Fragments* indicate that, although Shelley was one of her favorite poets, she strongly disagreed with or would have severely modified the religious views expressed in *A Defence of Poetry* and *Speculations on Morals*.[56] In political as in religious matters, Elizabeth

---

[54] *Ibid.*, p. 270.
[55] Browning, *An Essay on Percy Bysshe Shelley*, p. 19.
[56] James Thorpe, "Elizabeth Barrett's Commentary on Shelley: Some Marginalia", *MLN*, LXVI (November 1951), 455-458.

exercised a manner of supervision over Robert, much like Sarah Anna Browning's silencing of the contentious schoolboy.[57] She evidenced this corrective authority over Robert especially in relation to his essential hatred of tyranny in any form, and he was thus drawn by almost imperceptible degrees even farther from his initial affinity with Shelley.

Elizabeth belittled Robert's antagonism toward the tyrant Louis Napoleon as a "self-willed, pettish way".[58] Here may be a clue to the reason why Browning waited twenty years before he offered the public, in *Prince Hohenstiel-Schwangau*, the characteristically Browningesque apologia for his compromise with and failure to oppose Louis's conquest of Paris in December 1851.[59]

It is of interest to note that on the very night (4 December) when Louis Napoleon's forces were wiping out the last remnants of Republican opposition after the *coup d'état* of two days before, Browning was writing the final paragraphs of his essay on Shelley. Mrs. Miller conjectures:

It was while listening to the sound of Louis Napoleon's cannons, and remembering all the while on which side of the barricades Shelley himself would have been found, that Browning chose openly to recall the "signal service it was the dream of my boyhood to render to his fame and memory". The dream had long since faded, or been suppressed: as had the generous passion with which a Camberwell schoolboy proclaimed himself "Vowed to liberty". And here, in his fortieth year, his hair "already streaked with grey about the temples", the disciple of Shelley sat mute and unprotesting, while in the streets of Paris yet another tyrant silenced in cannon-fire the voice of liberty. Robert Browning, it is true, was not ready, like his wife, to "salve a tyrant o'er". Neither was he, as one of the unacknowledged legislators of the world, prepared to oppose himself to political tyranny.[60]

Elizabeth's admiration for Louis Napoleon was evidenced by her elation over the "grand spectacle" of the *coup d'état* which she

[57] Miller, p. 168.
[58] Letter to Mrs. Jameson, 12 April 1852. See her *Letters*, ed. Frederic G. Kenyon (New York, 1897), II, 67.
[59] Miller, p. 168.
[60] *Ibid.*, pp. 167-168.

and Robert had witnessed. Browning, no doubt, detested his wife's exaltation as strongly as he detested the *coup d'état* itself. Later he must have been yet more pained to hear her describe the republican resistance as "a little popular scum, cleared off at once by the troops", and to find that she accepted, in her "immoral sympathy with power", the censorship of the press as a "necessity of the dictatorship". In one of her letters she wrote of disagreements between Browning and herself on the subject of imperialism, pointing out that Browning hated "some imperial names".[61] Shelley, too, as his very nature reminds us, was a hater of imperialists. "Buonaparte", he wrote in 1812, "is to me a hateful and despicable being . . . . Excepting Lord Castlereagh, you could not have mentioned any character but Buonaparte whom I contemn and abhor more vehemently." [62] Browning's declaration of hatred toward "all Buonapartes, past, present, or to come",[63] is evidence that he always had this one basic characteristic in common with Shelley. Both poets had, in Shelley's words, an "irreconcilable enmity" to all forms of "domestic and political tyranny and imposture".

It is, therefore, all the more regrettable to receive the report of a friend that he heard him, in his later years, "speak slightingly of Shelley" and to learn that he contemptuously declared Shelley "not in his right senses – in the moon".[64] And it is not easy to avoid Mrs. Miller's conclusion that already in some earlier works and especially in *Childe Roland to the Dark Tower Came* (1852) Browning was aware of "the retribution appropriate to his own sin: the corruption and sterility that must claim one who has failed, like many another 'poor traitor' before him, to deliver to mankind the full burden of the message with which he has been entrusted".[65]

---

[61]   To Mrs. Martin, 11 December [1851]. See her *Letters,* II, 37.
[62]   To Thomas Jefferson Hogg, 27 December 1812. See Shelley, *Works,* IX, 37.
[63]   Elizabeth Barrett Browning to Mrs. Jameson, 12 April 1852. See her *Letters,* II, 67.
[64]   Miller, p. 271.
[65]   *Ibid.,* p. 168.

Sixty-one years after Shelley had written, at a lakeside of Montanvert near Mont Blanc, his sublime *Hymn to Intellectual Beauty*, Browning had so far departed from Shelley's emphasis on humanity and its potentialities that he could compose amid those very surroundings the poem, *La Saisiaz,* containing the following lines:

There is no reconciling wisdom with a world distraught,
Goodness with triumphant evil, power with failure in the aim . . .
If you bar me from assuming earth to be a pupil's place,
And life, time – with all their chances, changes – just probation-space.

                                        (266-267, 269-270)

This doctrine of earth's incompleteness as compared to heaven's perfect fulfillment became one of Browning's most frequently propounded emphases. He came to look upon life as a testing period in which variously handicapped individuals strive for the highest possible attainment within their own respective spheres. Universal perfection was to be achieved not by man's efforts but by divine intervention. The realism taken on by his visions of man's highest (though limited) attainments made them appear more substantial than Shelley's prophesies of the ultimate perfection of society. Browning's poetry, therefore, is more deeply involved in finite matters. Because of his exultation (forced though it was) in this word of evil as a "moral gymnasium", Browning, found that he must always be prepared to "bounce up joyously . . . to share immortal life with the Great Lover".[66]

He thought his vision of the infinite carried him, as a modern, beyond the finite rationalism of the Greeks . . . but the fact is that he stopped short of that. . . . In their various ways Keats and Shelley, Arnold and Tennyson, sought for philosophic unity, order, and meaning behind experience and appearances. Browning lustily buffeting the waves of flux, solves all problems by shouting "God! Life! Love!" [67]

Intellectual beauty alone could not, for Browning, as it always could for Shelley, suffice to make life honorable. Browning came, as he proclaims in *La Saisiaz,* to depend upon the rewards in a

---

[66] Bush, p. 359.
[67] *Ibid.,* pp. 384-385.

"second life" as compensation for the disappointments and short-comings he experienced in his earthly lot. In the optimism and morality of his old age, he had become virtually antithetical to the also optimistic and moral young Robert Browning – vegetarian, atheist, and Shelley enthusiast.

Two excerpts from Browning's essay on Shelley are perhaps the best explanation for the Victorian poet's continuing interest and trust in Shelley, long after he had broken with the latter's beliefs. They are:

Whatever Shelley was, he was with an admirable sincerity. It was not always truth that he thought and spoke; but in the purity of truth he spoke and thought always. Everywhere is apparent his belief in the existence of Good, to which Evil is an accident; his faithful holding by what he assumed to be the former, going everywhere in company with the tenderest pity for those acting or suffering on the opposite hypothesis.... And not only do the same affection and yearning after the well-being of his kind, appear in the letters as in the poems, but they express themselves by the same theories and plans, however crude and unsound. There is no reservation of a subtler, less costly, more serviceable remedy for his own ill, than he has proposed for the general one.

and

The key-note of the predominating sentiment of Shelley throughout his whole life – [was] his sympathy with the oppressed.[68]

It is the latter of these which had been the strongest tie with Shelley immediately after Browning's period of great devotion to him. That Browning, in his later years, came to place an increasing emphasis on the defects named in the first excerpt – "not always truth that he thought", "crude", "unsound" – and that he lost faith in Shelley's compensating virtues are the causes of his finally taking a stand so immeasurably removed from that of his early idol. Our conclusion must, however, not be that by relinquishing his Shelleyan ideals Browning forfeited his genius. It seems, rather, a marvel that, despite the tremendous alteration in his philosophy, he attained those heights of genius evidenced in his best poetry.

[68] Browning, *An Essay on Percy Bysshe Shelley*, pp. 21, 22.

III

SHELLEY AND DISRAELI

ATTRACTION TO SHELLEY

Like Browning, though not with equal abandonment, Benjamin Disraeli (1804-1881) experienced an early enthusiasm for Shelley and evidenced a basic affinity with the forces of liberty. These revolutionary tendencies, as Richard Garnett has pointed out, might have taken a free course in Disraeli's career, had he been debarred from practical politics. The necessities of political life and official position, however, suppressed that impulse which might have brought him fame as a keen, relentless assailant of many principles which, in actuality, he defended. Shelley, on his part, had he lived, would very probably have entered Parliament during the Reform Bill period. As parliamentary tactician he would have been no more successful than was Disraeli as poet, but he might have equaled the latter in oratorical prowess. He would have shown Disraeli's indomitable resolution, but without ever allowing it to make of him the conservative it made of Disraeli.[1]

The ideas of aristocracy and institutions were indelibly imprinted on Disraeli's thinking. He had grown up in an atmosphere of revolt, his father having left the Jewish religion, because of a quarrel with officials of his local congregation, in 1813 when Benjamin was nine years old. His own joining of the Anglican Church a few years later had, however, proved a first step to-

[1] Richard Garnett, "Shelley and Lord Beaconsfield", in *Essays of an Ex-Librarian* (London, 1901), p. 103. Garnett's paper was read to the Shelley Society in 1887.

ward conservatism; it had opened the way for him to hold political offices from which, as a Jew, he would in those years have
been barred. In 1832, young Disraeli was twice defeated as a
Radical candidate for a seat in Parliament. Then, with an audacious change of front, he came forward as a Tory, though main-
taining, in his pamphlet *What is He*, published not long afterwards, that it was possible honestly to be both a democrat and
a Tory.[2] This belief was one of his deepest and most lasting
political convictions, and in this respect, he remained a political
free-thinker all his life. But the conservatism which he had
adopted led Disraeli to actions and utterances far removed from
republicanism in any liberal sense. His Crystal Palace speech of
1872 conveniently marks the onset of modern British imperialism. In it Disraeli managed to associate the cause of social reform
with that of empire, and he denounced the Liberals for opposing
both.[3] His promotion in 1876 from the House of Commons to
the House of Lords, with the title Earl of Beaconsfield, is entirely
in accord with his aristocratic ideals.

That Shelley (as well as Byron) should hold a strong attraction
for a young man of Disraeli's capabilities, fluctuating between
the contending forces of conservatism and liberalism, is not surprising. The first noteworthy evidence of this attraction in Disraeli's writings appears in *The Revolutionary Epick* (1834),[4] a
long but fragmentary poem. And the outstanding demonstration
of Shelley's impact is the novel *Venetia* (1837), whose main
character, Marmion Herbert, is modeled primarily after Shelley
— numerous important Byronic traits also being clearly evident.
These two works constitute almost all the evidence we have of

[2] William Flaville Monypenny and George Earle Buckel, *The Life of
Benjamin Disraeli, Earl of Beaconsfield*, rev. ed. (London, 1929), I, 225-
231.
[3] See a discussion of the speech and excerpts from it in Monypenny and
Buckel, II, 533-536.
[4] See Disraeli's 1864 edition of *The Revolutionary Epick*. The poem
was never completed. In 1837, three years after the original publication,
and the same year in which *Venetia* appeared, Disraeli revised it but did
not republish it until 1864. For a discussion of Disraeli's idealization of
himself in the early 1830's as his country's potential liberator, see B. R.
Jerman, *The Young Disraeli* (Princeton, Univ. Press, 1960), pp. 136-139.

Shelley's direct influence on Disraeli's writings; and they form the basis for the discussion in the present chapter, in which I contend that Disraeli uses Shelley in a somewhat deceptive manner – not only in misrepresenting him to the public but also in furthering conservative thinking by an implied depreciation of the principles Shelley held most dear. Before studying the works themselves, however, we need to consider the sources of Disraeli's knowledge concerning Shelley.

As collector of information about Shelley's life and character, Disraeli was most fortunate in his friends and associates. He made the acquaintance of Trelawny the same year in which he began *Venetia*, and from this source, no doubt, came many of the personal touches in the character of Marmion Herbert.[5] Garnett says that he himself once met Trelawny and became convinced that the many anecdotes told by this man, who knew both Byron and Shelley equally well, were trustworthy, at least insofar as they concerned Shelley. Nothing had ever happened between him and Shelley to cloud his judgment of the poet, and his views of the feeling Shelley had towards Byron may well be taken as correct. That Disraeli came to know Trelawny and that he carried on a correspondence with him in 1836 – the time of the writing of *Venetia* – was undoubtedly of major importance to the novel.[6]

Another very likely source of information was Giovanni Battista Falcieri, who had once been Byron's personal servant. Shelley, in a letter to Mary, written from Ravenna on 10 August 1821, tells of his own contact with this Italian: "*Tita* [the] Venetian is here, and operates as my valet; a fine fellow, with a prodigious black beard, who has stabbed two or three people, and is the most good-natured looking fellow I ever saw." [7] Tita eventually came into the service of the elder Disraeli. Having been with Shelley for some time at Lerici, he is recorded to have known numerous anecdotes of him. Certainly, Disraeli would not have neglected Tita as a source of information for *Venetia*.

[5] Monypenny and Buckle, I, 366.
[6] Garnett, pp. 115-116.
[7] See *Works*, X, 305. For other references to Tita see pp. 385, 387, and 390 of the same volume.

Lytton Bulwer, as will be noted later, was also a likely source for the literary evaluation of Shelley. He was intimately connected with Disraeli for some time after the latter returned from his tour of the East in 1831. Though Bulwer's estimate of Shelley's poetry was not high, he had published, in the *New Monthly*, Hogg's reminiscences and was a friend of Mrs. Shelley.[8] He, no doubt, stimulated Disraeli's already-growing interest in Shelley.

Garnett concludes that, "looking at the character apart from the situation, we find that Herbert is drawn in conformity with the most orthodox Shelleyan tradition, precisely as Mrs. Shelley and Trelawny and Hogg and Medwin have agreed to represent the poet".[9] He goes on to say that Disraeli has delineated Shelley with substantial accuracy and has followed so closely the development of the poet's mind and the history of his writings that the pains taken to master the available biographical material are clearly evident. Disraeli's biographers, however, find that in one respect the portrait of Herbert is hardly faithful to its model: "It ignores too much perhaps the element in Shelley's character which made him describe himself as 'tameless and swift and proud'; but Herbert, it may be urged, is an older man than Shelley, and allowance must be made for the mellowing effect of age." [10] What the biographers do not mention is the possibility that Disraeli may have used the advanced age of the fictional poet as a device to propagate his own concerns and attitudes, many of which he found lacking in the historical Shelley.

In no other novel does Disraeli use Shelley's character and ideas as extensively as in *Venetia*. Garnett points out that Theodora of Disraeli's *Lothair,* in representing the author's highest conception of womanhood, has all the traits which Shelley valued most highly in women and is, in effect, a more mature Cythna than Shelley's.[11] In other Disraeli novels, expecially in *Sybil*,

---

8   Garnett, pp. 105-106.
9   *Ibid.*, pp. 107-108. Disraeli also sought the advice of Lady Blessington, who may have given him useful information regarding the Shelley-Byron relationship. See Jerman, p. 283.
10   Monypenny and Buckle, I, 367.
11   Garnett, pp. 103-104.

Shelleyan traits may be detected in various characters who concern themselves with social betterment. But *Venetia* is the novel in which Disraeli's thinking about Shelley and the ideas he derived from him are most clearly and adequately presented.

SHELLEY AND 'THE REVOLUTIONARY EPICK'

The impact of Shelley, however, is strong and unmistakable in *The Revolutionary Epick*, one of Disraeli's major poetic efforts. The inspiration derived from Shelley's true revolutionary epic, *The Revolt of Islam*, is unmistakable. A major characterization which proclaims the poem's obligation to *Prometheus Unbound* is Demogorgon, whom Disraeli presents as a Shelleyan rather than as a Miltonic character. Milton had represented Demogorgon as nothing more than an old anarch; Shelley had advanced him to the rank of a deity. He designated him, in fact, as the ultimate ground of divine existence.[12] Having early been a devoted student of Shelley, Disraeli patterns his poem after Shelley's in matter, machinery, and sentiment. But, unfortunately, the manner is not that of Shelley in his most inspired moments.

In the first two books of *The Revolutionary Epick* there are, in addition to Domogorgon, the rival genii Magros and Lyridon with a confusing assemblage of subordinate agents – all Shelleyan impersonations, but not comparable in quality to the impersonations in *Prometheus Unbound* or *Adonais*. As for content and implication, "Disraeli was able to remain at ease with his revolutionary theme through the space of a book or more, but he could not long have pursued it without acute spiritual discomfort".[13] Yet, the affinity of Disraeli's thought with that of Shelley, at least to a certain point, is further attested by a perfect analogy in the former's poem to Shelley's unfinished Prologue to *Hellas,* which Disraeli cannot have seen.[14] The incident is that in which Magros and Lyridon – the contending genii of Faith and

---

[12]   *Ibid.,* p. 118.
[13]   Monypenny and Buckle, I, 248-249.
[14]   See Garnett, pp. 118-119.

Freedom, certainly derived from the eagle-serpent struggle in *The Revolt of Islam* – plead their cause, rhetorically but not very poetically, before Demogorgon's throne. In Shelley's Prologue to *Hellas*, Christ and Mahomet play corresponding roles as advocates.

The Revolutionary Epick, despite Disraeli's obvious weakness in poetic ability and despite his attempting a task which would have been difficult even for Shelley, is given a freedom and largeness of treatment which save it from contempt. Disraeli, at a time when Shelley's imitators were generally copying only his style, chose in *The Revolutionary Epick* rather to neglect the style (his diction and versification being more akin to Milton's) to concentrate on the ideas. Although there are not many close verbal parallels, the poem gives evidence, in particular passages, that Shelley's work was in Disraeli's mind as he wrote. Section 21 of Book I clearly suggests a dependence upon Shelley's description of the Coliseum, which had been included in Medwin's *Shelley Papers*.[15] It may be of some value to compare the content of several passages from Disraeli's poem with thoughts expressed in Shelley's poetry.

Even in the first part of *The Revolutionary Epick*, where Magros pleads the cause of established institutions before Demogorgon's throne, the tone of the poetry is much like that of Shelley's works. As might be expected, the speech of the revolutionary Lyridon in part two is still more Shelleyan. It is surprising that Garnett, who compares some lines from the two respective poems of Shelley and Disraeli, has overlooked the following parallelisms. Echoing the declaration by Shelley's Spirit of the Hour that man, after the great transformation, remains "the king Over himself" (*P.U.*, III. 196-197), Lyridon says, "Behold man now Lord of himself" (*Rev. Ep.*, II. xxxv). The same speech in *Prometheus Unbound* contains the lines,

> None fawned, none trampled; . . .
> None frowned, none trembled,   (133, 137)

[15] *Ibid.*, pp. 120-121. For Shelley's description of the Coliseum see his *Works*, VI, 299-306. See also Thomas Medwin, *The Shelley Papers* (London, 1833), pp. 127-135.

from which Disraeli has borrowed freely for Lyridon's observation:

> None tremble where none frown; and none will fawn
> Where none can trample.   (II.xxxv)

Although there are numerous other instances of Shelleyan diction in *The Revolutionary Epick*,[16] the ideational influences of the Romantic poet are the more notable. The affinity throughout the poem is one of sentiment rather than of diction and is difficult to exhibit by any method other than a reading of both poets. The most Shelley-like aspect of the Lyridon section, for instance, is its aura of *Queen Mab*. Disraeli sensed Shelley's determination to set Liberty above all else and, as a young writer, responded by making the same emphasis in his poem.

THE PLOT OF 'VENETIA'

Garnett observes that the practical appreciation of Shelley, manifested in *The Revolutionary Epick* two years before *Venetia* was begun, gives us a basis for evaluating as genuine and sincere the interest which prompted Disraeli to introduce Shelley into the novel.[17] This observation, however, fails to identify the specific item of literature which was almost certainly the instigation and nucleus of the novel. The plot of *Venetia*, though set in the late eighteenth century, is based partly on the life of Byron as well as on that of Shelley. The suggestion for such a combination is

---

[16] Garnett, p. 123, finds *Alastor* to have been an influence on Disraeli's diction. On p. 124 he explains that *Alastor* was a scarce poem at the time and that Disraeli probably read it in the Galignani edition.

One verbal similarity which Garnett does not mention, but which is unmistakable, is the frequent use, by both writers, of the descriptive term "pale" in reference to eyes. Examples from Shelley are: "Your eyes look pale" (*Cenci*, V.iii.121); "his pale eyes ran with tears" (*Rosal.*, 250); "In those eyes grows pale with pleasure" (*Sophia*, III.2); and "On my lips and eyelids pale" (*Ind. Ser.*, III.4). Disraeli's *Revolutionary Epick* includes: "His idle sword each pale-eyed monarch seized" (I.xii); "That even eyes, to thrones angelic used, / Dropped their pale orbs" (I.xlvi); and "back To pale-eyed Paris (III.xvii).

[17] Garnett, p. 124.

clearly discernible throughout Thomas Medwin's memoir of Shelley, which appeared first in *The Athenaem* (1832) and the following year in *The Shelley Papers*, edited by Medwin. That Disraeli used Medwin's collection of Shelley's writings as a source will be proven by excerpts from it later in this chapter; that he got the very idea of the novel from Medwin's accompanying memoir seems highly probable. As Newman Ivey White points out, Trelawny also "was constantly drawing a comparison between Shelley and Byron, always to Shelley's advantage".[18] It is, of course, impossible to determine whether or not Trelawny mentioned the idea of the novel to Disraeli. If he did, he undoubtedly referred him to Medwin's memoir for elemental features of the plot.

Medwin, in the memoir, presents not only a picture of Shelley but also a comparative study of Byron. Almost invariably, in scenes from Shelley's life or in sketches of his character, Medwin makes comparisons with similar or (more frequently) contrasting aspects of Byron. The respective characterizations of Shelley and Byron are in thorough agreement with Disraeli's casting of Shelley in the role of the older man, Byron functioning as his youthful and less intellectual understudy. Several short excerpts will suffice to present Medwin's view of the two poets.

Having demonstrated Shelley's philosophic concerns by quoting from his essay *On Life*, Medwin comments, "Though congenial in their pursuits, there was little congeniality of sentiment between Shelley and Byron on these subjects. Byron was doubtless a sceptic; but why, he scarcely knew, or dared ask himself." [19] Shelley's superiority in dealing with practical matters Medwin asserts thus:

However visionary Shelley might be in his poetical theories, in the concerns of life he always showed a particular sagacity and rationality.... There was no one to whom a friend could better intrust his affairs, no one who displayed more judgment, prudence, and caution in their arrangement. This, Byron, who was not a man of business, knew, and latterly seldom acted without having recourse to Shelley – whose advice he generally adopted.[20]

[18]   *Shelley* (New York, 1940), II, 359.
[19]   *The Shelley Papers*, p. 39.
[20]   *Ibid.*, pp. 81-82.

Of Shelley's adeptness in logical discourse, as compared to Byron's, Medwin says:

In argument he was irresistible, always calm and unruffled; and in
eloquence surpassed all men I have ever conversed with. Byron was
so sensible of his inability to cope with him, that he always avoided
coming to any trial of their strength; for Shelley was what Byron
could not be, a close, logical and subtle reasoner, much of which he
owed to Plato, whose writings he used to call the model of a prose
style.[21]

The lengthy discussions – of a teacher-student or father-son nature
– between Marmion Herbert and Lord Cadurcis in the latter part
of the novel distinctly bear out these respective characterizations
of Shelley and Byron. Also noteworthy are the frequent references, in the conversations, to Plato and his influence on Herbert.
Thus it seems very likely that a reading of Medwin's memoir,
perhaps at Trelawny's instigation, first inspired Disraeli with the
central idea of *Venetia*.

In short, the story of the novel is as follows: Lady Annabel
Herbert has separated from her husband Marmion Herbert because of his subversive views on politics, religion, and morality.
Their daughter Venetia is brought up in ignorance of her father,
who, being a man of ability and character, has joined the American revolutionary forces and has become a general. Subsequently
he has settled in Italy. Venetia's devotion to her father, of whom
she has learned virtually nothing, increases when she discovers his
portrait and some of his poetry. She grows up in close association
with young Lord Cadurcis, a brilliant boy who presently adopts
the same subversive views as Herbert. Because of his liberal
ideas, Lady Annabel sets herself against his plans to marry Venetia. Soon Cadurcis's involvement in a social scandal obliges him
to leave England. Because of the ill health caused by her troubles,
Venetia travels with her mother in Italy. There they accidentally
encounter Herbert, and Venetia reconciles her parents. Cadurcis
joins them, quickly wins Herbert's affection, and is restored to
the esteem of Lady Annabel. The obstacles to the marriage of

Venetia and Cadurcis having been removed, the happiness of all appears complete; but suddenly Herbert and Cadurcis are drowned in a squall in the bay of Spezzia. The sorrowing mother and daughter return to England, where Venetia later marries a cousin of Cadurcis – thus becoming Lady Cadurcis after all.

In the dedication Disraeli says that he has "attempted to shadow forth, though as 'in a glass darkly', two of the most renowned and refined spirits that have adorned these our latter days".[22] He makes a complex, and at times curious, division of parts between the two poets. Byron's genius and personality are seen in Cadurcis; but incidents and circumstances of Byron's life are divided in almost equal proportions between Cadurcis and Herbert. To Cadurcis are assigned the wilful childhood, the foolish mother, the sudden success as poet, the episode with Lady Caroline Lamb (Lady Monteagle in the novel), and the sudden popular hostility which drove Byron from England. But Byron's unhappy marriage and subsequent relationship to Lady Byron and "Ada, sole daughter of my house and heart", are shifted to Herbert, who has Shelley's genius and personality. Shelley's death by drowning is the common end of both fictional poets.

The novel is most successful when dealing with the childhood scenes and with the relationship between Venetia and her father. Disraeli's biographers comment on this aspect of his writing: "He was almost the first writer 'who resolutely set himself to picture the child life' . . . . Even when Disraeli, greatly daring, tries to write verses for both Byron and Shelley, he is happiest when his subject is a father's love; for nowhere has he come nearer to real poetry than in the lines written by Herbert,'On the night our daughter was born'." [23] By his redistribution of the poets' characteristics, his attempts to write poetry for them, and his emphasis on childhood, Disraeli has effectively used his distorting glass to make the parts of his story fit together and to provide a link-to-link arrangement of characters.[24] Whatever the general weak-

[22] The First Earl of Beaconsfield, Benjamin Disraeli, *Venetia*, in *Works*, Bradenham ed., in 12 vols. (New York, 1927), VII. Hereafter, page references are parenthetically included in the text.
[23] Monypenny and Buckle, I, 367-368.
[24] Sylva Norman, *Flight of the Skylark* (London, 1954), p. 139.

nesses of the novel, Disraeli's skill in bringing Byron and Shelley together in a work of fiction is noteworthy.

Disraeli had less in common with Shelley than with Byron, but in strange admixture with Byron's ego-centered ambition he had some of Shelley's vision of the future. And he had studied Shelley's poetry as closely as Byron's. Disraeli's traveling companion, Meredith, kept a diary during their tour of the east and in it mentioned his friend's serious study of *The Cenci* during an enforced stay at Falmouth while enroute.[25] That Disraeli had later continued to pursue his Shelley studies is clearly shown by the *Revolutionary Epick.*

DISRAELI'S REPRESENTATION OF SHELLEY, AS SEEN
BY CRITICS

Venetia, by virtue of its distinguished authorship, marks not only a stage in the history of Shelley's reputation but also a satisfying episode in English literary history. Disraeli himself gained much by imitating Shelley's poetry within the novel as well as in his other verse; he thereby shows discernment, if not always felicity. And he gives evidence, by the estimate he makes of Shelley's character, that he has been able substantially to ascertain the actual man despite all the prejudice and misrepresentation surrounding him. Shelley profits by the fact that among the first to appreciate his character and reveal a sensitiveness to his influence was a brilliant man whose originality helped him to approach Shelley himself in efforts to avert from the nineteenth century the label of commonplace.[26] Disraeli was aware that the current judgment of Shelley was based largely on emotion. His own kinship of spirit with the poet led him to attempt in *Venetia* a more rational view.

The character of Shelley, as well as that of Byron, is clearly commented upon in the novel when Disraeli says of Marmion Herbert:

25   Monypenny and Buckle, I, 366.
26   See Garnett, pp. 124-125.

The general impression of the English public ... was, that Herbert was an abandoned being, of profligate habits, opposed to all the institutions of society that kept his infamy in check, and an avowed atheist; and as scarcely any one but a sympathetic spirit ever read a line he wrote, for indeed the very sight of his works was pollution, it is not very wonderful that this opinion was so generally prevalent. A calm inquirer might perhaps have suspected that abandoned profligacy is not very compatible with severe study ... that a solitary sage may be the antagonist of a priesthood without denying the existence of a God. But there never are calm inquirers. (pp. 229-230)

By this passage, as well as by the general portrait of Shelley in the novel, Disraeli places himself among the discerning critics who have defended Shelley when the prevailing opinion was against him. The biographers of Disraeli comment:

At the time *Venetia* was written Shelley was still something of a bugbear to the narrow and self-sufficient English world of the day; his fame as a poet had not yet won him forgiveness for his transgressions as a man, and still less for the crude and aggressive opinions which had brought him into such violent collision with orthodoxy as established in Church and State. To Disraeli's credit be it remembered that he was one of the first who had the courage to attempt to do him justice or, in defiance of popular prejudice, to present his personality in a sympathetic light.[27]

The portrait of Herbert's youth (reported as antecedent to the action of the novel) is a remarkably accurate partial résumé of Shelley's life and appears to be defective primarily in points with which Disraeli could hardly have been acquainted.

In his literary estimate, Disraeli is less reliable; yet it serves as evidence that his relatively favorable judgment of the man was not invalidated by an uncritical admiration of the poet.[28] "There is", the novelist makes Herbert say, "a radical fault in my poetic mind, and I am conscious of it. I am not altogether void of the creative faculty, but mine is a fragmentary mind; I produce no whole. Unless you do this you cannot last; at least you cannot materially affect your species" (p. 458). Of interest is a comparison between this remark and a criticism made in a

[27] Monypenny and Buckle, I, 367.
[28] See Garnett, pp. 111-112.

letter to Jefferson Hogg by Lytton Bulwer, then editor of the *New Monthly* and close associate of Disraeli: "You evidently admire him as a poet far more than I think criticism warrants us in doing. He is great in parts; but, the 'Cenci' excepted, does not, in my opinion, effect a great whole." [29] The indication is that Bulwer and Disraeli may have discussed the quality of Shelley's poetry and concluded erroneously that he had no unifying philosophy and, therefore, would not last as a poet.

Disraeli, if neither a disciple nor an adequate judge of Shelley, was a careful student of his writings. The most striking passages of conversation in *Venetia* are derived from the least known of Shelley's works, the borrowing being so direct that Disraeli might justly be accused of plagiarism if he had not put the excerpts into the mouth of Shelley himself.[30]

Cadurcis, in a conversation with Herbert, makes the comment, "The age of Pericles has passed away .... Solve me the problem why so unparalleled a progress was made during that period in literature and the arts, and why that progress, so rapid and so sustained, so soon received a check and became retrograde?" Herbert answers, "It is a problem left to the wonder and con-jecture of posterity. Nothing of the Athenians remains except their genius; but they fulfilled their purpose. The wrecks and fragments of their subtle and profound minds obscurely suggest to us the grandeur and perfection of the whole" (p. 456). Much of the conversation, which continues for some time in the same strain, is derived nearly verbatim, as is the above passage, from Shelley's *Discourse on the Manners of the Ancients*. This work was not published in authorized form until three years after the apperance of *Venetia*. Medwin, however had published a frag-ment of it, including the direct source for the above sentences, in his *Shelley Papers* (1833), most of which he had published by installments the previous year in *The Athenaeum*.[31] Disraeli must

[29] Quoted by Garnett, p. 106.
[30] Garnett, p. 112.
[31] For the fragment, which is entitled "The Age of Pericles: with Critical Notices of the Sculpture in the Florence Gallery", see Medwin, *The Shelley Papers*, pp. 135-152. The passage (pp. 135-136) which served as Disraeli's source reads: "Why that progress, so rapid and so sustained, so

have studied carefully Medwin's little book, or the same material as printed in *The Athenaeum*, and must have had resource to it while writing *Venetia*.[32] Still more striking is a quotation from the same source. Remembering that the *Defence of Poetry* was not published until 1840, the reader may be surprised in the middle of *Venetia*, to come upon one of its most memorable pronouncements: "Poets are the unacknowledged legislators of the world." This closing dictum from Shelley's essay is one which the poet frequently used in conversation, and Medwin, having often heard it from him, recorded it in *The Shelley Papers*.[33] Thus Disraeli gives evidence that his interest in Shelley's ideas, as expressed in the novel, was centered upon those works of Shelley which were included in Medwin's little book.

The Shelley Papers provides, also, another important piece of evidence pertaining to Disraeli's interest in the relationship between Byron and Shelley. Herbert, having just deplored the fragmentary character of his own work, says "What I admire in you, Cadurcis, is that, with all the faults of youth, of which you will free yourself, your creative power is vigorous, prolific, and complete; your creations rise fast and fair, like perfect worlds" (pp. 458-459). The source for this passage is Shelley's *Sonnet to Byron*, which was originally published, though imperfectly, in the *Shelley Papers*. In the sonnet Shelley says (according to Medwin's text, no other being accessible to Disraeli):

> My soul, which, as a worm may haply share
> A portion of the unapproachable,

---

soon received a check, and became retrograde, – are problems left to the wonder and conjecture of posterity. The wrecks and fragments of those subtle and profound minds, like the ruins of a fine statue, obscurely suggest to us the grandeur and perfection of the whole."

[32] As I have already shown, Disraeli very likely got the idea of the novel from Medwin's memoir, which appeared with "The Shelley Papers" in both *The Athenaeum* and Medwin's book. As later references in this chapter indicate, the selections which Medwin includes are the sources for most of Disraeli's direct borrowings from Shelley. Whether Disraeli used the magazine or the book is not discernible.

[33] See *Venetia*, p. 459. See also Medwin, *The Shelley Papers*, p. 73.

> Marks his creations rise as fast and fair
> As perfect worlds at the Creator's will.[34]

About the same time that he composed the sonnet, Shelley wrote to Gisborne concerning Byron's latest work: "What think you of Lord Byron now? Space wondered less at the swift and fair creations of God, when he grew weary of vacancy, than I at this spirit of an angel in the mortal paradise of a decaying body. So I think – let the world envy while it admires, as it may." [35] Garnett points out that "Disraeli's representation of Herbert, then, admiring without envy the more popular productions of his friend Cadurcis, and awarding him an unmerited superiority of genius, as well as pre-eminence in contemporary reputation, is perfectly in accordance with fact".[36]

Byron, however, is not the major concern of this chapter, and he figures in it only insofar as he is a model for Herbert or as the character of Cadurcis affects Herbert's views and actions. We need not, therefore, take up the various passages in which critics have found both Byron and Shelley clearly depicted. It is necessary, rather, to trace through the novel the representation of Marmion Herbert as a Shelleyan character and to detect any of his opinions which may also be Disraeli's own ideas, derived from Shelley or employed to refute Shelley.

Like the Romantic poet, young Herbert atends first Eton, then Oxford. At the latter he is ceaselessly in controversy with his tutor. Although he is not expelled as was Shelley, Herbert leaves Oxford, apparently without a degree, at the age of nineteen. Secluding himself in his castle for solitary study, he has what Disraeli calls "unfortunately a complete recurrence" to the heresies which his Oxford tutor supposed he had helped Herbert to overcome. He becomes "in politics a violent republican . . . and especially a strenuous antagonist of marriage, which he taught himself to esteem not only as an unnatural tie, but as eminently unjust towards that softer sex, who had been so long the victims

[34] *Shelley Papers*, p. 37. See also Shelley, *Works*, IV, 117, and Garnett, p. 114.
[35] Letter of 12 January 1822. See *Works*, X, 345.
[36] Garnett, p. 115.

of man" (pp. 223-224). Yet, like Shelley, he does marry. Also
as in Shelley's case, poetic expression triumphs over his impulse
toward non-poetic philosophical speculation.

Garnett has ably characterized and identified with its sources
Disraeli's description of Herbert's early poetic effort:

> The youthful poem attributed to Herbert is a fusion of two of Shel-
> ley's works. When we read that "he called into creation that society
> of immaculate purity and unbounded enjoyment which he believed
> was the natural inheritance of unshackled man", we are reminded of
> "Queen Mab"; but "the stanzas glittering with refined images and
> resonant with subtle symphony" are a description, and a very good
> description, of the "Revolt of Islam". With this poem also corre-
> sponds this further trait: – "In the hero he pictured a philosopher
> young and gifted as himself; in the heroine, his idea of a perfect
> woman." It is added, not unjustly as regards even the "Revolt of
> Islam", but with still closer application to "Prometheus Unbound":
> "These peculiar doctrines of Herbert, which, undisguised, must have
> excited so much odium, were more or less developed and inculcated
> in this work; nevertheless they were necessarily so veiled by the
> highly spiritual and metaphorical language of the poet that it re-
> quired some previous acquaintance with the system enforced to be
> able to discover and recognise the esoteric spirit of his muse." [37]

But Garnett fails to realize that it is precisely by insisting that
Shelley's spirit was basically esoteric that Disraeli finds an excuse
for not following the poet's ideas to their necessary conclusions.
Herbert, when reunited with his wife and daughter in Italy, appears as a mellowed elderly gentleman who holds to his beliefs
in an ideal society in the remote future but has relaxed, given up
his fervor for reform, and abandoned himself to the enjoyment
of the present. He has found, as Shelley never did, that his poetic
spirit is impractical and no longer worthy of his allegiance.
Critics, commenting on *Venetia,* have emphasized Disraeli's
achievement in presenting a relatively unbiased picture of Shelley
but have scarcely taken note of the love of aristocratic eminence
which yet manages to pervade the novel.

Disraeli's love for the aristocracy as one of the basic institutions of society repeatedly makes its impact, not only on *Venetia*

[37] *Ibid.*, pp. 109-110. The quotations from *Venetia* are taken from page
225 of the novel.

but also on his other novels. An outstanding example is the conclusion of the novel *Sybil*, where the heroine, who has been – both symbolically and actually – of and for the people, turns out to belong rightfully to the aristocracy. Sylva Norman has touched upon this emphasis as it is discernible in *Venetia*:

This Marmion Herbert (a descendant of Herbert of Cherbury) is undoubtedly a "gentleman", for all that blot upon his past when he left Lady Annabel, his wife, and exiled himself in Geneva to write heretical books and take a mistress. (Byron is apparently mixed in with this.) He is a gentleman in spite of the apparent betrayal of king and country that marked his heroic gesture for republicanism. . . . So, in boldly, and not insensitively, declaring Shelley's worth, the diplomatic author made it clear that what he praised was wholly admirable. There was queer behavior in his Herbert, but there could not and should not be that undying query which will never allow Shelley to rest securely poised between the estimates of saint and villain. Disraeli's was a novel; his technique was right when he made Herbert reappear, a heretic still, but wise with years and experience, to be reconciled as in a Shakespearean comedy to his half-faithful wife and wholly loving daughter, to meet Lord Cadurcis, who had long admired his work.[38]

Miss Norman then points out that the reviewer in *Fraser's* was delighted primarily with the manly and "truly *English* spirit" of the novel. The characters constituted for him a model of aristocracy to be held up before the provincials. The review, lauding as a "noble aspiration" the attempt to place Byron and Shelley "in a just light before their countrymen", was to serve as a "leg-up for the Tories". Miss Norman concludes, "We may smile again to think that Shelley the reformer has fallen, in this twisted way, into the Conservative camp for vindication." [39] It was the using of Shelley and remolding of him to fit the novelist's own purposes that made the *Fraser's* review possible.

Miss Norman is correct in suggesting that Disraeli misrepresents Shelley as a model gentleman and that he thus proves himself a capable technician of the novel. What she does not point out is that the author is more interested in defending English institutions than in restoring Shelley to his inheritance as an

---

[38] Norman, p. 139.
[39] *Ibid.*, p. 140. See also *Fraser's Magazine*, XV (June 1837), 774, 777.

aristocrat and that not only the *Fraser's* review, but also the novel itself is intended as a Tory "leg-up". Disraeli has gone over to the conservative camp; one of his basic concerns is to demonstrate that although an element of youthful agitation may be desirable in a society, the old forms, traditions, and institutions must remain unshaken. The mature Marmion Herbert has learned to recognize his youthful hopes as little more than juvenile fancies, and he lives so that they will no longer interfere with his present society.

The remainder of the present chapter, contending that Disraeli uses Shelley purposefully to show that the poet's liberalism is ineffective and impractical, goes beyond previous investigations of *Venetia*.

DISRAELI'S USE OF SHELLEY

Disraeli, both directly and through Lady Annabel's views, comments critically on the effect Herbert's beliefs had upon himself and his family. He calls attention to the results of Herbert's consistency of profession and action: "A mere sceptic, he would have been perhaps merely pitied; a sceptic with a peculiar faith of his own, which he was resolved to promulgate, Herbert became odious. A solitary votary of obnoxious opinions, Herbert would have been looked upon only as a madman; but the moment he attempted to make proselytes he rose into a conspirator against society" (p. 222). After the separation between Herbert and Lady Annabel, the English public takes extreme views regarding Herbert's character and his beliefs. Disraeli's own judgment is quite clearly presented later in the novel: "Great as might have been the original errors of Herbert, awful as in [Lady Annabel's] estimation were the crimes to which they had led him, they might in the first instance be traced rather to a perverted view of society than of himself" (p. 280). This basis for Herbert's faults the author contrasts with the idolatry of self which was the flaw in Cadurcis. Disraeli, it seems, despite his basic affinity with Herbert's ideas, is not willing to declare him justified in the stand he took. Obviously, Disraeli himself, had he followed Herbert's course, could not have risen in politics as he did.

It is with his marriage and subsequent separation that Herbert becomes a fusion of the characters of Byron and Shelley – the Byronic element becoming dominant for a time. The Shelleyan character comes to the fore, however, when Herbert, because he wants to devote himself entirely to the cause of freedom, renounces all things dear to him in England – even his own family. Byron's reason for a similar renunciation was more ego-centered. Herbert goes to America where he will most readily be able to apply his principles of freedom:

There seemed in the opening prospects of America, in a world still new, which had borrowed from the old as it were only so much civilization as was necessary to create and to maintain order; there seemed in the circumstances of its boundless territory, and the total absence of feudal institutions and prejudices, so fair a field for the practical introduction of those regenerating principles to which Herbert had devoted all the thought and labor of his life, that he resolved, after long and perhaps painful meditation, to sacrifice every feeling and future interest to its fulfilment. (p. 232)

Although Shelley never directly associated himself with America, the fiction thus far is true to the Shelleyan ideal. But Herbert's recruiting and commanding an American regiment is another Byronic element – an element diametrically opposed to Shelley's strong emphasis upon avoiding violence in the quest for social regeneration.

The Marmion Herbert, who, years later, is suddenly reunited with his wife and daughter is a changed man indeed, as the following excerpts prove:

Time had stilled his passions, and cooled the fervour of his soul. The age of his illusions had long passed. ... His heart melted to his daughter, nor did he care to live without her love and her presence. His philosophical theories all vanished. He felt how dependent we are in this world on our natural ties, and how limited, with all his arrogance, is the sphere of man. Dreaming of philanthropy, he had broken his wife's heart, and bruised, perhaps irreparably, the spirit of his child; he had rendered those miserable who depended on his love, and for whose affection his heart now yearned to that degree, that he could not contemplate existence without their active sympathy. . . . He had sacrificed his fortune, he had forfeited his country, he had alienated his wife, and he had lost his child; the home of his heroic ancestry, the ancient land whose fame and power they had created, the beauteous and gifted woman who would have clung for ever to his bosom, and her transcendent offspring worthy of all their loves! Profound philosopher! (pp. 380, 382, 384)

Here Disraeli gives evidence that his own liberalism goes only so far as Herbert's youthful enthusiasm for liberty. For Disraeli the consequences to the individual weigh very heavily.

Herbert, after the reunion with Lady Annabel and Venetia, gives little heed to Plato and Aeschylus; he prefers to read *Don Quixote* and other works which will please his family. Indeed, to please his wife and daughter is now his main object in life. Explaining his enthusiasm for the character of Don Quixote, Herbert says:

"In his hero, Cervantes has given us the picture of a great and benevolent philospher, and in his Sancho, a complete personification of the world, selfish and cunning, and yet overawed by the genius that he cannot comprehend: alive to all the material interests of existence, yet sighing after the ideal; securing his four young foals of the she-ass, yet indulging in dreams of empire."

"But what do you think of the assault on the windmills, Marmion?" said Lady Annabel.

"In the outset of his adventures, as in the outset of our lives, he was misled by his enthusiasm", replied Herbert, "without which, after all, we can do nothing. But the result is, Don Quixote was a redresser of wrongs, and therefore the world esteemed him mad." (p. 412)

It is difficult to avoid the conclusion that Disraeli here equivocates: Herbert sees the dangers in youthful enthusiasm but also the necessity for it; he observes that Don Quixote redressed wrongs and that he was, therefore, considered mad; but, in the wisdom of age, Herbert has withdrawn from the redressing of wrongs. Disraeli does not explain why, since age affirms its futility, enthusiasm is commendable in youth.

The common Victorian attitude that social evolution will work slowly of itself is voiced in Herbert's words to Cadurcis: "Mine were but crude dreams. I wished to see man noble and happy; but if he will persist in being vile and miserable, I must even be content. I can struggle for him no more . . . . I will not give up a jot of my conviction of a great and glorious future for human destinies; but its consumation will not be so rapid as I once thought, and in the meantime I die" (pp. 434-435). Disraeli is at fault not only in assuming that Shelley, as an older man, would have lost faith in the individual's effectiveness but also in interpreting Shelley's social philosophy as one of immediate and sudden Utopianism. As pointed out in the previous chapter, Browning apparently made the same mistake. Had they both read *Prometheus Unbound* with a careful attention to the length of the hero's struggle and to the warning that the cycle would need to be repeated unless men remained alert, they might have concluded otherwise, even without accessibility to the *Philosophical View of Reform*.

Much closer to Shelley's views, up to a point, is another statement by Herbert in the same conservation:

Life is the great wonder . . . into which all that is strange and startling resolves itself. The mist of familiarity obscures from us the miracle of our being. Mankind are constantly starting at events which they consider extraordinary. But a philosopher acknowledges only one miracle, and that is life. Political revolutions, changes in empire, wrecks of dynasties and the opinions that support them, these are the marvels of the vulgar, but those are only transient modifications of life. The origin of existence is, therefore, the first object which a true philosopher proposes to himself. Unable to discover it, he accepts certain results from his unbiased observation of its obvious nature, and on them he establishes certain principles to be our guides in all social relations, whether they take the shape of laws or customs. Nevertheless, until the principle of life be discovered, all theories and all systems of conduct must be considered provisional. (p. 435)

The opening sentences of this passage are taken almost word for word from Shelley's essay, *On Life* (ca. 1819), which begins:

Life and the world, or whatever we call that which we are and feel, is an astonishing thing. The mist of familiarity obscures from us the wonder of our being. We are struck with admiration at some of its transient modifications, but it is itself the great miracle. What are changes of empires, the wreck of dynasties, with the opinions which supported them; what is the birth and the extinction of religions and of political systems, to life? [40]

Shelley comes to the conclusion, as does Marmion Herbert after him, that the origin of being eludes even the true philosopher, who then must be content with what may be observed or perceived:

How vain is it to think that words can penetrate the mystery of our being! Rightly used they may make evident our ignorance to ourselves, and this is much. For what are we? Whence do we come? and whither do we go? Is birth the commencement, is death the conclusion of our being? What is birth and death?. . . .
    I confess that I am one of those who am unable to refuse my assent to the conclusions of those philosophers who assert that nothing exists but as it is perceived.[41]

Thus far Disraeli's older "Shelley" agrees with the actual Shelley of about 1819, but regarding the results of "unbiased observation", the two part company. Herbert expects the philosopher to establish institutions to guide the masses; Shelley is more concerned that the individual somehow find his own relationship to the universe. He seeks a unity which transcends institutionalism:

Whatever may be his true and final destination, there is a spirit within [man] at enmity with nothingness and dissolution. This is the character of all life and being. Each is at once the centre and the circumference; the point to which all things are referred, and the line in which all things are contained. Such contemplations as these, materialism and the popular philosophy of mind and matter alike forbid; they are only consistent with the intellectual system.[42]

Shelley, viewing the individual as a segment of the universal mind, disdains the laws and customs upon which Disraeli's Her-

---

[40] *Works,* VI, 193. Medwin, in *The Shelley Papers,* pp. 153-155, includes the opening section of *On Life.*

[41] *Ibid.,* p. 194. These two excerpts from Shelley's essay are not included in the portions Medwin used in *The Shelley Papers.* The more complete essay was not published until 1840, when Mrs. Shelley included it in *Essays, Letters from Abroad.* It is most unlikely that Disraeli was acquainted with any portions of *On Life* other than those published by Medwin.

[42] *Ibid.* See also Medwin, *The Shelley Papers,* pp. 38-39, where Medwin incorporates the passage in his Memoir of Shelley.

bert insists. And for Shelley the question of individual origins and destinies does not pose the problem it does for Disraeli, whose fictional poets become concerned, in their conversation, about the scientific possibility of the individual's endless life on earth.

Shelley remained, to the end, a foe of institutions and continued to insist upon perpetual change. One attitude of Herbert's with which Shelley would have been in full agreement is the following: "Why should we be surprised that the nature of man should change? Does not everything change? Is not change the law of nature?" (p. 436). It must be remembered, nevertheless, that for Herbert this potential change no longer depends in the least upon any efforts which he might put forth; he has given up all idealism about man's ability to help himself. Shelley's Demogorgon, on the other hand, remains inactive until Prometheus, the genius of human mind, finally achieves his victory.

Herbert's earlier declaration that he will no longer strive for men seems inconsistent with the following speech, which Disraeli improvised for Herbert by fusing verbatim portions of two excerpts from Shelley which are found in Medwin's *Shelley Papers*:[43]

---

[43] See *The Shelley Papers*, pp. 21-24 and 156-157. The former excerpt is Medwin's reprint of almost the entire essay *On Love*, and the latter is entered under the subtitle "Love" in a section entitled "Reflections". Disraeli's fusion of these two portions is conclusive proof that Medwin was his source.

Portions which Disraeli has adapted directly from *The Shelley Papers* are the following: "If we imagine, we would that the airy children of our brain were born anew within another's" (p. 22). "We are born into the world, and there is something within us which, from the instant we live and move, thirsts after its likeness. This propensity developes itself with the development of our nature" (p. 23; note that Disraeli follows Medwin's wording and omits the same parts Medwin has omitted). "The gratification of the senses is no longer all that is desired. It soon becomes a very small part of that profound and complicated sentiment which we call love, which is rather the universal thirst for a communion not merely of the senses, but of our whole nature, intellectual, imaginative, and sensitive" (pp. 156-157). "The discovery of its antitype ... is the invisible and unattainable point to which love tends" (p. 23).

The importance of sympathy is stressed also in Shelley's preface to *Alastor*.

We exist because we sympathise. If we did not sympathise with the air, we should die. . . . It is sympathy that makes you a poet. It is your desire that the airy children of your brain should be born anew within another's, that makes you create; therefore, a misanthropical poet is a contradiction in terms. . . . As for sexual love, . . . its quality and duration depend upon the degree of sympathy that subsists between the two persons interested. Plato believed, and I believe with him, in the existence of a spiritual antitype of the soul, so that when we are born, there is something within us which, from the instant we live and move, thirsts after its likeness. This propensity develops itself with the development of our nature. The gratification of the senses soon becomes a very small part of that profound and complicated sentiment, which we call love. Love, on the contrary, is an universal thirst for a communion, not merely of the senses, but of our whole nature, intellectual, imaginative, and sensitive. . . . If men were properly educated, and their faculties fully developed, the discovery of the antitype would be easy. (pp. 448-449)

The difficulty is that Herbert, as an old man, apparently no longer proposes to act upon these beliefs. Because of men's stubbornness, he does not intend to do anything more towards properly educating them or fully developing their faculties. One wonders how much of the author's opinion is implied in Herbert's declaration, "Once I sacrificed my happiness to my philosophy, and now I have sacrificed my philosophy to my happiness" (p. 438).

Greatly though Disraeli deserves to be appreciated for his insights into Shelley's true character and for his daring to present the poet in a favorable light when public opinion was antagonistic toward him, it is difficult to avoid the conclusion that he finally distorts Shelley's philosophy. In the first place, Disraeli pictures the older Herbert as a kind of superior Shelley, a poet whose maturity has given him insights which Shelley lacked. Secondly, by presenting Herbert as still retaining certain basically Shelleyan views but suppressing them because of disillusionment, Disraeli is actually declaring the poet ineffectual. The reader is thus led to wonder whether Shelley has not been favorably set up in the novel only to make his overthrow all the more noticeable and effective.

Disraeli's own view on social or governmental reform is clearly presented in his tract *The Spirit of Whiggism*, published in 1836, the very year he was writing *Venetia*. To know that he was studying Shelley for the novel at about the time he wrote the tract adds meaning to certain portions:

I would address myself to the English Radicals. . . . I mean those thoughtful and enthusiastic men who study their unstamped press, and ponder over a millennium of operative amelioration. Not merely that which is just, but that which is also practicable, should be the aim of a sagacious politician. . . .

There is no probability of ever establishing in England a more democratic form of government than the present English constitution. . . . The disposition of property in England throws the government of the country into the hands of its natural aristocracy. I do not believe that any scheme of the suffrage, or any method of election, could divert that power into other quarters. It is the necessary consequence of our present social state. . . .

Our revolutions are brought about by the passions of creative minds taking advantage, for their own aggrandisement, of peculiar circumstances in our national progress. They are never called for by the great body of the nation. Churches are plundered, long rebellions maintained, dynasties changed, Parliaments abolished; but when the storm is passed, the features of the social landscape remain unimpaired; here are no traces of the hurricane, the earthquake, or the volcano; it has been but a tumult of the atmosphere, that has neither toppled down our old spires and palaces, nor swallowed up our cities and seats of learning, nor blasted our ancient woods, nor swept away our ports and harbours. The English nation ever recurs to its ancient institutions – the institutions that have alike secured freedom and order; and after all their ebullitions, we find them, when the sky is clear, again at work, and toiling on at their eternal task of accumulation.[44]

In the light of this declaration of complacency, it is apparent that Disraeli, confronting himself with the character of Shelley as material for a novel, found it necessary, if he were not to denounce the poet outright, to depict him as an eventual deserter from his actual position. Medwin's characterization of Shelley as being far superior to Byron in intellect, philosophy, and practical insights presented Disraeli, no doubt, with the idea of Shelley as an elderly man. What better device than the process of aging to

[44]   Quoted by Monypenny and Buckle, I, 328-329.

make the change from radical revolutionary fervor to deliberate abandonment of concern about man's future seem plausible?

That Disraeli himself, at least in his youth, felt a basic affinity with the liberal point of view may not readily be denied; but that he allowed the attractions of high office, aristocracy, and institutionalism to suppress and overcome it seems equally clear. For Disraeli the mid-1830's had been years of difficult decision, of turning from an interest in Shelleyan liberalism toward a settlement with Tory conservatism. To his lawyer-friend Pyne he confided that *Venetia* contained evidence of his recent anxieties.[45] There is a gratuitous and partisan note in his biographers' comment: "To the end the revolutionary side was there; and it is just because Disraeli never lost his sympathy with the modern spirit, never felt any of that timorous shrinking from new political ideals which afflicts Conservatives of a narrower type, that his conservatism is so sane, so robust, and so fruitful." [46] The equivocal use made in *Venetia* of Shelley's ideals may hardly be considered more commendable than would have been a "timerous shrinking" from them.

Insofar as the technique of the novel is concerned, Disraeli manipulates the Shelley material very well; but we may scarcely conclude, in view of his own political status in 1836 and 1837 and the ideas expressed in *The Spirit of Whiggism*, that he employed the Shelley theme in the novel for technical reasons alone. Indeed, it appears that he found the nucleus of the novel already formed for him in Medwin's joint treatment of Byron and Shelley. When once he realized that he could present Shelley in an ostensibly favorable light and yet disqualify his liberal ideas, Disraeli must have had little trouble getting his novel underway.

[45] See Hesketh Pearson, *Dizzy: The Life and Personality of Benjamin Disraeli, Earl of Beasonsfield* (New York, 1951), p. 62.
[46] Monypenny and Buckle, I, 249.

IV

SHELLEY IN KINGSLEY'S THREE SOCIAL NOVELS

Charles Kingsley's essay, *Thoughts on Shelley and Byron* [1] is so abusive an outburst against Percy Bysshe Shelley that the reader is startled at the author's daring to apply the term "hysterical" to Shelley. Kingsley's disapproval of the Romantic poet is so clearly established that critics have not noted the rather paradoxical Shelleyan influence in his three social novels. Nevertheless, in *Yeast* (1848), *Alton Locke, Tailor and Poet* (1850), and *Two Years Ago* (1857),[2] the evidence of Kingsley's dependence upon Shelley for some of the major ideas is unmistakable. The direct quotations from and allusions to Shelley, as well as the creation of several characters obviously modeled after the poet, are clear indications that Shelley was constantly in Kingsley's mind during the composition of the novels. Although numerous anti-Shelley views are directly expressed, one of the major Shelleyan concepts – that of an extended search after an ideal – is a prominent feature of the novels.

The purpose of this chapter, therefore, is to examine Kingsley's use of quotations from Shelley, Shelleyan characters, direct criticism of the poet, and especially the *Alastor*-like pursuit of an ideal, as they appear in the three social novels. That Kingsley (1819–1875) had come to any consistent view regarding the poet or that he was even attempting a consistent expression of a

---

[1] See his *Miscellanies* (London, 1860), I, 304-324. The essay first appeared in *Fraser's Magazine*, November 1853.
[2] The edition of the novels used in this chapter is *The Life and Works of Charles Kingsley*, 19 vols. (London, 1901). Unless otherwise indicated, all footnote or parenthetical references to Kingsley's novels are to this edition.

philosophy in the novels may not be demonstrable, but it may be possible to evaluate, at least to some extent, the power of Shelley's expressed convictions on even so outspoken an antagonist as was Kingsley.

DIFFERENCES AND SIMILARITIES

In *Thoughts on Shelley and Byron* Kingsley denounces his "mesmerising, table-turning, spirit-rapping, Spiritualising, Romanising generation, who read Shelley in secret, and delight in his bad taste, mysticism, extravagance, and vague and pompous sentimentalism". To him the age seems an effeminate one which "can well afford to pardon the lewdness of the gentle and sensitive vegetarian". As for the real Shelley, "if once his intense self-opinion had deserted him, [he] would have probably ended in Rome, as an Oratorian or a Passionist" (p. 311). This las judgment seems extreme and unfounded until one takes into consideration Kingsley's strong antagonism to the Roman Catholic Church and the basis for it.

Kingsley, like many other young men of the university, had developed serious doubts while at Cambridge. But unlike most of these students who experienced a gradual drift toward disbelief, Kingsley, characteristically, had passed through a quite sudden period of troubled and intense soul-searching. At first his revolt from childhood faith had led him to a denial of all religious authority – after which he was conversely drawn toward Roman Catholicism. The latter temptation must have been of short duration, but Kingsley often in later life reiterated that he had known Rome's attraction as well as any convert. It may be that his memory exaggerated the difficulty of resistance, or perhaps the very sense of having safely avoided a danger was responsible for the illogical disdain for Catholicism which he evidenced from 1841 to the end of his life.[3] But there seems to be another reason for this antagonism. In 1849 Kingsley wrote to a young clergy-

---

[3]   Robert Bernard Martin, *The Dust of Combat: A Life of Charles Kingsley* (London, 1959), pp. 38-39.

man who was about to become a Romanist: "If by Holiness you mean 'saintliness', I quite agree that Rome is the place to get that, and a poor pitiful thing it is when it is got – not God's ideal of a man, but an effeminate shaveling's ideal. Look at St. Francis de Sales, or St. Vincent Paul's face, and then say, does not your English spirit loathe to see *that*? God made man in His image, not in an imaginary Virgin Mary's image." [4] Undoubtedly at least a part of Kingsley's hatred of Rome was sexually motivated. In his own marriage he had found a security which made him contemptuous of the celibate life; but there is, beyond this, a frightened and hysterical note in his repeatedly attributing to Roman Catholicism the characteristics of effeminacy and abnormality.[5] These same traits he saw as the basis for Shelley's unorthodox – and to Kingsley, abhorrent – views of marriage.

The ethical difference between Byron and Shelley, he maintains, is that the former has an intense, awful sense of moral law; whereas the latter has little if any – perhaps less than any other known writer who ever dealt with moral questions. Shelley's whole life appears to Kingsley as a substitution of internal sentiment for the external law which he denied. The law made Shelley miserable; therefore he held that it should be abolished. Quoting the poet's "custom and faith the foulest birth of time" [6] as an example of his anti-marriage views, Kingsley holds that "lawless love" is Shelley's expressed ideal of relationship between the sexes and that his justice, benevolence, and pity are equally lawless. To the essayist it appears that Shelley's one law is "Follow your instincts", except when the instincts lead to the eating of animal food or to tyranny over fellow-men; then the rule is "Follow the instincts of Percy Bysshe Shelley". Sentimental Shelley is unable to recognize facts other than those which please his taste.

[4]   *The Life and Works of Charles Kingsley*, I, 212. Mrs. Kingsley's *Charles Kingsley: His Letters and Memories of His Life* constitutes the first four volumes of this edition.

[5]   Martin, p. 107.

[6]   Shelley, "Feelings of a Republican on the Fall of Bonaparte", *Works*, I, 206.

Kingsley contends that, had the eighth stanza of the *Ode to Liberty* been written by anyone but Shelley, with an equal degree of knowledge, it would have been called "a wicked and deliberate lie". In Shelley's case it occasions a sigh but nothing more. "For Shelley's nature is utterly womanish. Not merely his weak points, but his strong ones, are those of a woman. Tender and pitiful as a woman: and yet, when angry, shrieking, railing, hysterical as a woman. . . . The lawlessness of the man, with the sensibility of the woman" (pp. 314-315). Thus it appears that Kingsley's hatred of Catholicism and his aversion to Shelley are similar, at least to some extent, in point of origin and that the one is perhaps the basis for the other. Distinguishing between Shelley and Byron on the ground of "healthiness", Kingsley appears to have reasoned that Shelley's introspection was to be equated with effeminacy – and, hence, with a natural inclination toward Roman Catholicism.[7]

And that the timid British public has gradually sipped more and more from Shelley's once-dreaded fountain and has found its "magic water" more favorable than Byron's "fiercer wine" is a source of severe agitation to the robust Kingsley. He considers that nine-tenths of the bad influence charged against Byron is really of Shelley's doing. Byron, unlike Shelley, never attempted to establish his own sin as a religion and the worship of uncleanness as mankind's highest ethical development. Nor did he, finding himself at moments in hell, try to convince his public that, if they could but see aright, they would know it to be heaven.[8] Such prejudiced pronouncements sometimes merely alienated Kingsley's readers, one of whom, George Gilfillan, wrote in his journal after he had read the essay: "His judgments on Byron and Shelley as poets are most unjust. Tennyson is his idol. He talks of Shelley being 'girlish', etc., which was not the case. Childlike is a far truer epithet. He was to the end an impassioned and inspired child, and this is perhaps as good as 'muscular Christian'. Again, what Kingsley says about his exquisite lines written in dejection at Naples, is absolutely contemptible. Al-

---

7   See Martin, p. 164.
8   *Thoughts on Shelley and Byron*, pp. 310-311.

together, I begin to think Kingsley destitute of true taste." [9] Kingsley's criticism of *Stanzas, Written in Dejection near Naples* is, indeed, narrow and unjust. He finds only one instance of Shelley's seeing the truth about himself, the remainder of the poem being clouded over with sentiment. It is to such criticism that Mrs. Campbell objects when she puts upon the Victorians the blame for some of the artistic failures of her own generation and asks, "Why did Kingsley never look within for false principles?" [10]

Writing of critics with principles other than his own – the scholars and "poetasters" who imitated Shelley – Kingsley has this to say: "They found it easy to curse and complain, instead of helping to mend. So had he. They found it pleasant to confound institutions with the abuses which defaced them. So had he .... They found it pleasant to believe that the poet was to regenerate the world, without having settled with what he was to regenerate it. So had he." [11] Although contending that, of all the Romantic poets, Shelley was the greatest sinner against the canons of good taste, Kingsley yet recognizes that this tactless poet most clearly saw and most boldly proclaimed the truth about the decaying European social order which was ripe for reform. Using the label of "hysterical", Kingsley classes Shelley with Rousseau as one of the bad men or fools whom God uses to do His work, and do it "right well". Whereas Byron had focused on the decay and rottenness of the old world, Shelley had been attracted to the possible glory of the new. And the same attraction was strong in Kingsley. It is, however, only insofar as ends are concerned that Kingsley could apply the judgement of "right well" to Shelley's work; to the essentials of Shelley's means he was radically opposed.

Yet Kingsley and Shelley were surprisingly alike in their youthful responses when confronted with extreme poverty and other social problems. Shelley's enthusiasm over the Tremadoc Em-

[9] R. A. and E. S. Watson, *George Gilfillan: Letters and Journal, with Memoir* (1892), pp. 321-322.
[10] Olwen Ward Campbell, *Shelley and the Unromantics* (New York, 1924), pp. 8-9.
[11] *Thoughts on Shelley and Byron*, pp. 315-316.

bankment project for reclaiming land from the ocean is well
known, as are his efforts on behalf of the Irish and his distribution
of food, clothing, and fuel to the poor at Tremadoc. Virginia
Woolf has succinctly summarized this aspect of Shelley: "He
became the champion of every down-trodden cause and person.
Now it was an embankment; now a publisher; now the Irish
nation; now three poor weavers condemned for treason; now a
flock of neglected sheep." [12] Very similar to these enterprises was
the action taken by the young clergyman Kingsley and his friends
when they observed the deplorable living conditions in the slum
area known as Jacob's Island. Their first objective was to convince either the landlords or local authorities to supply sanitary
drinking water and adequate drainage for the area; their method
was agitation. Although their speeches and pamphlets attracted
attention, they took even more immediate action – doling out
drinking water from carts and setting up waterbutts for a reserve
supply. Being both innocent and idealistic, the young clergymen
brought large, well-built butts fitted with brass cocks which could
be opened only by keys given to the tenants. On the assumption
that there would be a general objection to a return to the use of
ditch-water, the plan was that the butts be blown up after the
tenants had enjoyed the fresh water for ten months. But not only
did the inhabitants refuse to believe that the ditchwater was un-
healthy; they began almost immediately to steal the brass cocks.
The final blow to the project was the disappearance of the large
butts themselves.[13] Though, in the cases of both Shelley and
Kingsley, projects such as these were evidences primarily of
youthful enthusiasm, they foreshadowed a continuing concern in
both men.

No other poet serves Kingsley's purposes in the three social
novels as frequently, as readily, or as effectively as does Shelley.
Much though he might emphasize a character's conquest of an
early Shelley influence and strongly though his own essay denounces the poet, Kingsley could not write fiction about the

---

social problems of England without taking Shelley's ideas into account. Nor did he trouble himself to disguise his use of the poetry for which he professed so intense a dislike.[14] That his quarrel with Shelleyan views was apparently over the means by which social reform was to be brought about has already been indicated. It now becomes necessary to define more clearly what this difference of opinion involved.

Kingsley does, in his essay, make some effort to credit Shelley with a limited poetic virtue: "In spite of bombast, horrors, maundering, sheer stuff and nonsense of all kinds, there is a plaintive natural melody about this man, such as no other English poet has ever uttered, except Shakespeare in some few immortal songs .... Yes, when he will be himself – Shelley the scholar and the gentleman and the singer, and leave philosophy and politics which he does not understand, and shriekings and cursings, which are unfit for any civilized and self-respecting man, he is perfect .... His true power lies in his own 'native wood-notes wild'. " [15] The same view is presented in *Alton Locke* when, in answer to the suggestion by Dean Winnstay (Kingsley's mouthpiece) that neither Shakespeare nor any of the great poets of the last thirty years were politicians, Alton cites Southey, Shelley, and Burns as evidence to the contrary. The dean, after dismissing Southey as a mere "verse-maker", maintains that the worst portions of the poetry and practice of Burns and Shelley were dictated to them by their politics. Of the latter poet he says, "Shelley, what little I have read of him, only seems himself when he forgets radicalism for nature" (II, 29-30). The lone virtue Kingsley sees in Shelley is that of being capable of writing genteel verse

---

[14] The detested poetry of Shelley also appears to have exerted a direct influence on Kingsley's own poetry outside the novels, as evidenced by the following excerpt from *Palinodia*:

> Thou sea, who wast to me a prophet deep
> Through all thy restless waves, and wasting shores,
> Of silent labour, and eternal change; ...
> To me alike thy frenzy and thy sleep
> Have been a deep and breathless joy: Oh hear!

See Kingsley, *Poems* (London, 1875), p. 266.

[15] *Thoughts on Shelley and Byron*, pp. 317-318.

– a patently absurd evaluation in view of Shelley's eloquent and incisive poetry opposing injustice and inequality.

Shelley knew that pauperism is not an unaccountable or sporadic phenomenon, but necessarily and logically a counterpart of wealth. For this reason he could not avoid the conclusion that eventually Great Britain's entire social and economic system must be completely renovated. Kingsley, too, was concerned about society devouring the laboring classes, but he was appalled at the drastic changes which Shelley envisioned. It appears that, in his novels, he quoted from such poems as *Song to the Men of England* and *The Masque of Anarchy* in order to show that Shelley, good though his analysis of social and political problems might be, was dangerously radical in the solutions he proposed. Thus his extreme vituperation against Shelley, despite the common ground of their major concerns, is at least partially clarified.

SHELLEY IN THE NOVELS

Instances of Kingsley's simultaneous attraction to and disapprobation of Shelley's works are the numerous direct quotations from Shelley scattered throughout the three social novels. A short look at each of these quotations and the context in which it is used will give an indication of the breadth of Kingsley's concern with Shelley's works and will demonstrate some of his interpretations of the poems.

Published in the Year of Revolutions, *Yeast*, Kingsley's first novel, is a crude work by literary standards. It deals with such social and religious problems as the game laws, the miseries of the rustic poor, and the Tractarian movement. Consisting mainly of sociological discussions between the hero and various other people, it allows for but little plot. The principal character in this limited narrative is Lancelot Smith, a generous but impulsive young man of society, who reacts to the influences of the various people about him. *Yeast* contains less direct quotation from Shelley than do the two later novels, but there are in it various imitations and borrowings from Shelley.

The first of the three direct Shelley quotations in *Yeast* appears in the opening passage. The journal or "soul-almanack" which Lancelot kept as a youth contains an entry which reads in part: "As I watched the beetles, those children of the sun, who, as divine Shelley says, 'laden with light and odor, pass over the gleam of the living grass' [*The Sensitive Plant*, I, 82-85], I gained an Eden-glimpse of the pleasures of virtue." Kingsley comments that the journal was "very bad", but that "to do justice to Lancelot, he had grown out of it by the time when my story begins. . . . Lancelot had found Byron and Shelley pall on his taste" (p. 2).[16]

Later in the novel, the artist Claude Mellot explains to Lancelot his Platonic view of art: "Truth of form, color, chiaroscuro. They are worthy to occupy me a life; for they are eternal – or at least that which they express; and if I am to get at the symbolized unseen, it must be through the beauty of the symbolizing phenomenon. If I, who live by art, for art, in art, or you either, who seem as much a born artist as myself, am to have a religion, it must be a worship of the fountain of art – of the

> 'Spirit of beauty, who doth consecrate
> With his own hues whate'er he shines upon.'"
> *(Hymn to Intellectual Beauty,* 13-14)

"As poor Shelley has it; and much peace of mind it gave him!" is Lancelot's reply. "I have grown sick lately of such dreary tinsel abstractions" (p. 43). It appears that Lancelot, who has distinctly Shelleyan social reform ideas, has lost all respect for Shelley's theory of poetry.

One more direct quotation from Shelley occurs in the description of the persistence of lovely Argemone's presence in Lancelot's mind (pp. 74-75). To emphasize her influence upon Lancelot, Kingsley quotes a passage from *Alastor:*

> When his regard
> Was raised by intense pensiveness, two eyes,
> Two starry eyes hung in the gloom of thought,

[16] It will be noted that many of Kingsley's quotations are inaccurate. Apparently the novelist often quoted from memory or took the freedom to make alterations as he saw fit.

> And seemed, with their serene and azure smiles,
> To beckon him.   (lines 488-492)

Alton Locke is a novel of more definite structure and, comparatively, less declamation. Young Alton, raised and educated by his puritanical widowed mother and later apprenticed to a sweating tailor, realizes the misery of the working classes, becomes a poet, and (after some wavering) emerges as an enthusiastic Chartist. That the original of Alton Locke was Thomas Cooper – friend of Kingsley, poet, shoemaker, Chartist orator, and one-time prisoner – has been fully established.[17] But that a large measure of Shelley is blended into the characterization is also clearly evident.

In this novel the old Scotsman Sandy Mackay, commenting on the tragic lives of some working-class women whom he and Alton have just seen, gives his version of two Shelley lines:

> With hues as when some mighty painter dips
> His pen in dyes of earthquake and eclipse.
>
> (*Revolt of Islam,* V, xxiii, 8-9)

His comment on them is, "Ay, Shelley's gran'; but Fact is grander – God and Satan are grander. All around ye, in every gin-shop and costermonger's cellar, are God and Satan at death grips . . . and will ye think it beneath ye to be the 'Peoples' Poet?'" (I, 207). Alton does take the peoples' part and, as a result, spends three years in prison. It is with the first stanza of Shelley's *Ode to Liberty* that Kingsley opens the chapter telling of Alton's release from imprisonment (II, 163). And on the next page, commenting on the tradition of freedom in England, he quotes again from the same poem:

> The shadow of her coming fell
> On Saxon Alfred's olive-tinctured [*sic*] brow.   (IX, 2-3)[18]

---

[17] See Louis Cazamian *Kingsley et Thomas Cooper: Étude sur une Source d'Alton Locke* (Paris, 1903). See also W. Henry Brown, *Charles Kingsley: The Work and Influence of Parson Lot* (London, 1924), p. 95-104, and Stanley E. Baldwin, *Charles Kingsley* (Ithaca, Cornell Univ. Press, 1934), pp. 99-105.

[18] The error (*tinctured* for *cinctured*) is present in the first edition of *Alton Locke* (London, 1850), II, 149.

Alton's musings about liberty continue as follows:

But were there no excuses for the mass? Was there no excuse in the
spirit with which the English upper classes regarded the continental
revolutions? No excuse in the undisguised dislike, fear, contempt,
which they expressed for that very sacred name of Liberty, which
had been for ages the pride of England and her laws –

> The old laws of England, they
> Whose reverend heads with age are grey –
> Children of a wiser day –
> And whose solemn voice must be
> Thine own echo, Liberty!
>
> [*Masque of Anarchy*, LXXXIII]

for which according to the latest improvements, is now substituted a
bureaucracy of despotic commissions?   (II, 165)

In the next chapter, Crossthwaite, Alton's friend who favors active revolt, also quotes from Shelley's *Masque of Anarchy*,
forming one stanza from parts of two:

> Men of England, heirs of glory,
> Heroes of unwritten story,
> Rise, shake off the chains like dew
> Which in sleep have fallen on you!
> Ye are many, they are few!   (II, 174) [19]

Supplementing these direct quotations is Alton's crucial speech
to the mob (II, 129-131). In urging parliamentary representation
of the working classes, fairer taxation, and adequate remuneration
for labor, it is a typical Chartist oration and a close parallel to
Shelley's various social tracts. Its final outburst against the evil
system which withholds bread from the hungry people is reminiscent of the righteous anger which Shelley exhibited in *The
Masque of Anarchy, Song to the Men of England,* and *England
in 1819.*

Kingsley also acknowledges a parody of Shelley: "As society
is now, the brutes are masters – the horse, the sheep, the bullock,
is the master, and the labourer is their slave. 'Oh! but the brutes
are eaten!' Well; the horses at least are not eaten – they live like
landlords, till they die. And those who are eaten, are certainly

[19] See Shelley's *Masque of Anarchy*, stanzas XXXVII and XXXVIII.

not eaten by their human servants. The sheep they fat, another kills, to parody Shelley; and after all, is not the labourer, as well as the sheep, eaten by you, my dear Society?" (II, 118).[20] And later in the novel he employs Shelleyan terms to define this voracious nature of English society: "The great fish, and the great estates, and the great shopkeepers, eat up the little ones of their species – by law of competition, lately discovered to be the true creator and preserver of the universe" (II, 203).

Two Years Ago is more episodic than *Alton Locke* and has several minor plots (one involving a denunciation of slavery in the United States). Set primarily in nineteenth-century England, the novel has as its central incident an attack of cholera in a small Cornish village. The character who is of primary importance to our study is John Briggs, an effeminate poet who goes by an assumed name for the sake of his career. His ineffectual nature is contrasted with the virile personality of Tom Thurnall, an adventuresome and arrogant young doctor. Briggs marries unfortunately, deserts his wife and two children, longs to escape to Italy, and is finally drowned in the surf.

Two Years Ago gives further evidence of Kingsley's reliance upon Shelley's poetry to make impressive certain scenes and actions. The first instance is that of Grace Harvey, standing and looking out to sea on the stormy night of the shipwreck. "Thus she stands long, motionless, awe-frozen, save when a shudder runs through every limb, with such a countenance as that 'fair terror' of which Shelley sang:

> Its horror and its beauty are divine;
> Upon its lips and eyelids seem to lie
> Loveliness like a shadow, from which shine,
> Fiery and lucid, struggling underneath,
> The agonies of anguish and of death."
>
> (*On the Medusa of Leonardo da Vinci*, I, 4-8) [21]

---

[20]   The poetry parodied here is *Song, To the Men of England*, stanza V.
[21]   *Two Years Ago*, I, 60. Kingsley's use of the verb "seem" instead of "seems" (line 6 of Shelley's poem) is an indication that he may have used the uncorrected 1824 edition of the *Posthumous Poems* of Shelley. See Charles A. Taylor, Jr., *The Early Collected Editions of Shelley's Poems* (New Haven, Yale Univ. Press, 1958), p. 68.

In another scene, Valentia (sister of Lucia Vavasour) sings for an assembled group, and Kingsley, quoting stanza II of *To Constantia Singing*, remarks that not one of the guests, had he been poetically gifted, but might have expressed the same thoughts with Shelley (II, 32). Near the end of the novel a poetizing barfly, from whom Tom Thurnall and Major Campbell try to learn the whereabouts of the poet Elsley (note the Shelley anagram) Vavasour, tells of Elsley's having taken to opium and emphasizes the fact by quoting:

> Our Adonais hath drunk poison; Oh!
> What deaf and viperous murderer could crown
> Life's early cup with such a draught of woe?
>
> (*Adonais*, stanza XXXVI)

And Kingsley, perhaps in an attempt to save his own artistic integrity, presents Cambell's loss of self-possession and his cry of disgust at the fool: "As I live, sir, you may rhyme your own nonsense as long as you will, but you sha'nt quote the Adonais about that fellow in my presence" (II, 222-223).

Some of Kingsley's attitudes toward Shelley are revealed, in the novels, through minor incidents in which the latter's poetry or character figures prominently, though without direct quotation. One such incident occurs in *Alton Locke* when Dean Winnstay, criticizing a poem by Alton, says, "I am sorry to see that Shelley has had so much influence on your writing. He is a guide as irregular in taste, as unorthodox in doctrine: though there are some pretty things in him now and then. And you have caught his melody tolerably here, now –." It is the beautiful but ineffective Lillian who interrupts with, "Oh, that is such a sweet thing! . . . How very fond of beautiful things you must be, Mr. Locke, to be able to describe so passionately the longing after them" (I, 272). Later, after becoming a successful author, Alton begins lecturing to working men on literary and social subjects. Because he has been persuaded by aristocratic friends to take the social impact out of his poetry in order to get it published, the audiences at these lectures have lost faith in him, and they grow increasingly hostile. Finally, as Alton himself later tells it:

In the middle of a lecture on Shelley, I was indulging, and honestly too, in some very glowing and passionate praise of the true nobleness of a man whom neither birth nor education could blind to the evils of society; who for the sake of the suffering many, could trample under foot his hereditary pride, and become an outcast for The People's Cause.

I heard a whisper close to me, from one whose opinion I valued, and value still – a scholar and a poet, one who had tasted poverty, and slander, and a prison, for The Good Cause –

"Fine talk: but it's 'all in his day's work.' Will he dare to say that to-morrow to the ladies at the West End?"

No – I should not. I knew it. . . .   (II, 106)

And Alton rushes from the room in utter confusion.

That Kingsley could genuinely eulogize Shelley, as he does in Alton's words above, and that he yet found it necessary to write his violent essay against the poet, indicates that he himself saw the logical consistency of Shelley's profession and action but dared not proclaim it before "the ladies at the West End". Having chosen to take the more secure stand of defending the established order, Kingsley, in his diatribe against so iconoclastic a poet as Shelley, perhaps had a motivation similar to that of Alton's exit from the lecture room.

Early in *Two Years Ago*, the young John Briggs (later known as Elsly Vavasour), in a conversation with his older friend, Dr. Edward Thrunall, remarks that he does not wish to wait, like Wordsworth, through long years of obscurity, misunderstanding, and ridicule, for his day of success. He wants to make the world immediately confess "that another priest of the beautiful has arisen among men". Kingsley's comment is: "Now, it can scarcely be denied that the good doctor was guilty of a certain amount of weakness in listening patiently to all this rant. Not that the rant was very blamable in a lad of eighteen; for have we not all, while we are going through our course in Shelley, talked very much the same abominable stuff, and thought ourselves the grandest fellows upon earth on account of that very length of ear which was patent to all the world save our precious selves; blinded by our self-conceit, and wondering in wrath why everybody was laughing at us?" (I, 29-30). Here the implication is that

Kingsley was carried away, in his youth, by an enthusiasm for Shelley; and in his case it may well have taken the form of extreme optimism about the early effectiveness of practical social-improvement projects – such as the water-butt episode.

In the same novel another item which touches upon Kingsley's reaction to Shelley, is the letter received by young Tom Thurnall from Marie, the former slave whom he has helped to freedom. She writes from Montreal on the subject of freedom and dependence: "But to tell you the truth, I pay a price for this dependence. I must needs be staid and sober; I must needs dress like any Quakeress; I must not read this book or that; and my Shelley – taken from me, I suppose, because it spoke too much 'Liberty', though, of course, the reason given was its infidel opinions – is replaced by 'Law's Serious Call' " (I, 127-128). Kingsley's attitude seems equivocal, but perhaps this passage in Marie's letter is only the novelist's view of what a society must demand in return for certain freedoms it can offer.

MAJOR SHELLEYAN CHARACTERIZATIONS

The influence Shelley had upon Kingsley is revealed not only by quotations, references, and specific incidents; it is apparent also in several major characterizations in the novels. Aspects of the Shelleyan stereotype, as Kingsley saw it, are prominent in those characters who are intended as men of artistic temperament.

We have already noted Shelleyan characteristics in Lancelot Smith. The prime example, however, is the artist Claude Mellot who appears first in *Yeast* and later in *Two Years Ago*. Not that Mellot is an out-and-out Shelleyan character; Kingsley has given him some traits which are quite unlike Shelley's. But, in physical appearance as in philosophy, the likenesses to the poet are unmistakable. Being termed a "general favorite" and "general guest", Mellot is described as "a tiny, delicate-featured man, with a look of half-lazy enthusiasm about his beautiful face, which reminds you much of Shelley's portrait; only he has what Shelley had not, clustering auburn curls, and a rich brown beard, soft as silk. You set him down at once as a man of delicate susceptibility, sweetness, thoughtfulness; probably (as he actually is) an artist" (I, 2). The description coincides with Kingsley's dictum that Shelley should not have left his rightful place as an "artist" for that of a political and social reformer. A passage in *Yeast*, characterizing Mellot, clearly presents Kingsley's concept of the effeminate artist; the author makes references to Mellot's "delicate woman-like limbs", to Prometheus and the nymphs, and to guitar music (p. 233) – all of which point to his having Shelley in mind.

In both *Yeast* and *Two Years Ago* Mellot is depicted as a transient, unsettled, and ineffectual person. He and his wife appear on the scene intermittently. Their life is always quite removed from the reality in which the other characters find themselves. Mellot does not accomplish anything in either novel, and in both instances he is merely lost sight of in the end. What more implicit commentary could Kingsley have made on his regard of Shelley and his work? But, whereas Claude Mellot is ineffectual because he does not use the beautiful and natural as his model exclusively (thus not remaining the "artist"), the other poet, Elsley Vavasour, fails because he removes himself from the real and contemplates the ideal. In *Two Years Ago* Kingsley tells of Vavasour's long poem on the noble subject of Mariotti's tragedy about Fra Dolcino and Margaret – a poem which, he declares, should draw cannon balls or at least hanging for the poet. The section – which ends with a direct reference to Shelley's influence – can scarcely be read without calling to mind numerous criticisms Kingsley has made of Shelley:

[Vavasour] had conceived (and not altogether ill) a vision in which wandering along some bright Italian bay, he met Dolcino sitting, a spirit at rest but not yet gloried, waiting for the revival of that dead land for which he had died; and Margaret by him. . . . There they were to prophesy to him such things as seemed fit to him, of the future of Italy and of Europe, of the doom of priests and tyrants, of the sorrows and regards of genius unappreciated and before its age; for Elsley's secret vanity could see in himself a far greater likeness to Dolcino than Dolcino – the preacher, confessor, bender of all hearts, man of the world and man of action, at last crafty and all but unconquerable guerilla warrior – would ever have acknowledged in the self-indulgent dreamer. However, it was a fair conception enough; though perhaps it never would have entered Elsley's head, had Shelley never written the opening canto of the 'Revolt of Islam'.   (I, 205-206)

In his life, too, Elsley evidences this self-indulgence and dreaminess; and Kingsley points out the basis for these characteristics. He depicts Elsley's dread, more nervous than cowardly, of infectious diseases and tells of his dislike (on which Elsley prides himself) of all that is terrible or horrible – sickness, disease, wounds, death, anything which jars with that "beautiful" which is his ideal (I, 212). The "manliness" in Kingsley's character objected to everything which seemed to him effeminate; the early sympathy he felt for Shelley's objection to all violence had given way to the influence of Carlyle's more obviously robust "hero worship" ideas.

In marriage Elsley has also been the victim of idealism; Kingsley's description of the home life of Elsley and Lucia Vavasour is an unmistakable allusion to the relationship of Shelley and Harriet Westbrooke. Having been motivated by feeling and romance to run away with Elsley to be married, Lucia soon reveals that little real intellect underlies her passionate sensibility. After the sensibility is burned out and replaced by family and household cares, Elsley finds his wife to be commonplace and without her former good looks and good temper. The "vain, capricious, over-sensitive" Elsley, who craves admiration and distinction, wants more than a homemaker; he wants his wife to serve as an appreciative public whenever he is hungry for praise. She is to worship him, live for him, and talk sentiment with him, no matter how severe have been the cares of the day. Therefore, they quarrel a great deal. Finally, Elsley, having conceived a delusion of her unfaithfulness to him, leaves Lucia. She remains with their two children while he wanders into the mountains on a stormy night. After he has been found unconscious on a high bluff, Elsley has visions of an escape to the Apennines or Calabria. "Yes! He would escape thither, and be at peace; and if the world heard of him again, it should be in such a thunder-voice as those with which Shelley and Byron, from their southern seclusion, had shaken the ungrateful motherland which had cast them out" (II, 181). At every opportunity Kingsley emphasizes the delusions of the weak, vacillating, irresponsible Elsley.

As in the case of Claude Mellot, the biographical and ideational details regarding Elsley Vavasour do not always fit when applied to Shelley. But that Kingsley's concept of Shelley was liberally drawn upon in the creation of both characters seems scarcely disputable. It is noteworthy that, whereas in the earlier novels the Shelleyan characteristics are given to persons whom the author treats more or less kindly, by the time of *Two Years Ago* (four years after *Thoughts on Shelley and Byron*), Kingsley has nothing but contempt for the Shelleyan character.

SHELLEYAN SYMBOLS AND KINGSLEY'S SOCIAL VIEWS

Kingsley also drew on Shelley for some of the major symbols in his novels – one being that of "twin stars" or "twin spheres of light", attracting each other and achieving together some good for humanity. Shelley repeatedly used the symbol of twin stars as a correlate to his concept of soul partnership. It may be helpful, before examining Kingsley's use of the idea, to consider some of its recurrences in Shelley's poetry. In *Alastor* the symbol is employed twice, in two different ways, both implying an attraction toward fulfillment. The setting for its first occurrence (see Kingsley's quotation of the passage, *Yeast*, pp. 74-75) is the emaciated poet's arrival at the serene, densely vegetated shore of the river along which his boat has taken him. There, beckoning to him, "two eyes. Two starry eyes hung in the gloom of thought" (lines 489-490). In the scene of the poet's death the symbol is used again. His very last sight is of the sinking great new moon, after the major portion of the crescent has disappeared below the horizon. It appears to him as "two lessening points of light alone" (line 654), gleaming through the darkness.

The "twin stars" symbol appears also in *The Revolt of Islam*. The "Dedication" of that revolutionary poem ends with the lines:

> Thou and I,
> Sweet friend! can look from our tranquility
> Like lamps into the world's tempestuous night, –
> Two tranquil stars, while clouds are passing by
> Which wrap them from the foundering seaman's sight,
> That burn from year to year with unextinguished light.
>
> (stanza XIV)

And in Canto I the symbol represents the spiritual unity of Laon and Cythna. The scene is the arrival of the poet and the Woman at Laon's throne room:

> Then first, two glittering lights were seen to glide
> In circles on the amethystine floor,
> Small serpent eyes trailing from side to side,
> Like meteors on a river's grassy shore,
> They round each other rolled, dilating more
> And more – then rose, commingling into one. (stanza LVI)

In *Epipsychidion* Shelley uses the symbol most effectively. Apparently indicating Emily and Mary, he says:

> Twin Spheres of Light who rule this passive Earth,
> This world of love, this *me*; and into birth
> Awaken all its fruits and flowers, and dart
> Magnetic might into its central heart. . . .
> So ye, bright regents, with alternate sway
> Govern my sphere of being, night and day!
>
> (lines 345-348, 360-361)

Finally, in his closing exhortation to Emily, Shelley distinctly equates the "twin stars" symbol with the idea of the "soul of my soul":

> We shall become the same, we shall be one
> Spirit within two frames, oh! wherefore two?
> One passion in twin-hearts, which grows and grew
> Till like two meteors of expanding flame,
> Those spheres instinct with it become the same,
> Touch, mingle, are transfigured; ever still
> Burning, yet ever inconsumable. (lines 573-579)

That Kingsley derived from these passages his symbol for the relationship between Argemone and Lancelot in *Yeast* may be shown by a few excerpts from that novel. Early in the narrative

there appears a distinct reflection of the Emily-Mary influence
upon Shelley, personified here in Argemone and her sister Honoria, "the two poles of beauty .... Look at them! Honoria the
dark – symbolic of passionate depth; Argemone the fair, type of
intellectual light! Oh, that I were a Zeuxis to unite them instead
of having to paint them in two separate pictures, and split perfection in half, as everything is split in this piecemeal world!"
(p. 32).[22] Reminiscent of the Alastor poet's "excess of love" (lines
181-182) for the veiled maid of his vision – for him the "type
of intellectual light" – is Lancelot's half-apologetic longing for
Argemone, whom he has first met in a setting not totally unlike
a vision.

The ideas of the *Epipsychidion* passages which use the "twin
stars" concept, as well as their terminology, are unmistakable in
Lancelot's arguments and in Argemone's poetry. Taking his cue
from one of the key ideas in *Epipsychidion*, Lancelot lectures
Argemone on the nature of love and the pursuit of intellectual
beauty as found in the affinity of two souls for each other:

Love is like a flame – light as many fresh flames at it as you will, it
grows, instead of diminishing, by the dispersion.... But, oh, how
miserable and tantalizing a thought ... to know that a priceless spirit
is near them [two lovers], which might be one with theirs through
all eternity, like twin stars in one common atmosphere, forever giving
and receiving wisdom and might, beauty and bliss, and yet are barred
from their bliss by some invisible adamantine wall, against which
they must beat themselves to death, like butterflies against the win-
dow-pane, gazing, and longing, and unable to guess why they are forbidden to enjoy!   (pp. 95-96)

The ideals which Lancelot and Argemone have found in each
other eventually encounter the very "wall" of which Lancelot
speaks. Argemone dies as a result of her humanitarian efforts,
but she leaves her final poem for Lancelot – a poem which distinctly echoes the same Shelleyan lines which inform the above

---

[22]   See *Alastor*, lines 454-456 as a possible source:
　　　　　　Through the dell,
　　　Silence and twilight here, twin-sisters keep
　　　Their noonday watch.

speech by Lancelot. The first stanza of the poem is sufficient to
show the similarity:

> Twin stars, aloft in ether clear,
> Around each other roll away,
> Within one common atmosphere
> Of their own mutual light and day.   (p. 250)

To compare poetry of this calibre with that of Shelley is certainly
to Kingsley's disadvantage; but that he did no better, considering
the extent to which he obviously was acquainted with Shelley's
work, reflects on either his taste or his poetic ability.

That Kingsley, the advocate of "Muscular Christianity", despised the actions of the fictional poet in *Alastor* is eminently
clear. But whether the highly-contrived passage, depicting Argemone after her first evening visit with Lancelot, is a satire on
Shelley's poem in particular or only on what Kingsley considered
the poet's effeminacy in general, may be open to some question.
Feeling needless, lonely, and out of tune with self and nature,
Argemone sits listlessly in the window and reads over to herself
a fragment of her own poetry, entitled "Sappho". Concluding the
long, dreary passage, she reproaches it for its prosody; and Kingsley then inserts his criticism of her purpose in writing the poem:

Sweet self-deceiver! Had you no reason for choosing as your heroine
Sappho, the victim of the idolatry of intellect – trying in vain to fill
her heart with the friendship of her own sex, and then sinking into
mere passion for a handsome boy, and so down into self-contempt
and suicide? . . .
 "After all", [Argemone] said pettishly, "people will call it a mere
imitation of Shelley's 'Alastor'. And what harm if it is? Is there to
be no female Alastor? Has not the woman as good a right as the man
to long after ideal beauty – to pine and die if she cannot find it; and
regenerate herself in its light?"   (p. 24)

Whatever was Kingsley's intent in presenting this obvious parody,
his novels give serious treatment to the theme of a sudden vision
which irresistibly draws the seer in pursuit – the theme of
Alastor. Love being a prominent topic throughout *Alastor*, the
tendency is strong to combine the love of universal truth with
the love for an ideal mate. It is not, however, a perfect combi-

nation, the love of truth being predominant. There is a constant tendency to shift the emphasis, first from truth to beauty, then to love itself. In the essay *On Love* and in *Epipsychidion* Shelley makes the combination more effectively and convincingly, and *The Triumph of Life* marks his highest achievement in this poetic tendency.[23]

A sense of incompleteness accompanies the vision of the veiled maid in *Alastor*; it, combined with the attractiveness of the perfect mate, compels the Poet's search. Kingsley employs a similar formula in the incident involving Argemone's absurd *Alastor* imitation. But rather than obviously pursuing Lancelot, who represents the "vision" in her experience, Argemone seeks the ideal of alleviating as much social distress as she can. This choice directly illustrates Kingsley's view that the fortunate members of society must be willing to sacrifice for the benefit of the less fortunate classes – which is his definition of the "love and brotherhood" by which Shelley meant a complete discarding of all barriers to equal status for all. Argemone, though her ministering to the plague-stricken poor finally brings about her own death, always gives to the needy in a spirit of benevolence, not of unequivocal social equality.

Likewise in *Alton Locke*, Kingsley maintains the concept of "association" but scarcely implies more thereby than a willingness on the part of the aristocracy to help the poor. There is a lofty and commendable tone in his declaration: "The battle [against 'Mammon' and 'that accursed system of competition, slavery of labor', etc.] remains still to be fought; the struggle is internecine; only no more with weapons of flesh and blood, but with a mightier weapon – with that association which is the true bane of Mammon – the embodiment of brotherhood and love" (II, 168). But there are certain limitations on the extent to which this "brotherhood and love" may be applied. Alton Locke, a member of the lower classes who seeks to associate with the elite and to raise his fellow-laborers to a higher level, is utterly defeated. It is Eleanor, the "high-born countess", who points the way in

23   Frederick L. Jones, "The Vision Theme in Shelley's *Alastor* and Related Works", *SP*, XLIV (Januari 1947), 124.

Kingsley's philanthropic world by establishing an asylum for unfortunate girls and by sending Alton to tropical America with the
smiling words, "You are my servant now, by the laws of chi-
valry, and you must fulfil my quest. I have long hoped for a
tropic poet .... Go for me, and for the people" (II, 264).

Increasingly, Shelley saw the idea of brotherhood as a matter
of total commitment, not limited to actual physical assistance in
areas of obvious need. It was, for him, rather a condition of mind
and being, whatever the appearances might indicate. An observation by Professor F. L. Jones is pertinent in this respect: "It
is significant that after *Alastor* Shelley never again represents the
poet as guilty and deserving of punishment because he is a solitary who neglects human fellowship. The inconsistency of *Alastor*
proves his uneasiness on that point, and the complete reversal in
Prince Athanase reveals the reconciliation of thought and feeling.
Prince Athanase is as much of a solitary as the Poet of *Alastor,*
but he is represented as loving mankind and devoting himself to
its improvement, as Shelley himself did." [24]

Eleanor's exultant speech to the slowly dying Alton Locke
contains some very similar ideas; but a distinctly Kingsleyan twist
entirely alters the effect: " 'See!' she said, 'Freedom, Equality, and
Brotherhood are come; but not as you expected .... Realize
them in thine own self, and so alone thou helpest to make realities for all. Not from without, from Charters and Republics, but
from within, from the Spirit working in each; not by wrath and
haste, but by patience made perfect through suffering, canst thou
proclaim their good news to the groaning masses, and deliver
them, as thy Master did before thee, by the cross, and not the
sword. Divine Paradox!' " She continues, pointing out how the
"tyranny of Mammon" contains its own suicidal elements, by
which it is already crumbling, and that labor shall be free after
the self-destruction of tyranny is complete. Thus far, there is
much of Shelleyan philosophy in what Eleanor says. But in her
clerical terminology, she deviates from it to imply that the individual should be concerned only with the salvation of himself and of those with whom he can deal directly – that agitation

[24] *Ibid.*, pp. 122-123.

on the larger, political scene is ineffective and even wrong (II, 266-267). Her objective is to make life tolerable for the lower classes: to strengthen them in religion and to deliver them from cruel oppression – but not to permit their gaining mastery over themselves. Shelley, on the other hand, would give the initiative to the people and would assist, wherever he could, their attainment of self-mastery.

SHELLEY AND KINGSLEY'S RELIGIOUS VIEWS

In 1848, at the height of Chartism's greatest effort, Kingsley went to London to make the acquaintance of Maurice's friend, the barrister John Ludlow, who had experienced two French revolutions. Ludlow pointed out to him that French socialism was not necessarily atheistic and that the people's religious respect increased with the degree of their power. As a boy in Paris in the revolution of 1830, Ludlow had witnessed a great antagonism toward the Church; however, during the months just past when he had been back in Paris and had observed the revolutionary deposition of Louis Philippe in its first stages, he had seen priests and Sisters of Charity treated without hostility and even with affectionate sympathy. In Kingsley's mind, to be sure, there was a great distinction between French tolerance of Roman Catholic priests and the respect of honest Englishmen for their church. But he became convinced that socialism must be entirely Christianized if it were not to be a threatening alternative which could shake the very foundations of organized Christianity. The Church and the forces of social action must work together, not against each other. The danger to the Church was that if it remained antagonistic toward socialism, one of the two might have to go, and it could prove to be Christianity.[25]

Kingsley, gripped by this deep concern for both Christianity and social improvement, appears to have examined closely the religion of Shelley, whose social views he knew. And Shelley did,

[25] *Martin,* pp. 83-84.

from the very first, involve Christianity with his ideas of social progress and the means of its achievement. Already in *An Address, To the Irish People* (1812) he wrote "Anything short of unlimited toleration, and complete charity with all men, on which . . . Jesus Christ principally insisted, is wrong." [26] Historically this creed, practised by the early Christians, was abandoned because of envy and avarice after the first glow of enthusiasm had faded. Moral improvement had not preceded the new system. Shelley, in letters and pamphlets as early as 1811-1813, insisted that political improvement is impossible until after a moral revolution has occurred. But Shelley does not look to conventional theology for the source of this moral revolution. In *Prometheus Unbound* he agrees with Aeschylus that the long-drawn process of time holds hope for man's release. Time and mechanism, two categories of the understanding, affect the onward movement of life, both individual and cosmic. But they have meaning only insofar as they are servants of purpose, and they are, therefore, not final. When man also acknowledges himself a servant to the great cosmic design, purpose becomes both freedom and hope.[27] This hope Shelley holds out to Society in the essay *On Life*, as well as in his most lofty poetry. It must be classed a religious hope, but it is not the orthodoxy of Kingsley.

Kingsley's hope for society is perhaps most clearly elucidated by one of the final pronouncements in *Yeast*. The old prophet Barnakill, who speaks for the author, instructs Lancelot: "Don't believe Catholic [not Roman Catholic, to be sure] doctrine unless you like; faith is free. But see if you can reclaim either society or yourself without it; see if He will let you reclaim them. Take Catholic doctrine for granted; act on it; and see if you will not reclaim them!" (p. 265). In the final analysis, it is this confident but vague expression of belief in the efficacy of established religion which is Kingsley's answer to social problems. In his essay he blames Shelley's less pious and (to Kingsley) more effemi-

[26]   *Works*, V, 221.
[27]   James S. Thomson, "The Unbinding of Prometheus", *UTQ*, XV (April 1946), 16.

nately foolhardy approach for much of the unrest and unhealth seen in sensitive young men for many succeeding years:

> Must we not thank the man who gives us fresh hope that this earth will not be always as it is now? His notion of what it will be may be, as Shelley's was, vague, even in some things wrong and undesirable. Still, we must accept his hope and faith in the spirit, not in the letter. So have thousands of young men felt, who would have shrunk with disgust from some of poor Shelley's details of the "good time coming". And shame on him who should wish to rob them of such a hope, even if it interfered with his favorite "scheme of unfulfilled prophecy". So men have felt Shelley's spell a wondrous one – perhaps, they think, a life-giving, regenerative one. And yet what dream at once more shallow, and more impossible?[28]

The many criticisms of and severe recriminations against the Church in Kingsley's novels are made with the sole purpose of rejuvenating and strengthening it as *the* institution which could cope with the issues of the day. Shelley's contention that old institutions needed to be eliminated or replaced was as objectionable to Kingsley as were the effeminate characteristics he saw in the poet. These two aspects of his difference with Shelley appear to have become more pronounced as Kingsley's writing career progressed. Whereas *Yeast* and *Alton Locke* give evidence of a strong attraction to the Shelleyan philosophy of achieving reform by non-violent means, Kingsley's last three novels (*Westward Ho!*, 1855; *Two Years Ago*, 1857; and *Hereward the Wake*, 1866) are compounded almost exclusively of the virtues of martial fervor, manly strength, ennobling warfare, extreme Protestant bias, and heroic deeds on behalf of the England of tradition. If social improvement were to come, Kingsley believed, it must be found by the aristocracy and handed down to the poor, ignorant masses. He saw a need for improvement in the system of priests and tyrants but was terrified by Shelley's consistent argument that

---

[28]   *Thoughts on Shelley and Byron*, pp. 316-317. The use of the phrase "good time coming" in this discussion of Shelley lends added support to the view that Shelley's ideas are of basic concern in *Alton Locke*. The novel closes with Alton's death in Texas. He has written a final poem extolling social change; but his last utterance emphasizes his belief that there is a "Good Time Coming" – that it has, in fact, already begun and is progressing according to God's good time (II, 270-271).

this order must be superseded and that men must build an ideal society in which truth and beauty would replace authority and power.

Kingsley found Shelley's belief to have been disillusioning. Having, in *Yeast*, just quoted lines from *Hymn to Intellectual Beauty*, he has Lancelot say, "And much peace of mind it gave him! ... When you look through the glitter of the words, your 'spirit of beauty' simply means certain shapes and colors which please you in beautiful things and in beautiful people." Then, speaking for the author by pointing out the void left by Shelley's religion, Lancelot says: "I don't care sixpence now for the ideal! ... If I must have an ideal, let it be, for mercy's sake, a realized one" (p. 43). Similarly, Alton Locke says, "I had utterly given up the whole problem of religion as insoluble. I believed in poetry, science, and democracy – and they were enough for me then; enough, at least, to leave a mighty hunger in my heart, I knew not for what" (II, 61). Later, in prison, Alton longs for the coming of true religion (and the terminology, at least, is much like Shelley's): "When shall we see a nation ruled, not by the law, but the Gospel; not in the letter which kills, but in the spirit which is love, forgiveness, life?" (II, 151).

To all these questings and yearnings, especially to the demand for a "living, loving person" or a "realized" ideal, Kingsley gives his answer at the close of his first novel – the old prophet Barnakill speaking to Lancelot, who has totally lost his way:

Had you never the sense of a Spirit in you – a will, an energy, an inspiration ... and you heard the sound of it ringing through your consciousness, and yet you knew not ... why it drove you on to dare and suffer, to love and hate. ... But did it never seem to you that this strange wayward spirit, if anything, was the very root and core of your own personality? And had you never the craving for the help of some higher, mightier spirit, to guide and strengthen yours; to regulate and civilize its savage and spasmodic self-will; to teach you your rightful place in the great order of the universe around; to fill you with a continuous purpose and with a continuous will to do it? Have you never had a dream of an Inspirer? – a spirit of all spirits?

There is a very probable reference to Shelley in Lancelot's confession, "I have been irreverent to the false, from very longing to worship the true; I have been a rebel to sham leaders, for very desire to be loyal to a real one." Finally the old prophet Barnakill asks the question which leads to Lancelot's conversion: "Did you ever mistake these substitutes, even the noblest of them, for the reality? Did not your very dissatisfaction . . . show you that the true inspirer ought to be . . . the Spirit of order, obedience, loyalty, brotherhood, mercy, condescension?" (pp. 262-264). And thus Kingsley brings together the Shelleyan ideals of the soul partners or "twin stars", of the vision, and of the search for Intellectual Beauty; he has the answer to all questions regarding them; and this answer suffices also in the two later social novels. As the prophet leads Lancelot off to his own strange land, the reader senses that this land has much in common with – no doubt, it *is* – a rejuvenated Church of England, and that "grace" is depended upon to accomplish that in which Shelley's ideals seemed to Kingsley utterly ineffective.

V

SHELLEY AND OTHER EARLY AND MID VICTORIANS

Creative writers of the early and middle periods of the Victorian era were predominently non-Shelleyan. Generally, they either opposed him or were not sure enough of his ideas to be greatly influenced by them. A notable exception is George Eliot, whose view of Shelley, reflected in one character in one of her novels, is discussed later in this chapter. The epitome of disregard for Shelley is evidenced by Matthew Arnold, whose pronouncement against the earlier poet is perhaps still accepted more widely than any other judgment of him.

JOHN STUART MILL

Among those who had studied Shelley seriously before Queen Victoria ascended to the throne was John Stuart Mill (1806-1873). Yet, though his concern for liberty and social progress was affected by Shelley, he appears not to have considered the poet's views adequately matured. Although, late in his life, Mill one evening read to his friends Shelley's *Ode to Liberty* and "got quite excited and moved over it rocking backwards and forwards and nearly choking with emotion",[1] it may be that before the age of about 24 he had never studied Shelley. Harriet Taylor, whose acquaintance he made in 1830 and whose few minor poems reflect her interest in Shelley, convinced Mill to read him with

---

[1] *The Amberly Papers: The letters and Diaries of Bertrand Russell's Parents,* ed. Bertrand and Patricia Russell, 2 vols. (New York, 1937), II, 375.

some care.[2] Mill and Harriet soon fell in love; she became his valued consultant and pre-publication critic and, in 1851 (after the death of her first husband), his wife.

In his *Autobiography* Mill gives a description of Harriet which indicates not only his knowledge of Shelley's personality and ideas but also his view that Shelley had not had time to mature in his thinking. The enumeration of Harriet's qualities begins:

In her, complete emancipation from every kind of superstition (including that which attributes a pretended perfection to the order of nature and the universe), and an earnest protest against many things which are still part of the established constitution of society, resulted not from the hard intellect, but from strength of noble and elevated feeling, and co-existed with a highly reverential nature. In general spiritual characteristics, as well as in temperament and organisation, I have often compared her, as she was at this time [the early 1830's], to Shelley: but in thought and intellect, Shelley, so far as his powers were developed in his short life, was but a child compared with what she ultimately became.[3]

It is important to remember that Mill has in mind this comparison to Shelley as he continues the description of Harriet:

Alike in the highest regions of speculation and in the smaller practical concerns of daily life, her mind was the same perfect instrument, piercing to the very heart and marrow of the matter; always seizing the essential idea or principle.... Her intellectual gifts did but minister to a moral character at once the noblest and the best balanced which I have ever met with in life. Her unselfishness was not that of a taught system of duties, but of a heart which thoroughly identified itself with the feelings of others, and often went to excess in consideration for them by imaginatively investing their feelings with the intensity of its own. The passion of justice might have been thought to be her strongest feeling, but for her boundless generosity, and a lovingness ever ready to pour itself forth upon any or all human beings who were capable of giving the smallest feeling in return. The rest of her moral characteristics were such as naturally accompany these qualities of mind and heart: the most genuine modesty combined with the loftiest pride; a simplicity and sincerity

[2]   Michael St. John Packe, *The Life of John Stuart Mill* (London, 1954), p. 134.
[3]   Mill, *Autobiography* (New York, Columbia Univ. Press, 1924), pp. 130-131.

which were absolute, towards all who were fit to receive them; the utmost scorn of whatever was mean and cowardly, and a burning indignation at everything brutal or tyrannical, faithless or dishonourable in conduct and character, while making the broadest distinction between *mala in se* and *mala prohibita* – between acts giving evidence of intrinsic badness in feeling and character, and those which are only violations of conventions either good or bad, violations which whether in themselves right or wrong, are capable of being committed by persons in every other respect lovable or admirable.

Despite the stated belief that Shelley lacked development, the above lines indicate a good understanding of and contain a high tribute to the poet's character and motivations.

In a passage which he eventually did not include in the *Autobiography*, Mill wrote:

The first years of my friendship with her [Harriet] were, in respect of my own development, mainly years of poetic culture. It is hardly necessary to say that I am not now speaking of written poetry, either metrical or otherwise; though I did cultivate this taste as well as a taste for paintings & sculptures, & did read with enthusiasm her favorite poets, especially the one whom she placed far above all others, Shelley.[4]

And with enthusiasm he accepted Shelley's main principle – freedom of thought and action. Having read G. H. Lewes's essay on Shelley before it appeared in the *Westminster Review* of April 1841, Mill wrote to Lewes, stating one of his criticisms thus:

I would say that the idea of a vindicator should be abandoned. Shelley can only be usefully vindicated from a point of view nearer that occupied by those to whom a vindication of him is still needed. I have seen very useful and effective vindications of him by religious persons and in a religious tone: but *we,* I think, should leave that to others, and should take for granted, boldly, all those premises respecting freedom of thought and the morality of acting on one's own credo which to anyone who admits them carry Shelley's vindication with them.[5]

Although Shelley did not replace Wordsworth as Mill's favorite

[4] See Jack Stillinger, ed., *The Early Draft of John Stuart Mill's Autobiography* (Urbana, Univ. of Illinois Press, 1961), p. 199.
[5] See Anna Theresa Kitchel, *George Lewes and George Eliot: A Review of Records* (New York, 1933), pp. 28-29.

poet, Mill wrote in 1837 to E. Lytton Bulwer complementing him on his article, "The Works of Thomas Gray" (*London and Westminster Review*, July 1837), but not agreeing wholly with Bulwer's low rating of Shelley. Mill says of the article:

I have hardly found a sentence which has not my heartiest concurrence, except perhaps some part of what you say of Shelley, and *there* I am not sure that there is any difference, for all that you say to his disparagement I allow to be true, though not, I think, the whole truth. It seems to me that much though not most, of Shelley's poetry is full of the truest passion; and it seems to me hardly fair to put Shelley in the same *genus* as Gray, when the imagery of the one, however redundant and occasionally far-fetched, is always true to nature, and that of the other, as you say yourself, drawn from books and false; the one, the exuberant outpouring of a seething fancy, the other elaborately studied and artificial.

But perhaps you think all this as well as I; if so, and only if so, would not some little addition or qualification give a truer impression? [6]

In 1833 Mill had written two essays on poetics, "What is Poetry" and "Two Kinds of Poetry". The latter refers to Shelley as "perhaps the most striking example ever known of the poetic temperament",[7] by which Mill means a poet in whom emotions completely control ideas. It appears that Harriet was able to convince Mill of Shelley's greatness in technique and imagination but, even though Shelley's main principle was wholly congenial, not of his full reliability in subject matter. In 1849, replying to Harriet's criticism of a particular sentence in one of his manuscripts and agreeing to delete the sentence, Mill explained to her that he meant, in regard to social and political improvement, that only experience can assure us of the results of innovations. The letter continues:

I do not say that you cannot realize and judge of these things – but if you and perhaps Shelley and one or two others in a generation can, I am convinced that to do so requires both great genius and great experience and I think it quite fair to say to common readers that the present race of mankind (speaking of them collectively) are

[6]   *The Letters of John Stuart Mill*, ed. Hugh S. R. Elliot, 2 vols. (London, 1910), I, 107.
[7]   Mill, *Early Essays*, ed. J. W. M. Gibbs (London, 1897), p. 226.

not competent to it. I cannot persuade myself that you do not greatly overrate the ease of making people unselfish. Granting that in "ten years" the children of the community might by teaching be made "perfect" it seems to me that to do so there must be perfect people to teach them. You say "if there were a desire on the part of the cleverer people to make them perfect it would be easy ["] – but how to produce that desire on the part of the cleverer people? I must say I think that if we had absolute power tomorrow, though we could do much to improve people by good laws and could even give them a very much better education than they have ever had yet, still, for effecting in our time anything like what we aim at, all our plans would fail from the impossibility of finding fit instruments. To make people really good for much it is so necessary not merely to give them good intentions and conscientiousness but to unseal their eyes – to prevent self flattery, vanity, irritability and all that family of vices from warping their moral judgements as those of the very cleverest people are almost always warped now.[8]

Evidently Harriet had been urging Mill to consider these Shelleyan ideas of social progress. She may have been excessively optimistic about the rapidity with which improvement would come, thus aiding and abetting Mill's view of Shelley as a poet with noble and desirable ideas but yet a visionary who was unrealistic about their implementation. In his insistence upon the slowness of social evolution, Mill was nearer Shelley's actual philosophy than he appears to have realized. He was moved and inspired by Shelley's ideas, but his works do not indicate demonstrably that he accepted the poet as relevant to practical applications of reform theories. How much Mill's ideas, however, were molded and modified by Shelley's influence on Harriet Taylor remains largely a matter of conjecture.

THOMAS CARLYLE

A contemporary of Shelley but a writer also of the early and middle Victorian periods, Thomas Carlyle (1795-1881) is one of

---

[8] F. A. Hayek, *John Stuart Mill and Harriet Taylor: Their Correspondence and Subsequent Marriage* (Chicago, Univ. of Chicago Press, 1951), pp. 145-146.

those who saw Shelley only in terms of their one dominant impression of him. Adulating naked force in the character of Frederick the Great, he was most vituperative in his denunciation of Shelley. He judged the poet to be "weak in genius, weak in character (for these two always go together); a poor, thin, spasmodic, hectic, shrill and pallid being; – one of those unfortunates, of whom I often speak, to whom 'the talent of silence', first of all, has been denied".[9] On one occasion, when William Bell Scott was rhapsodizing about Shelley, Carlyle rudely interrupted him to declare, "Yon man Shelley was just a scoundrel, and ought to have been hangèd".[10] In a longer and more comprehensive tirade he summoned all his force of eloquence and overstatement to express his dislike for Shelley:

Poor Shelley always was, and is, a kind of ghastly object; colourless pallid, without health or warmth or vigour; the sound of him shrieky, frosty, as if a ghost were trying to "sing to us"; the temperament of him, spasmodic, hysterical, instead of strong or robust; with fine affectations and aspirations, gone all such a road: – a man infinitely too weak for that solitary scaling of the Alps which he undertook in spite of all the world.[11]

And in his *Characteristics*, Carlyle gives clear evidence that the Romantic poets (especially Shelley) were the antithesis of the hero who was taking shape in his mind:

The Godlike has vanished from the world: and they [poets], by the strong cry of their soul's agony, like true wonder-workers, must again evoke its presence.... Our land yet knows not of it. Behold a Byron, in melodious tones, "cursing the day".... Hear a Shelley filling the earth with inarticulate wail; like the infinite, inarticulate grief and weeping of forsaken infants.[12]

Yet Carlyle's views on the Romantic idea of the artist in society are basically those of Shelley. Of his "Man-of-Letters Hero" he writes: "Whence he came, whither he is bound, by what ways he

[9]   See his *Letters to John Stuart Mill, John Sterling and Robert Browning*, ed. Alexander Carlyle (New York, 1923), p. 292.
[10]   See Newman Ivey White, *Shelley* (New York, 1940), II, 413.
[11]   *Reminiscences*, ed. James Anthony Froude (London, 1881), II, 325.
[12]   *Critical and Miscellaneous Essays,* in vols. XXVI to XXX of Centenary Ed. of *Works* (London, 1899), iii, 31.

arrived, by what he might be furthered on his course, no one asks. He is an accident in society. He wanders like a wild Ishmaelite, in a world of which he is as the spiritual light, either the guidance or the misguidance." [13] However, Shelley may well have been the model for the "unregenerate Prometheus Vinctus of a man" of whom Carlyle says, "It is ever the bitterest aggravation of his wretchedness that he is conscious of Virtue, but he feels himself the victim not of suffering only but of injustice."[14] And this sensitiveness to suffering and injustice Carlyle cannot endure. In his opinion it designates Shelley as the "misguidance" rather than the "guidance" of the world. Carlyle does not recognize the unselfishness of Shelley's concern about suffering and injustice; and if he did, he would still object, because the Carlylean hero – misplaced wanderer though he may be – does not question and ponder; he gets to work.

Thus Carlyle's reaction to Shelley is seen to differ from that of Browning, Disraeli, and Kingsley in that he never was enthusiastic about him. Shelley's ideas about social improvement had little impact on the writer who saw no solution to the problems of Victorian society but the return of an effective, compelling power system.

JOHN RUSKIN

That Carlyle had in John Ruskin (1819-1900) an acknowledged follower is well known, but what is perhaps the prime example of that pupil's surpassing his master has only recently been published. As a display of sheer emotion and venom a passage once intended for Ruskin's autobiography [15] far exceeds even Carlyle's outbursts. That in a more rational moment Ruskin should cancel the passage was only to be expected of a man of his stature. It's

---

13   *On Heroes, Hero-Worship and the Heroic in History*, in the Centenary Ed. of *Works* (London, 1897), V, 159.

14   *Sartor Resartus*, Book II, Chap. vii. See *Works*, I, 130.

15   See Samuel E. Brown, "The Unpublished Passages in the Manuscript of Ruskin's Autobiography", *Victorian Newsletter*, No. 16 (Fall 1959), p. 12.

cumulative effect can be demonstrated only by a presentation of the whole diatribe:

This is the first time I have mentioned Shelley, and I interrupt my story to say all I want to, and be done with him. My Father read nothing in poetry but Milton, Pope, Scott and Byron, but I was not allowed Byron for my own, while I was allowed, to my sorrow, a large octavo close printed volume, containing Coleridge – Shelley – and Keats. The latter puzzled me and I let him alone – Coleridge I read as a duty because I had heard he was a philosopher. But with Shelley's descriptions of sea and mountain I had complete sympathy – and after I had once been in Italy, I imagined Pisa and Lucca and La Spezia from him as I did Venice from Byron. In my nascent and vulgarly sensuous taste, liking richness and sweetness, by eyes and lips alike, – as Dr. Andrews' velvet cushion – and Christmas plum cake, Shelley was to me like a grocer's shop full of barley sugar – and I fed upon him like a fly, till I was sick and sticky. He clogged all my faculties and infested all my imagination – he is to me now comparable in memory only to a dream I had – prolonged through the whole of a weary and miserable day in first recovering after my Matlock illness (inflammation of bowels) – a dream of putrid apple-blossoms with a smell which was to that of real appleblossom as that of rotten cabbage to fresh lettuce. Worse than this, I began in my own verses to imitate his affected diction, and to make myself miserable over the plots of the *Cenci* and *Prometheus*; mixed up with deadly arsenic out of the juvenil [*sic*] blasphemies of *Queen Mab*. Voltaire by himself, in his Satanic strength – and Satanic ugliness, will do no one any harm but Voltaire powdered and mixed with red currant jelly and jalap – and swallowed in table spoonfuls! needed something of a constitution to stand against. *Revenons a nos moutons.*

As a true Carlylean hero, Ruskin thus throws off a youthful in-fatuation – not recognizing that it has become repulsive not so much because of the substance of its object as because of the cramped childhood which nourished it. For the soul-searching of the disillusioned Browning, Disraeli, and Kingsley, Ruskin sub-stitutes a "clean break" of which Carlyle himself might well have been proud.

WALTER BAGEHOT

Another severe critic who had formed one basic mind-set regard-ing Shelley and allowed it to control his every thought concerning the poet's ideas was Walter Bagehot (1826-1877). His influential essay, "Percy Bysshe Shelley" (1856), by its assumption throughout that Shelley was motivated by pure impulse in all that he did and in all that he wrote, immediately disqualifies its author as a valid critic of the poet. An example of Bagehot's irresponsible conjectures is his imaginary placing of Shelley as a violent fighter for liberation in the French revolution and his conclusion: "Who can think that he would have been scrupulous how he attained such an end? It was in him to have walked toward it over seas of blood." [16] When declaring Shelley "defective in the sensations of conscience",[17] Bagehot can scarcely have taken into consideration the letters to Godwin which indicate Shelley's devotion, because of Godwin's commendable characteristics, to his disillusioning father-in-law. And Bagehot's attributing to Shelley an "abstract intellect" which was "self-enclosed, self-absorbed" [18] indicates a narrow range of study and a lack of insight regarding Shelley's social ideas. Bagehot ends by finding in Shelley's work – which he considers only fragmentary – little but occasional aesthetic excellence.

ALFRED LORD TENNYSON

There were those Victorians who were vaguely and transiently challenged by Shelley's social ideas but who seemed never actually to grasp their import. Alfred Lord Tennyson (1809-1892) wrote that Byron and Shelley, "however mistaken they may be, did yet give the world another heart and new pulses". He added the observation, "And so we are kept going. Blessed be those that grease the wheels of the old world, insomuch as to move on is better than to stand still." [19] This comment, by its unconcern with the direction of progress, indicates that Tennyson was not

[16]   Bagehot, *Literary Studies,* ed. Richard Holt Hutton (London, 1891), I, 80.
[17]   *Ibid.,* p. 90.
[18]   *Ibid.,* p. 99.
[19]   Hallam Tennyson, *Alfred Lord Tennyson: A Memoir by His Son* (New York and London, 1897), I, 141, hereafter referred to as *Memoir.*

familiar enough with Shelley's social ideas to deal with them except in broad generalities. He found a good deal of Shelley to be only "a great wind of words" and declared that "he is often too much in the clouds for me". "One must", he said, "distinguish Keats, Shelley, and Byron from the great artists, like Aeschylus, Shakespeare, Dante, and Goethe".[20] In Shelley's poetry he found "splendid imagery and colour", but also "a sort of tenuity".[21]

It was as a writer of blank verse, and not as a thinker, that Tennyson admired Shelley. In this regard he considered him "perhaps the most skillful of the moderns".[22] His choice of a favorite from among Shelley's poems indicates that the prosody, rather than the thought, of the Romantic poet appealed to him: "Nobody admires Shelley more than I once did, and I still admire him. I think I like his 'Epipsychidion' as much as anything by him." [23] Yet Tennyson found Shelley, as contrasted with Keats, too ethereal. He cited the lyric *Life of Life* as an example of those poems in which Shelley "seemed to go up, and burst".[24] Tennyson's limited appreciation of Shelley is best illustrated by the fact that this most characteristic of Shelley's lyrics was prevented by his opposition from appearing in *The Golden Treasury*.[25]

Tennyson's first volume, *Poems of Two Brothers* (1827), gives ample evidence that he had read Byron and Ossian, but no indication that he had become acquainted with either Shelley or Keats. Very likely the "Apostles", of whom both he and Henry Hallam were members at Cambridge, first introduced him to Shelley.[26] Tennyson himself says of *The Lover's Tale* (wr. about

---

[20]   *Ibid.*, II, 69, 285, 287.
[21]   See Hallam Tennyson, ed., *Tennyson and His Friends* (London, 1911), p. 269.
[22]   *Memoir*, II, 70.
[23]   *Ibid.* See also p. 285 for Tennyson's listing of *Epipsychidion, Alastor, Adonais,* and some short lyrics as works of Shelley which he admires.
[24]   *Ibid.*, p. 500.
[25]   B. Ifor Evans, "Tennyson and the Origins of the Golden Treassury", *TLS,* 8 December 1932, p. 941.
[26]   George H. Ford, *Keats and the Victorians: A Study of His Influence and Rise to Fame 1821-1895* (New Haven, Yale Univ. Press, 1944), pp. 23-24.

1826; pbl. 1833), "That was written before I had ever seen a Shelley, though it is called Shelleyan." [27] Precisely when Tennyson first became acquainted with Shelley's poetry is not certain, but we must conclude that it was not before 1826.

The 1830 volume, *Poems Chiefly Lyrical*, evidences no interest in Shelley other than a Shelleyan variety of melody and what may be an occasional, somewhat artificial echo of his humanitarian concerns. But in the poems written during 1831 and 1832, Tennyson's social consciousness appears to deepen. *The Palace of Art* is most significant among the poems devoted to the social theme.[28] Hoxie N. Fairchild points out the following lines of *Queen Mab* as the probable germ for *The Palace of Art*:

> "Spirit!" the Fairy said,
> And pointed to the gorgeous dome,
> "This is a wondrous sight
> And mocks all human grandeur;
> But, were it virtue's only meed, to dwell
> In a celestial palace, all resigned
> To pleasurable impulses, immured
> Within the prison of itself, the will
> Of Changeless Nature would be unfulfilled.
> Learn to make others happy."   (II, 55-64)

Professor Fairchild finds other lines in *Queen Mab* which may have inspired certain lines in Tennyson's poem and concludes, "Even if the resemblance is coincidental it is an interesting illustration of the fact that the ethical purposiveness of Victorian poetry is an outgrowth of romantic benevolism rather than a reaction against the romantic spirit." [29]

---

[27] *Memoir*, II, 285. See also p. 239 for Hallam Tennyson's statement that his father wrote the poem at the age of seventeen. Arthur Waugh, in his *Alfred Lord Tennyson: A Study of His Life and Work* (New York, 1892), p. 63, evidences a stereotyped view of Shelley and is mistaken about Shelley's influence on Tennyson: "The voluptuous affection for nature, the warm overloaded phraseology, and the long-drawn eloquence of melancholy passion are indisputable signs of an early study of Shelley."

[28] Lionel Stevenson, "Tennyson, Browning, and a Romantic Fallacy", *UTQ*, XIII (January 1944), 180, 182.

[29] Hoxie N. Fairchild, "Tennyson and Shelley", *TLS*, 11 January 1947, p. 23.

But Tennyson scarcely extended his poetic involvement in social concerns beyond the expression of them in *The Palace of Art*. Various critics have pointed out other similarities between the poetry of Shelley and that of Tennyson, but these likenesses are limited to diction, symbolism, and poetic art. Arthur Waugh finds that Tennyson's *Hero and Leander* is startlingly like Shelley's poetry in its passionate declaration of love.[30] And Lionel Stevenson contends that Tennyson's frequently used theme of a high-born maiden, who secludes herself from others in order to contemplate the future, is influenced chiefly by Shelley's *Revolt of Islam* and *Queen Mab,* as well as by *To a Skylark, Epipsychidion,* and *The Witch of Atlas.*[31]

Tennyson himself, however, denied all direct indebtedness to Shelley. Writing to S. E. Dawson about Dawson's edition of *The Princess,* he declared:

It is scarcely possible for anyone to say or write anything in this late time of the world to which, in the rest of the literature of the world, a parallel could not somewhere be found. But when you say that this passage or that was suggested by Wordsworth or Shelley or another, I demur; and more, I wholly disagree.[32]

A recent article [33] employs this comment to refute attributions by several critics of Shelleyan influence upon Tennyson's "The Poet", first published in *Poems Chiefly Lyrical.* In the above statement Tennyson is, of course, not denying any general, pervasive influences.

In Memoriam (1850), more clearly than any other of Tennyson's works, gives evidence of a conscious effort to parallel Shelley's poetry. It follows in the train of both Milton's *Lycidas* and Shelley's *Adonais.* It seems significant, in this regard, that Arthur Henry Hallam himself had brought the latter poem to England from Italy to be printed later (1834) in the Cambridge Union's

---

[30] Waugh, pp. 41-42.
[31] Lionel Stevenson, "The 'High-Born Maiden' Symbol in Tennyson", *PMLA,* LXIII (March 1948), 234-243.
[32] *Memoir,* I, 256-257.
[33] George O. Marshall, Jr., "Tennyson's 'The Poet': Mis-seeing Shelley Plain", *PQ,* XL (January 1961), 156-157.

Transactions. Other poems by Shelley which have been suggested as influential on the diction and tone of *In Memoriam* are the *Cenci* and *Queen Mab*.[34] Beyond these similartities, little affinity with Shelley is revealed in Tennyson's poetry.

It is apparent that the ideational influence of Shelley upon Tennyson was slight and transient. The Avelings, in their strongly partisan essay, compare Shelley's "fiery outbursts of practical teaching" with "the uncertain sound and bated breath of the washed-out, emasculated, effeminated Shelley, Tennyson". In their opinion, "the breath is bated in this latter case because it is that of a respectable gentleman, and the sound is uncertain ... because Lord Tennyson does not grasp the real meaning of the relative positions of man and woman in today's society".[35] Despite all its overstatement and slanting, this declaration is essentially correct. Even in his early poetry, Tennyson does not declare himself specifically and clearly where the sociological subject matter seems to demand that he do so. And in later years, what social emphasis there is tends strongly toward conformity, unquestioning patriotism, and security.

MATTHEW ARNOLD

The expressed views of Matthew Arnold (1822-1888) on Shelley have led critics to believe that he did not at all understand the earlier poet's ethical and moral philosophy. But it is not certain that because he chose to emphasize repeatedly Shelley's beautiful ineffectiveness, he did not know of his poetry's deeper implications.

In the concluding paragraph of his essay on Byron (1881), Arnold wrote, "I for my part can never even think of equalling with them [Wordsworth and Byron] any other of their contemporaries; – either Coleridge ... or Shelley, beautiful and in-

---

[34]   J. D. Jump, "Shelley and Tennyson", *N & Q,* CXCVI (8 December 1951), 540-541.
[35]   Edward and Eleanor Marx Aveling, *Shelley's Socialism: Two Lectures,* a reprint from 1888 ed. (Manchester, England, 1947), p. 14.

effectual angel, beating in the void his luminous wings in vain." [36]
Seven years later, in the *Nineteenth Century* (January 1888), appeared his essay on Shelley, which draws toward its close with:

Let no one suppose that a want of humour and a self-delusion such
as Shelley's have no effect upon a man's poetry. The man Shelley,
in very truth, is not entirely sane, and Shelley's poetry is not entirely
sane either. The Shelley of actual life is a vision of beauty and ra-
diance, indeed, but availing nothing, effecting nothing.

The essay ends with a direct quotation of the earlier dictum:
"In poetry, no less than in life, he is 'a beautiful and *ineffectual
angel,* beating in the void his luminous wings in vain'." [37] The
public appears to have liked this expression as much as did Arnold himself; for, although it was already protested by Stopford
Brooke in his Shelley Society inaugural address, it has continued
to be among the best-known and most influential critical pronouncements on Shelley.

Arnold had much more to say, in a similar vein, concerning
Shelley. On 28 October 1852 he wrote to Arthur Hugh Clough,
stressing the importance of content in modern-day poetry and
severely taking Shelley to task for neglecting content in favor of
"exuberance of expression", "charm", and "exquisite bits and
images".[38] In poetry, too, he proclaimed Shelley's ineffectuality:

> What boots it, Shelley! that the breeze
> Carried thy lovely wail away,
> Musical through Italian trees
> Which fringe thy soft blue Spezzian bay?
> Inheritors of thy distress,
> Have restless hearts one throb the less? [39]

The English poetry of the first quarter of the nineteenth century,
with all its energy and creative force, says Arnold in *The Function
of Criticism* (1864), "did not know enough" – and this is why

---

[36]   See Matthew Arnold, *Works*, Edition de Luxe (London, 1903), IV,
149-150. Hereafter cited as *Works*.
[37]   *Ibid.*, p. 185. The italics are Arnold's.
[38]   See *The Letters of Matthew Arnold to Arthur Hugh Clough*, ed. H.
F. Lowry (London and New York, 1932), p. 124.
[39]   *Stanzas from the Grande Chartreuse*. See *Works*, I, 291.

Shelley was so "incoherent".[40] In his essay on Heinrich Heine, published about the same time, he writes:

In the literary movement of the beginning of the nineteenth century the signal attempt made to apply freely the modern spirit was made in England by two members of the aristocratic class, Byron and Shelley. Aristocracies are, as such, naturally impenetrable by ideas; but their individual members have a high courage and a turn for breaking bounds; and a man of genius, who is the born child of the idea, happening to be born in the aristocratic ranks, chafes against the obstacles which prevent him from freely developing it. Byron and Shelley did not succeed in their attempt. . . . The resistance to baffle them, the want of intelligent sympathy to guide and uphold them were too great. . . . Their literary creation . . . is a failure [comparatively]. The best literary creation of that time proceeded from men who did not make the same bold attempt as Byron and Shelley. . . . Wordsworth, Scott, and Keats have left admirable works; far more solid and complete works than those which Byron and Shelley have left. But their works have this defect – they do not belong to that which is the main current of the literature of modern epochs, they do not apply modern ideas to life. . . . Byron and Shelley will long be remembered, long after the inadequacy of their actual work is clearly recognized, for their passionate, their Titanic effort to flow in the main stream of modern literature; their names will be greater than their writings.[41]

When Arnold, in this passage, takes up the poet's revolt against aristocracy, he shows that he understands a great deal about Shelley's ideas; his accusation against the resisting forces of ignorance seems well directed. But when he then identifies the "bold attempt" to flow "in the main current" of modern literature as merely something to remember Byron and Shelley by, he implies that these poets were not suited to social criticism and that both were constitutionally limited to the composition of that harmless lyrical poetry which Arnold emphasizes throughout his criticism of Shelley.

In *The Study of Poetry* (1880) Arnold reverts to his characteristic description of Shelley's beauty and ineffectiveness. He employs the terms "beautiful spirit" and "many-coloured haze of

[40] See *Works*, III, 8.
[41] *Ibid.*, pp. 193-194.

words and images"; and to point out the superiority of Burns, he compares the lines –

> On the brink of night and the morning
> My coursers are wont to respire,
> But the Earth has just whispered a warning
> That their flight must be swifter than fire –

of *Prometheus Unbound* with the entirely unrelated lines from *Tam Glen:*

> My minnie does constantly deave me
> And bids me beware o' young men;
> They flatter, she says, to deceive me;
> But wha can think sae o' Tam Glen? [42]

Considering Arnold's insistence upon content, his respective evaluation of these two passages is surprising. For, unless one absolutely rejects metaphor in poetry, one can hardly fail to find more content in the selection from Shelley.

The following year Arnold published the essay on Byron, which implies that Shelley seldom wrote about anything but clouds and sunsets:

All the personal charm of Shelley cannot hinder us from at last discovering in his poetry the incurable want, in general, of a sound subject-matter, and the incurable fault, in consequence, of insubstantiality. Those who extol him as the poet of clouds, the poet of sunsets, are only saying that he did not, in fact, lay hold upon the poet's right subject-matter; and in honest truth, with all his charm of soul and spirit, and with all his gift of musical diction and movement, he never, or hardly ever, did. . . . I doubt whether his delightful Essays and Letters, which deserve to be far more read than they are now, will not resist the wear and tear of time better, and finally come to stand higher, than his poetry. [43]

In view of the insight revealed in the already noted comment, in the essay on Heine, regarding Shelley's social views, it seems very probable that the above passage is an attempt to conceal Shelley's true subject matter, rather than an indication that Arnold was unaware of it.

[42]   *Ibid.*, IV, 39-40.
[43]   *Ibid.*, pp. 121-122.

His essay on Shelley was Arnold's reaction to a reading, in 1888, of Dowden's highly sentimental biography. He was angered and disappointed by the story of Shelley's life and the incongruities it presented to the picture of a beautiful angel which he had so carefully built up. As Professor Baker points out, Arnold's essay makes no attempt to present a complete picture of Shelley but, in its absorption in accusations, wholly neglects the last four years of the poet's life – the years of his great poetry.[44] Relying heavily on the inadequate adjectives *beautiful, lovable, charming,* Arnold again gives the impression (perhaps intentional) that he is unaware of the strongly ethical content of Shelley's mature work. It is incredible that a man of Arnold's capacities and sensibilities should find in a reading of Shelley only aesthetic values. Disagreeing fundamentally with the ethical values he found in Shelley, Arnold may well have decided to combat them by neglecting them and by diverting the readers' attention from them.

In the essay Arnold puts great emphasis on Shelley's nonconforming associates: "What a set! What a world! is the exclamation that breaks from us as we come to the end of this history." Having used the French word *bete* to describe Shelley's letter to Harriet after his elopement with Mary, Arnold declares, "For the world in which we find him I can only use another French word, *sale*."[45] On this judgment Mrs. Campbell has keenly remarked, "It had apparently never entered his head that Shelley might have wholeheartedly agreed with him." And she points out that Shelley was pained by the "sordid horror" of Godwin's house, by Hogg's deceit, Byron's selfishness, Mr. Timothy Shelley's "cringing snobbery", and the Duke of Norfolk's drunkenness. Her point is that "to judge of this world from the safe respectability of mid-Victoria, is a very different thing from growing up, a sensitive, friendless, passionate nature, in the midst of it".[46] But Arnold's purpose in stressing the company Shelley

---

[44] Carlos Baker, "The Permanent Shelley", *Sewanee Review,* XLVIII (October-December 1940), 512-513.

[45] See *Works,* IV, 175.

[46] Olwen Ward Campbell, *Shelley and the Unromantics* (New York, 1924), p. 69. In a footnote Mrs. Campbell quotes Mrs. Shelley's letter to

kept is that it enables him to come round to the conclusion that
we need not look to such a poet for any ethical guidance and that
we are fortunate to get what aesthetic enjoyment he provides.

Yet, underneath, a kindred feeling draws Arnold to Shelley,
and it may be that his case was similar to Browning's – that Shelley pointed him to a course he had foresworn. As Mrs. Campbell
has shown,[47] there are striking similarities between the longings,
the inspirations, the major interests, and the poetry of Arnold
and Shelley. And his understanding of the purposes of poetry is
similar to Shelley's, making him a most formidable adversary.
For Arnold's suffering was much like that of Shelley:

> There rises an unspeakable desire
> After the knowledge of our buried life;
> A thirst to spend our fire and restless force
> In tracking out our true original course;
> A longing to enquire
> Into the mystery of this heart which beats
> So wild, so deep in us – to know
> Whence our lives come and where they go.[48]

Shelley, beginning with *Alastor* and throughout his poetry and
prose, evidenced the same motive in his art. He progressed toward the affirmative belief in humanity which is most eloquently
and imaginatively expressed in *Prometheus Unbound*. Arnold, on
the other hand, deserted imagination for an intellectual philosophy, thus seeking an avenue of escape from his despair over
modern life. He finds himself one of the

> Light half-believers of our casual creeds,
> Who never deeply felt, nor clearly will'd,
> Whose insight never has borne fruit in deeds,
> Whose vague resolves never have been fulfill'd;
> For whom each year we see
> Breeds new beginnings, disappointments new;
> Who hesitate and falter life away,
> And lose to-morrow the ground won today.[49]

---

her husband, in which she refers to their friends and enemies alike as
"all a bad set".
[47] *Ibid.*, pp. 3-4.
[48] *The Buried Life.* See *Works*, II, 108.
[49] *The Scholar Gipsy.* See *Works*, I, 234-235.

Because of this wide divergence from Shelley's imaginative hopes, Arnold dwelt upon the Romantic poet's mistakes and doubted his motives. He either could not or would not believe that so outspoken an idealist could hold practical views. Shelley's "Arise, and will!" [50] did not move the author of the lines:

> The thoughts that reign their steady glow
> Like stars on life's cold sea,
> Which others know, or say they know –
> They never shone for me.[51]

Like Shelley, Arnold could not accept the traditional beliefs; but deserting them, he gave up also the willingness or the ability to grasp a new belief. Perhaps it is only natural that he should mistrust Shelley and should seek to cover up by a false emphasis a social message which, to him, was only another heresy. It is regretable, nevertheless, that he did not sort out and confront himself directly, in his essays, with the essential elements of Shelley's philosophy.

WILLIAM MICHAEL ROSSETTI AND DANTE GABRIEL ROSSETTI

The Rossetti brothers are of only minor concern in the present study. William Michael Rossetti (1829-1919) is noteworthy as a devoted Shelley scholar rather than as a creative artist, and Dante Gabriel Rossetti (1829-1882) liked neither Shelley's tendency toward abstraction nor his concern with revolutionary philanthropy. His work was, therefore, little, if at all, influenced by Shelley.

On one occasion William argued with his brother, who considered Keats the greatest modern poet, and for a short time convinced him of Shelley's greater excellence.[52] Gabriel, however, soon reverted to his dislike for Shelley and later wrote, "I have been reading again Hogg's *Shelley*. S. appears to have been as

---

[50] *The Revolt of Islam*, canto viii, stanza 16.
[51] *Despondency*, lines 1-4. See *Works*, II, 53.
[52] William Michael Rossetti, *Rossetti Papers, 1862 to 1870* (London, 1903), p. 499.

mad at Keswick as everywhere else, but not madder; – that he could not compass." [53]

William Rossetti, however, deserves mention not only for the great service he did to the cause of Shelley's reputation and to Shelley scholarship but also for his *Democratic Sonnets*, which give evidence of Shelley's strong influence upon him. He published articles on Shelley (some of them ranking among the best interpretations of the poet's works) during the thirty-five-year period from 1868 to 1903, prefixed to his edition of Shelley's works (1870) an excellent *Memoir* of Shelley, and contributed an even better article on the poet to the 1886 edition of the *Encyclopedia Britannica*. From the founding of the Shelley Society in 1886 until it was dissolved in 1895, William Rossetti served as its "Chairman of Committee" (equivalent to presidency).[54] In his letters, also, he evidences a sincere interest in the promulgation of Shelley's ideas.

Throughout the two small volumes of his *Democratic Sonnets* there is a strongly Shelleyan concern with liberty and brotherhood. Perhaps most clearly evidencing Shelley's influence are the last lines of the sonnet "Socialism, 1848":

> Though these things now be dreams
> They are the dreams of some millenial age,
> An age when love of man to man shall burn
> A world-wide light, no more a glimpse of gleams.[55]

Rossetti refers to Shelley directly in two other sonnets. In "Mary Shelley, 1851" he praises Mary with the designation,

> Heart-mate and wife of one who, burning red
> With world-embracing love, forever draws
> Into his orbit the thrilled globe, and awes
> With visioned poesy each highest head
> Of song for aye.[56]

[53] T. Hall Caine, *Recollections of Dante Gabriel Rossetti* (Boston, 1883), p. 275.
[54] Harris Chewning, "William Michael Rossetti and the Shelley Renaissance", *K-SJ*, IV (Winter 1955), p. 92. Chewning's article (pp. 81-96) is a remarkably complete survey of Rossetti's contribution to the Shelley cause.
[55] William M. Rossetti, *Democratic Sonnets* (London, 1907), I, xxviii.
[56] *Ibid.*, p. xv.

And "Leigh Hunt, 1859" begins:

> The friend of Shelley. Thirty-seven years' space
> Divides him from that day of dark July
> When Spezia's widow watched with sateless eye
> For the doomed bark which sinking left no trace.[57]

The sonnet goes on to point out that Hunt, like his friend, was "the trenchant champion of our freemen's cause".

Although their artistic quality is not great, these sonnets attest to the power wich Shelley's ideas exerted on William Rossetti. The subject matter of the sonnets is precisely that which one would expect in the creative works of an enthusiastic Shelley scholar.

GEORGE HENRY LEWES AND GEORGE ELIOT

Another of Shelley's admirers who, like his friend W. M. Rossetti, was a literary man, but not of the creative kind, was George Henry Lewes (1817-1878). In 1837, at the instigation of Leigh Hunt, Lewes wrote an introductory letter to William Bell Scott, beginning, "Sir – Leigh Hunt tells me that as cordial natures we ought to know each other. How far that is the case I know not, but this much I do know, that we both agree in heartily loving Shelley." [58] The following year, as a young student in Germany, Lewes wrote to his friend Leigh Hunt, reasserting his deep interest in Shelley, seeking more information about him, and announcing that he was writing a critical biography of him. On 21 December 1839 he asked Mary Shelley to read the manuscript of his study. However, his "Life of Percy Bysshe Shelley", which was advertised in 1838 as already being in the press, never appeared; the Lewes family has neither record nor knowledge of it.

Lewes is known to have helped W. M. Rossetti in 1869 with the preparation of his *Memoir of Shelley*, and some of its ideas and evaluations may have been drawn from Lewes's proposed Life of Shelley. It is also likely that parts of the proposed book

[57]   *Ibid.*, p. xvii.
[58]   Kitchel, p. 12.

have been preserved in Lewes's excellent forty-one-page critical review of *The Poetical Works of Percy Bysshe Shelley*, which appeared in the April 1841 issue of the *Westminster Review*.[59] Referring to the Carlyle lectures on *Heroes and Hero-Worship*, given less than a year before, Lewes declares Shelley one of the two great nineteenth-century Englishmen and presents him as "the original man, the hero", deserving of hero-worship.

During his many years of association with Leigh Hunt, Lewes had ample opportunity to learn about Shelley – both the man and his ideas. As a youth Lewes had aspired to become a contributor to Hunt's periodicals and thus had first become acquainted with the friend and supporter of Shelley. Around the year 1837, when he was still only twenty-two, Lewes was among the many young progressives who frequented Leigh Hunt's house at Chelsea – as a tribute to the older man's personality and his pioneer efforts for reform. In William Bell Scott's autobiography there appears an etching which shows Lewes as an eager member of a fireside group gathered around Leigh Hunt. And Lewes later recalled his excited expectation of and anxiety for the success of Hunt's play *A Legend of Florence*, whose première at Covent Garden he attended in 1840.[60]

---

[59]   Newman Ivey White, *Shelley* (New York, 1940), II, 402-403. See also the review by G. H. L[ewes], in *The Westminster Review*, XXXV (April 1841), 303-344 – hereafter cited as G. H. L[ewes].

[60]   Edmund Blundon, *Leigh Hunt: A Biography* (London, 1930), p. 282. Also of interest is Lewes's close association throughout the 1840's and into the 1850's with Leigh Hunt's eldest son, Thornton. The younger Hunt, as a boy, had known Shelley, and he later wrote about him, the most extensive of these commentaries being his article, "Shelley; By One Who Knew Him", *The Atlantic Monthly*, XI (February 1863), pp. 184-204. In 1850 Thornton Hunt and Lewes co-edited a liberal journal, *The Leader*. Some years previously Lewes and his attractive young wife, Agnes, had been associated with the unconventional Philanstery, an experiment in cooperative housekeeping which was conducted in the Queen's Road, Bayswater, by a number of couples of the Hunt and Gliddon families (Thornton had married Kate Gliddon, and one of his sisters had married Kate's brother John). However, by 1852, if not earlier, Lewes had learned of an affair between his wife and Thornton Hunt. The result was the estrangement (though not divorce) of Lewes and Agnes – the situation which prevailed in 1854 when Lewes met Marian Evans.

Several items of correspondence [61] indicate that Leigh Hunt and G. H. Lewes continued their friendship well into the decade of the 1850's; and this friendship very likely had not diminished when Hunt died in 1859. Meanwhile, Hunt maintained his interest in Shelley. He wrote an extensive letter in 1858 to his publisher friend, Edmund Ollier, regarding Charles S. Middleton's newly-published Life of Shelley.[62] Appropriately, Hunt's final published works were two short articles on Shelley in *The Spectator* of 1859, and his last personal letter was addressed to Shelley's daughter-in-law, Lady Jane Shelley. Leigh Hunt undoubtedly provided Lewes with a considerable insight into Shelley's personality and ideas. Very probably Lewes, in turn, aroused George Eliot's interest in the poet.

In her comments on Lewes's early novel, *The Apprenticeship of Life,* Anna Kitchel observes, "One cannot help getting from some of the passages of this book sidelights on the views of its author . . . . The ideas of Shelley and Godwin on the subject of 'free love' . . . seem to be fairly well represented in the attitude of Armand toward matrimony." [63] And that the well-known liaison between Lewes and George Eliot – Marian Evans (1819-1880) – had much in common with Shelley's relationship to Mary Godwin can scarcely be denied. In the winter of 1852, when Lewes was despondent about the break-up of his marriage, Herbert Spencer introduced him to George Eliot. These new friends and fellow journalists were strongly attracted to each other and in 1854 decided upon a relationship which became a marriage in all but the legal sense. It appears very likely, then, that Lewes and George Eliot frequently discussed Shelley and that Will Ladislaw, the Shelleyan character in *Middlemarch*, may have evolved largely from Lewes's ideas about Shelley.

That George Eliot had Shelley in mind as she created the character of Ladislaw is indicated by several direct references in the novel. The first of these occurs in a passage describing the

[61]   See Luther A. Brewer, *My Leigh Hunt Library: The Holograph Letters* (Iowa City, State Univ. of Iowa Press, 1938), pp. 334, 358.
[62]   *Ibid.*, pp. 113-114.
[63]   Kitchel, p. 55.

early stages of Ladislaw's affiliation with Dorothea's politically-minded uncle, Mr. Brooke, in various projects of reform, including the editing of the liberal *Pioneer*:

> It seemed that Will was not only at home in all those artistic and literary subjects which Mr Brooke had gone into at one time, but that he was strikingly ready at seizing the points of the political situation, and dealing with them in that large spirit which, aided by adequate memory, lends itself to quotation and general effectiveness of treatment.
>
> "He seems to me a kind of Shelley, you know", Mr Brooke took an opportunity of saying, for the gratification of Mr Casaubon. "I don't mean as to anything objectionable – lexities or atheism, or anything of that kind, you know – Ladislaw's sentiments in every way I am sure are good – indeed, we were talking a great deal together last night. But he has the same sort of enthusiasm for liberty, freedom, emancipation – a fine thing under guidance – under guidance, you know. I think I shall be able to put him on the right tack." [64]

By means of Mr. Brooke's cautious endorsement of Ladislaw's radicalism, George Eliot shrewdly inserts a comment upon the general reaction of declared English liberals to Shelley's views – an avowal of agreement, but with definite reservations. In a later passage, showing a keen perception of the poet's readiness to accept whatever limited reforms become obtainable, there is a second direct reference to Shelley:

> "You know there are tactics in these things", said Mr. Brooke; "... but we sometimes cut with rather too sharp a knife, Ladislaw. These ten-pound householders, now: why ten? Draw the line somewhere – yes: but why just at ten? That's difficult question, now, if you go into it."
>
> "Of course it is", said Will, impatiently. "But if you are to wait till we get a logical Bill, you must put yourself forward as a revolutionist, and then Middlemarch would not elect you, I fancy. As for trimming, this is not a time for trimming."
>
> Mr Brooke always ended by agreeing with Ladislaw, who still appeared to him a sort of Burke with a leaven of Shelley. (II, 317-318)

---

[64] George Eliot, *Middlemarch,* in 3 vols., in Rosehill Limited Edition of *Works* (Boston, 1894), II, 121-122. Hereafter page and volume numbers referring to this edition are given parenthetically in the text.

It is not difficult to detect the "leaven of Shelley" in Ladislaw's impatient retort to Mr. Brooke, for Shelley's *Philosophical View of Reform* contains the following declarations: "If Reform shall be begun by the existing government, let us be contented with a limited *beginning,* with any whatsoever opening; . . . it is no matter how slow, gradual and cautious be the change; we shall demand more and more with firmness and moderation. . . . Nothing is more idle than to reject a limited benefit because we cannot without great sacrifices obtain an unlimited one." (*Works,* VII, 46)[65]

In 1819 Shelley had written to Lewes's friend Leigh Hunt: "The great thing to do is to hold the balance between popular impatience and tyrannical obstinacy . . . . You know my principles incite me to take all the good I can get in politics, for ever aspiring to something more. I am one of those whom nothing will fully satisfy, but who [are] ready to be partially satisfied [by] all that is practicable." (*Works,* X, 130-131)[66] And George Eliot presents Ladislaw and Mr. Brooke in the following conversation:

"If you go in for the principle of Reform, you must be prepared to take what the situation offers", said Will. "If everybody pulled for his own bit against everybody else, the whole question would go to tatters."

"Yes, yes, I agree with you – I quite take that point of view. I should put it in that light. I should support Grey, you know. But I don't want to change the balance of the constitution and I don't think Grey would."

"But that is what the country wants", said Will. "Else there would be no meaning in political unions or any other movement that knows what it's about. It wants to have a house of Commons which is not weighted with nominees of the landed class, but with representatives

[65]   Proffessor Kenneth Neill Cameron, in two articles, points out that Shelley not only synthesized the ideas of reformers of his time but also originated certain reform ideas – in some respects surpassing the other reformers. See "Shelley, Cobbett and the National Debt", *JEGP,* XLII (April 1943), 197-209 and "Shelley and the Reformers", *ELH,* XII (March 1945), 62-85.

[66]   For early printings of the letter, see Leigh Hunt, *Lord Byron and Some of His Contemporaries,* 2 vols. (London, 1828), I, 399-402; and Percy Bysshe Shelley, *Essays, Letters from Abroad,* etc., ed. Mary Shelley, 2 vols. (London, 1840), II, 255-258. The latter work was reprinted in 1845 and again in 1852. Mary Shelley dates the letter November 1819.

of the other interests. And as to contending for a reform short of that, it is like asking for a bit of an avalanche which has already begun to thunder." (II, 261)

Turning back to Shelley's *Philosophical View of Reform*, we find: "The House of Commons ought questionless to be immediately nominated by the great mass of the people. The aristocracy and those who unite in their own persons the vast privileges conferred by the possession of inordinate wealth are sufficiently represented by the House of Peers and by the King" (*Works*, VII, 43). And in his *Proposals for Putting Reform to the Vote Throughout the Kingdom* Shelley had declared:

Every one is agreed that the House of Commons is not a representation of the people. The only theoretical question that remains is, whether the people ought to legislate for themselves, or be governed by laws and impoverished by taxes originating in the edicts of an assembly which represents somewhat less than a thousandth part of the intire community. . . . The question now at issue is, whether the majority of the adult individuals of the United Kingdom of Great Britain and Ireland desire or no a complete representation in the Legislative Assembly. . . . The House of Commons does not represent the will of the people of the British Nation; . . . that House should originate such measures of Reform, as would render its Members the actual Representatives of the Nation. (*Works*, VI, 63-66)

In an argument about the methods and conditions of reform, Ladislaw maintains that one cannot always find immediately the best methods or the most effective means but that one "must begin somewhere". Nor can one afford to refrain from doing anything because he has not found "immaculate men to work with" (II, 269-270).

So practical an outlook was certainly not in accord with the public image of a Shelleyan character. But a serious nineteenth-century student of Shelley could readily assimilate this view of the poet's ideas. Although copies of Shelley's original (1817) edition of *Proposals for Putting Reform to the Vote* were undoubtedly scarce by 1860 or 1870, Middleton in 1858 had presented extensive excerpts from it in his two-volume work.[67] *A*

[67]   Charles S. Middleton, *Shelley and His Writings* (London, 1858), II, 107-115. These excerpts include the passages quoted above. An explana-

Philosophical View of Reform had not been published, but Mary Shelley had made a transcript of it with a view to publication,[68] and had mentioned it in the Preface to her 1840 edition of Shelley's *Essays, Letters from Abroad*, etc. Leigh Hunt certainly knew of the essay, for Shelley had written to him on 26 May 1820 as follows:

One thing I want to ask you. Do you know any bookseller who would publish for me an octavo volume, entitled "A Philosophical View of Reform"? It is boldly but temperately written – and I think readable. It is intended for a kind of standard book for the philosophical reformers politically considered, like Jeremy Bentham's something, but different and perhaps more systematic. I would send it sheet by sheet. Will you ask, and think for me? (*Works*, X, 172)

The succeeding letters from Hunt to Shelley – those which we have – indicate that Hunt at the time was overworked, ill, and concerned about his brother's impending trial. How extensively (or whether at all) he exerted himself to get the essay published we do not know. But his own great interest in political reform would scarcely have allowed him to forget it. Whatever the extent of Hunt's acquaintance with *A Philosophical View of Reform*, he no doubt knew that Shelley held the views expressed therein, and during the years from 1837 onward, he must have discussed these ideas with young Lewes, the would-be biographer of Shelley.

In addition to this direct evidence of Shelley's ideas and characteristics, Lewes and George Eliot had access to various biographical accounts dealing with aspects of the poet which are also present in the character of Ladislaw. One facet of Ladislaw's personality closely parallels the major struggle in Shelley's being:

It is undeniable that but for the desire to be where Dorothea was, and perhaps the want of knowing what else to do, Will would not at

---

tory comment by Leigh Hunt serves as a footnote on page 112. That copies of the original editions of Shelley's *Proposals* were scarce is attested by W. M. Rossetti, a careful scholar, who states that he has not seen it (*Memoir*, in *Poetical Works*, 1870, I, ciii).

[68]   Professor Kenneth Neill Cameron considers it not unlikely that Mary Shelley consulted Leigh Hunt regarding this contemplated publication.

this time have been meditating on the needs of the English people or criticising English statesmanship: he would probably have been rambling in Italy sketching plans for several dramas, trying prose and finding it too jejune, trying verse and finding it too artificial ... while in politics he would have been sympathising warmly with liberty and progress in general. . . .

Ladislaw had now accepted his bit of work, though it was not that indeterminate loftiest thing which he had once dreamed of as alone worthy of continuous effort. His nature warmed easily to the presence of subjects which were visibly mixed with life and action, and the easily-stirred rebellion in him helped the glow of public spirit. . . . He was a sort of gypsy, rather enjoying the sense of belonging to no class; he had a feeling of romance in his position, and a pleasant consciousness of creating a little surprise wherever he went. (II,262-264)

Shelley likewise was torn between an inclination for close personal relationships and an equally strong urge to devote himself unreservedly to his art and the cause of liberty.

Several other characteristics of Ladislaw also bring Shelley to mind. One of his peculiarities was that "in houses where he got friendly, he was given to stretch himself at full length on the rug while he talked, and was apt to be discovered in this attitude by occasional callers" (II, 266). Shelley, in his Oxford days, had a very similar habit, often falling asleep on the hearth-rug. Shelley's strong attraction to little children may well have influenced George Eliot to write of Ladislaw: "He had a fondness, half artistic, half affectionate, for little children – the smaller they were on tolerably active legs, and the funnier their clothing, the better Will liked to surprise and please them." [69] The description continues, "In Rome he was given to ramble about among the poor people, and the taste did not quit him in Middlemarch" (II, 265-266). Lewes, in his *Westminster Review* article, strongly

[69] Middleton, in his *Shelley and His Writings* (I,84) relates Shelley's practice of reclining on the hearth-rug. In the same volume (pp. 93-97) he tells of the poet's intense love for and attraction to little children. He notes especially Shelley's surprising visit to the tent of two gipsy children and the pleasure he provided for one of them by giving him an orange. Thomas Hogg's *Life of Shelley*, also published in 1858, records the same actions and characteristcs of Shelley. Hogg had related them earlier in his "Reminiscences of Shelley at Oxford", *New Monthly Magazine,* 1832.

emphasizes Shelley's benevolent excursions to help the poor and the hospitalized.[70]

In addition to stressing Shelley's benevolence, Lewes makes a strong point in his article of the poet's refusal to alter his principles for the sake of the money and social position which would legally have been his, had he bowed to the will of his father.[71] Ladislaw clearly expresses a similar refusal in the following two conversations with Dr. Lydgate and old Mr. Bulstrode, respectively:

"But as to money and place in the world", Will ended, tossing back his head, "I think it is pretty clear that I am not determined by considerations of that sort."

"You quite mistake me, Ladislaw", said Lydgate, surprised.... "I beg your pardon for unintentionally annoying you. In fact, I should rather attribute to you a romantic disregard of your own worldly interests." (II, 271)

"The business was established before I became connected with it, sir; nor is it for you to institute an inquiry of that kind", [Bulstrode] answered, not raising his voice, but speaking with quick defiantness.

"Yes, it is", said Will, ... "It is eminently mine to ask such questions, when I have to decide whether I will have transactions with you and accept your money.... You shall keep your ill-gotten money.... What I have to thank you for is that you kept the money till now, when I can refuse it. It ought to lie with a man's self that he is a gentleman."   (III, 129-130)

And Ladislaw's declaration of willingness to face the world without the backing of money or prestige leads Dorothea to comment upon his other attributes.

"There will be a great deal of political work to be done by-and-by, and I mean to try and do some of it. Other men have managed to win an honourable position of themselves without family or money."

"And that will make it all the more honourable", said Dorothea, ardently. "Besides, you have so many talents. I have heard from my uncle how well you speak in public, so that every one is sorry when

---

[70] G. H. L[ewes], pp. 310, 313. Middleton (II, 96-97) also describes Shelley's visits to hospitals and his giving provisions to the poor.
[71] G. H. L[ewes], pp. 313, 317.

you leave off, and how clearly you can explain things.[72] And you care that justice should be done to every one. I am so glad. When we were in Rome, I thought you only cared for poetry and art, and the things that adorn life for us who are well off. But now I know you think about the rest of the world." (III, 11-12)

It is his ability, despite his youthful appearance, to speak forcefully before an audience which brings down upon him the wrath of his enemies in newspaper reviews highly reminiscent of those which Shelley's writings received.

It was disgusting to Keck [editor of the conservative *Trumpet*] to see a fellow, with light curls round his head, get up and speechify by the hour against institutions "which had existed when he was in his cradle." And in a leading article of the "Trumpet", Keck characterised Ladislaw's speech at a Reform meeting as "the violence of an energumen – a miserable effort to shroud in the brilliancy of fireworks the daring of irresponsible statements and the poverty of a knowledge which was of the cheapest and most recent description."   (II, 265)

But the views of others have little effect upon Ladislaw's opinions. Dorothea asks "What is *your* religion?" and explains her question, "I mean – not what you know about religion, but the belief that helps you most?" Ladislaw makes a response which sounds very Shelleyan: "To love what is good and beautiful when I see it." And he continues with a still more Shelleyan explanation: "But I am a rebel: I don't feel bound, as you do, to submit to what I don't like" (II, 166-167).

Ladislaw's idea of poetic inspiration and the poet's sensitivity or quickness to feel agrees closely with that expressed by Shelley in his *Defence of Poetry*. Shelley says:

Poetry is not like reasoning, a power to be exerted according to the determination of the will. . . . For the mind in creation is as a fading coal, which some invisible influence, like an inconstant wind awakens to transitory brightness. . . . The intervals of inspiration . . . may be frequent without being durable. . . . [The poet] is more delicately organized than other men, and sensible to pain and pleasure, both

---

[72] See Thomas Medwin, *The Shelley Papers* (London, 1833), p. 105, where Medwin says of Shelley, "In argument he was irresistible, always calm and unruffled; and in eloquence surpassed all men I have ever conversed with."

his own that of others, in a degree unknown to them. (*Works*, VII, 135, 139)

To Dorothea's sugestion that he become a poet, Ladislaw replies:

That depends. To be a poet is to have a soul so quick to discern that no shade of quality escapes it, and so quick to feel, that discernment is but a hand playing with finely-ordered variety on the chords of emotion – a soul in which knowledge passes instantaneously into feeling, and feeling flashes back as a new organ of knowledge. One may have that condition by fits only. (I, 309-310)

Thus it appears that George Eliot's two direct references to Shelley in her presentation of Will Ladislaw are more than incidental. Although many aspects of his career do not correspond to Shelley's background and life, Ladislaw seems to have been intended as a strongly Shellyan character. That George Eliot relied greatly on the ideas of G. H. Lewes for this characterization is most probable. There are indications in *Middlemarch* that George Eliot had a better understanding and more genuine appreciation of Shelley as ethical and social thinker than did most of the creative writers of her generation.

VI

SHELLEY AND SOME LATE VICTORIANS

The late Victorian creative writers took Shelley more seriously than had their immediate predecessors. The rise of socialism and the achievement, in British government and society, of various other goals which Shelley had set forth were undoubtedly factors in his advancing influence on literary men. Not that Shelley was no longer generally considered ineffectual or visionary; but there were some writers who were newly inspired by the long-disregarded Shelleyan views on society and its improvement.

It must be noted, however, that several mid and late Victorians who are known as ardent Shelleyites gave little or no evidence, in their works, of influence by Shelley's social concerns. James Thomson (B.V.) (1834-1882), Algernon Charles Swinburne (1837-1909), and Francis Thompson (1859-1907) were all greatly interested in Shelley, but their enthusiasm was aroused almost exclusively by his aesthetics, symbolism, and poetic technique; and in this respect he was a strong inspiration to their poetry. Although Swinburne valued Shelley for his concern with moral ideas and with life,[1] none of the three poets produced any work appreciably informed by Shelley's sociological ideas. Francis Thompson, for example wrote an essay which makes of Shelley a naively angelic being whose wisdom was purely instinctive – "to the last" an "enchanted child",[2] Indeed, in their

[1] In *The Swinburne Letters,* ed. Cecil Y. Lang, 6 vols. (New Haven, Yale Univ. Press, 1960), there are many allusions to Shelley, a number of them giving evidence of Swinburne's general agreement with Shelley's social views.
[2] Francis Thompson, *Shelley* (London, 1909), 30, 45. Paul van Kuykendall Thomson, in his *Francis Thompson: A Critical Biography* (New

idolatrous praise of Shelley as the ethereally and aesthetically supreme poet, some enthusiasts did considerable damage to his reputation.

Among the socially-concerned late Victorian writers is George Gissing (1857-1903), upon whom Shelley's influence was of an important but almost undefinable nature. Gissing was especially conscious of what Shelley had proclaimed in *A Defence of Poetry* about the relation of literary art to moral and social reform. This consciousness is evident in numerous of Gissing's novels and essays; but the influence of Shelley in these works is so generally pervasive that it would be difficult to deal more specifically with the subject than has Professor Korg in his fourteen-page article.[3] Similarly, in the creative works of both Oscar Wilde (1854-1900) and H. G. Wells (1866-1946), although both indicate that they have studied and appreciated Shelley, evidence that various ideas are distinctly or specifically Shelleyan seems inconclusive.

WILLIAM MORRIS

The socialism of William Morris (1834-1896) easily leads one to expect in him a greater affinity with Shelley than is actually apparent. In many ways Morris was himself a radical, but instead of allowing his intense social passion to draw him into a struggle with the immediate problems faced by the masses, he escaped, in his poetry, to the pleasant, mythological land of Greece.[4] Of his days at Oxford he said, "Our clique was much influenced by Keats, who was a poet who represented semblances, as opposed to Shelley who had no eyes, and whose admiration was not

---

York, 1961), gives numerous indications regarding the range of Thompson's interest in Shelley.

[3] Jacob Korg, "Division of Purpose in George Gissing", *PMLA*, LXX (June 1955), 323-336. Professor Korg's thesis is that, although Shelley's essay convinced Gissing that direct social reform was not the province of art, he could not refain from allowing his views on society to intrude into his novels.

[4] Douglas Bush, *Mythology and the Romantic Ttradition in English Poetry* (Cambridge, Harvard Univ. Press, 1937), p. 398.

critical but conventional." [5] Morris considered Shelley to be too much concerned with the actual future of mankind to write the poetry of detachment which the later Victorian age valued.

Shelley's "golden age" was an inspiring vision of the future. The Victorian, seeing men bound by continual and joyless labor, finds the golden age to have returned to its old place in the infancy of civilization.[6] Morris, in his verse, presents it as a hopeless dream, the Shelleyan millenium having dwindled to

> a little garden close
> Set thick with lily and red rose,
> Where I would wander if I might
> From dewy dawn to dewy night,
> And have one with me wandering. (*Jason*, iv. 577-561)

In the best-known lyric of *The Earthly Paradise*, Morris's excuse for not attempting to set straight the affairs of society is that he is only constructing

> a shadowy isle of bliss
> Midmost the beating of the steely sea,
> Where tossed about all hearts of men must be.

This lyric presents Morris's poetic dream world, which had nothing to do with propaganda or with life and was far less substantial than Shelley's.

There was, however, another side to Morris – an earnest and steady humanitarianism which he always kept separated from his dream-world. Early in his literary career he chose to devote himself to his dreams: "I can't enter into politico-social subjects with any interest, for on the whole I see that things are in a muddle, and I have no power or vocation to set them right in ever so little degree. My work is the embodiment of dreams in one form or another." [7] Later in his life this view seems to have changed considerably, as is evidenced by his active part in the Social Democratic Federation and the Socialist League. *News from Nowhere* (1891) has something in common with Shelley's hopes for

---

[5] William Morris, *Collected Works,* ed. May Morris (London, etc., 1910-1915) XXII, xxxii.
[6] Bush, p. 312.
[7] J. W. Mackail, *The Life of William Morris* (London, New York, and Bombay, 1901), I, 107; cf. II, 25.

a better world. It does not, however, give evidence of direct influence by Shelley. A major difference from the Shelleyan idea of achieving a perfected society is Morris's reliance on a forceful revolution to bring about the change. This view does not agree with Shelley's insistence that the approach to a peaceful world must itself be peaceful.

Morris failed to find in Shelley any human touch. He was too earthbound to participate in the skylark's flight – too much concerned with the here and now to see any profit in poetry which depicts mankind's better future as actually attainable. His complaint was that *To a Skylark* "doesn't bring up any thoughts of humanity".[8] Morris, a leader in the Socialist movement, thus gave evidence that Shelley was not to him what he was to certain other proponents of Socialism.

WILLIAM BUTLER YEATS

A late-Victorian poet upon whom Shelley had a strong, enduring effect was the Irishman, William Butler Yeats (1865-1939). At the age of about seventeen Yeats began his serious study of Shelley.[9] But this was not his first acquaintance with the poet. His grandfather "constantly read Shelley",[10] and his father used to read aloud passages of *Prometheus Unbound*. The first models for the youthful Yeats were the *Alastor* poet ("my chief of men"), whose melancholy he longed to share, and the Wandering Jew of *Queen Mab*. His "mind gave itself to gregarious Shelley's dream of a young man, his hair blanched with sorrow, studying philosophy in some lonely tower, or of his old man, master of all human knowledge, hidden from human sight in some shell-strewn cavern on the Mediterranean shore".[11]

[8]   Quoted by George H. Ford, *Keats and the Victorians: A Study of His Influence and Rise to Fame 1821-1895* (New Haven, Yale Univ. Press, 1944), p. 151.
[9]   Letter of 5 November [1922] to Charles Ricketts. See William Butler Yeats, *The Letters,* ed. Allen Wade (London, 1954), p. 691.
[10]   Joseph Hone, *W. B. Yeats* (New York, 1943), p. 7.
[11]   William Butler Yeats, *The Autobiographies* (London, 1955), p. 171. On the next page Yeats quotes at length Shelley's passage telling of the

His father's high regard for dramatic poetry caused Yeats to write numerous plays in imitation of Shelley and Spencer. The result was that his poetry became "too full of the reds and yellows Shelley gathered in Italy",[12] which condition he then attempted to cure by fasting and sleeping on a board. Yeats's early absorption in Shelley is set forth by Katherine Tynan's recollection of his "holding an umbrella at the wrong angle over her in a driving rain while he enthusiastically recited 'The Sensitive Plant' into her ear".[13] And, although his loyalties shifted, Yeats never lost his interest in Shelley. On 29 July 1938, six months before his death, he wrote to Dorothy Wellesley that the previous day he had visited Field Place, Shelley's boyhood home, and that he planned soon to visit the pond where Shelley sailed paper boats.[14]

Prometheus Unbound, especially, became the book for which Yeats longed when in a mood of romance. He called it "my sacred book" and used it as an example in his proposal that the finest affirmations of the great poets were "the nearest we could come to an authoritative religion".[15] But much of the Shelleyan influence upon Yeats, manifested in a kind of mystic symbolism, is not within the scope of the present study. Various critics have ably and comprehensively discussed the primary influence of Shelley on Yeats in relation to his mystic concepts as well as his imagery and symbolism.[16]

---

supernaturally aged Jew who, surviving "cycles of generation and of ruin", has attained sovereignty over great secrets which are accessible to only the few brave souls.

[12] William Butler Yeats, *Ideas of Good and Evil*, in *Collected Works* (London, 1908), VI, 3.

[13] Roger McHugh, ed. "Introduction", *Letters of W. B. Yeats to Katherine Tynan* (London, 1953), p. 12.

[14] William Butler Yeats, *Letters on Poetry from W. B. Yeats to Dorothy Wellesley* (London, New York, Toronto, 1940), p. 200.

[15] Yeats, *Autobiographies*, 87-90.

[16] In Giorgio Melchiori, *The Whole Mystery of Art: Pattern into Poetry in the Work of W. B. Yeats* (London, 1960), see especially pp. 104-108, 207-211, and 229-230. Articles of importance in this regard are: Donald Weeks, "Image and Idea in Yeats' The Second Coming", *PMLA*, LXIII (March 1948), 281-292; Howard Baker, "Domes of Byzantium", *Southern Rev.*, VII (1942), 639-650; and A. Norman Jeffares, "Yeats's 'The Gyres': Sources and Symbolism", *The Huntington Library Quarterly*, XV (November 1951), 87-97.

Yeats, however, also admired Shelley's ideas about social regeneration. In November 1901, he wrote to Mrs. Patrick Campbell:

In London the subjects which people think suitable for drama get fewer every day. Shelley said that when a social order was in decay, the arts attached themselves to the last things people were interested in – imaginatively interested in. Here people look on the world with more and more prosaic eyes, as Shelley said they did in dying Greece.[17]

A challenging faith that this condition of society could be remedied he found in Shelley's masterpiece:

I have re-read *Prometheus Unbound* ... and it seems to me to have an even more certain place than I had thought, among the sacred books of the world. I remember going to a learned scholar to ask about its deep meanings, which I felt more than understood, and his telling me that it was Godwin's *Political Justice* put into rhyme, and that Shelley was a crude revolutionist, and believed that the overturning of kings and priests would regenerate mankind. I quoted the lines which tell how the halcyons ceased to prey on fish, and how poisonous leaves became good for food, to show that he foresaw more than any political regeneration.[18]

It seems to me, indeed, that Shelley had re-awakened in himself the age of faith, though there were times when he would doubt, as even the saints have doubted, and that he was a revolutionist, because he had heard the commandment, 'If ye know these things, happy are ye if ye do them.' I have re-read his *Prometheus Unbound* for the first time for many years, in the woods of Drim-da-rod, among the Echte hills, and sometimes I have looked toward Sliev-nan-Orr, where the country people say the last battle of the world shall be fought till the third day, when a priest shall lift a chalice, and the thousand years of peace begin. And I think this mysterious song utters a faith as simple and as ancient as the faith of those country people, in a form suited to a new age, that will understand with Blake that the holy spirit is 'an intellectual fountain', and that the kinds and degrees of beauty are the images of its authority.[19]

But, except in the somewhat Shelleyan prophecy of *The Gyres,*

---

[17] See *Letters*, pp. 360-361.
[18] Yeats, *Ideas of Good and Evil*, p. 72.
[19] *Ibid.*, p. 87.

Yeats could not muster Shelley's optimism about man's ability to realize this dream. In his group of poems, *Meditations in Time of Civil War*,[20] Yeats evidences a Shelleyan insight into the emptiness of revenge and retaliation as social renovators but sees no hope for overcoming these evil traits. One of the poems, "The Stare's Nest by My Window", tells of the confusion and waste caused by warfare and comes to the conclusion that

> We have fed the heart on fantasies,
> The heart grows brutal from the fare,
> More substance in our enmities
> Than in our love.

Another poem in the group bears the long title, "I See Phantoms of Hatred and of the Heart's Fullness and of the Coming Emptiness." The poet tells of climbing a tower and there having a vision of a battle:

> "Vengence upon the murderers", the cry goes up
> "Vengence for Jacques Molay." In cloud pale rags, or in lace,
> The rage driven, rage tormented, and rage hungry troop,
> Trooper belabouring trooper, biting at arm or at face,
> Plunges towards nothing, arms and fingers spreading wide
> For the embrace of nothing; and I my wits astray
> Because of all that senseless tumult, all but cried
> For vengence on the murderers of Jaques Molay.

Though realizing the evil of it all, the poet sees in his youthful, Shelleyan hopes for a better way nothing but abstract images:

> I turn away and shut the door, and on the stair
> Wonder how many times I could have proved my worth
> In something that all others understand and share;
> But oh, ambitious heart had such a proof drawn forth
> A company of friends, a conscience set at ease,
> It had but made us pine the more. The abstract joy,
> The half read wisdom of daemonic images,
> Suffice the aging man as once the growing boy.[21]

Perhaps the closest parallel between the poetry of Yeats and that

---

[20] See *The London Mercury,* VII (January 1923), 232-238.
[21] The last five lines bring to mind Matthew Arnold's "What boots it, Shelley! ... Have restless hearts one throb the less?"

of Shelley is to be found in respective passages dealing with the decadent condition of unregenerated men. Shelley says of them:

> In each human heart terror survives
> The ruin it has gorged. . . .
> They dare not devise good for man's estate,
> And yet they do not know that they do not dare.
> The good want power, but to weep barren tears.
> The powerful goodness want; worse need for them.
> The wise want love; and those who love want wisdom.
>
> *(P.U.*, I, 618-631.)

And Yeats declares:

> The blood-dimmed tide is loosed, and everywhere
> The ceremony of innocence is drowned;
> The best lack all conviction, while the worst
> Are full of passionate intensity.
>
> (*The Second Coming*, 5-8)

The primary fault which Yeats seems to find in Shelley's program for the reform, on a grand scale, of this sad condition is that it is not specific enough. Even in *Queen Mab,* which the laboring-class Chartists had found pertinent to their cause, Yeats does not find the practical advice he desires. In 1921 he wrote:

Had some young Greek found Shelley's "Ahasuerus" in that shell strewn cavern, the sage would not have talked mathematics or even "those strong and secret thoughts ... which others fear and know not" but given I think very simple advice, not indeed fitted to any momentary crisis but fitted perhaps for the next fifty years.[22]

For poets who do not participate in his mysticism, Yeats seems to advise a Browingesque concern with the foreseeable future.

In some respects Yeats found Keats to be a greater poet than Shelley, and he explains: "If you accept metempsychosis, Keats was moving to greater subjectivity of being, and to unity of that being, and Shelley to greater objectivity and to consequent break-up of unity of being." [23] That in later life he came to feel that, as a young man, he had over-estimated Shelley is indicated in the

---

[22] Letter of 29 March [1921], to George Russell. See *Letters,* pp. 666-667.
[23] Letter to J. B. Yeats, 17 October [1918]. See *Letters,* p. 653. See also another letter to J. B. Yeats, 14 March [?1916], *Letters,* p. 608.

following excerpt from a letter (postmarked 9 February 1931)
to Olivia Shakespeare:

I write very much for young men between twenty and thirty, as at
that age, and younger, I wanted to feel that any poet I cared for –
Shelley let us say – saw more than he told of, had in some sense seen
into the mystery. I read more into certain poems than they contained,
to satisfy my interest.[24]

When in his 1933 essay, somewhat misleadingly entitled "Prometheus Unbound", Yeats traced the influence of Shelley on his life
and society, he expressed regret that it had been so great:

When I was in my early twenties Shelley was much talked about,
London had its important "Shelley Society". The Cenci had been
performed and forbidden, provincial sketching clubs displayed pictures by young women of the burning of Shelley's body. . . . He had
shared our curiosities, our political problems, our conviction that
despite all experience to the contrary, love is enough; and unlike
Blake, isolated by an arbitrary symbolism, he seemed to sum up all
that was metaphysical in English poetry. When in middle life I
looked back I found that he and not Blake, whom I had studied
more and with more approval, had shaped my life, and when I
thought of the tumultuous and often tragic lives of friends or acquaintance I attributed to his direct or indirect influence their Jacobin
frenzies, their brown demons.[25]

Yeats's concern with mystic religion seems to have clouded his
view of Shelley, for he unreasonably finds him "terrified of the
Last Day like a Victorian child".[26] By the statement, "It was
many years before I understood that we must not demand even
the welfare of the human race, nor traffic with divinity in our
prayers," [27] Yeats implies that Shelley was asking favors of a
supernatural being rather than relying on mankind's ability to
reform itself. He detects a selfishness in Shelley's humanitarianism:

Shelley was not a mystic, his system of thought was constructed by
his logical faculty to satisfy desire, not a symbolical revelation received after the suspension of all desire. . . . Shelley's art shows that

[24]   See *Letters*, p. 781.
[25]   See *The Spectator*, CL (17 March 1935), 367.
[26]   *Ibid.*, p. 366.
[27]   *Ibid.*, p. 367.

he was an unconverted man though certainly a visionary, what people called a 'psychic'.... He was the tyrant of his own being ... as though he knew the shortness of his life.[28]

The mysticism of Yeats required that all desire and striving be relinquished. He declared that Balzac saved him from the Shelleyan "pursuit of a beauty that seeming at once absolute and external requires, to strike a balance, hatred as absolute".[29] But neither did he find in Balzac a complete solution; for that, he believed, could be found in religion alone. And great writing, like religion, he instists, requires a "preocupation with evil", not Rousseau's or Shelley's resolution to dwell only upon the good.

For them human nature has lost its antagonist.... Is it that these men, who believe what they wish, can never be quite sincere and so live in a world of half belief? But no man believes willingly in evil or in suffering. How much of the strength and weight of Dante and of Balzac comes from unwilling belief, from the lack of it how much of the rhetoric and vagueness of all of Shelley's poetry that does not arise from personal feeling.[30]

Yeats did not find in Shelley the comprehensive "vast humanity" which he considered necessary for great poetry. Therefore he needed to admit that to him Shelley had "always seemed a little crazy, a little of a fanatic".[31]

"We are never satisfied with the maturity of those whom we have admired in boyhood", wrote the aging Yeats; "and, because we have seen their whole circle – even the most successful life is but a segment – we remain to the end their harshest critics." [32] But it is not certain that Yeats had seen the "whole circle" of Shelley. Ideed, despite his access to the *Philosophical View of Reform* and enlightened criticism on Shelley's social and political views, Yeats fell prey to the great delusion about the poet: "Prometheus is set free, nature purified. Shelley the political

---

[28]   *Ibid.,* pp. 366-367.
[29]   *Ibid.,* p. 367.
[30]   Quoted by Morton Dauwen Zabel, "The Thinking of the Body: Yeats in the Autobiographies", *Southern Rev.,* VII (1942), pp. 587-588.
[31]   Quoted by Hone, p. 36.
[32]   William Butler Yeats, *Autobiography* (New York, 1938), p. 211.

revolutionary expected miracle, the Kingdom of God in the twinkling of an eye like some Christian of the first century."[33] Small wonder that, with such a concept of Shelley's social and political views, Yeats came to regret the poet's earlier influence upon him. Had he perceived the nature of Shelley's struggle for the welfare of humanity, he could perhaps have maintained his youthful enthusiasm for Shelley.

THOMAS HARDY [34]

Surprising though it may be, Yeats's contemporary, the fatalistic Thomas Hardy (1840-1928), found himself closer to Shelley's social optimism at the close of his career than did Yeats. Emotionally, Hardy was in accord with Shelley and could detect the error of the Victorian view which saw in his poetry nothing pertinent to nineteenth-century life. Taking little account of popular opinion, Hardy shared Shelley's ideas and employed them in his works. As an English poet who based his poetry on a comprehensive world view which did not depend upon a profession of established Christianity, Shelley had stood almost entirely alone. Hardy, although his cosmology seems more detachable from his poetry, is one of the very few poets of later years who approach Shelley's position in this respect.[35] And, like Shelley, he did not hesitate to apply his ideas to the social scene about him.

---

[33] "Prometheus Unbound", *Spectator,* p. 366. A related misunderstanding of Shelley's deep sympathy with the sufferings of humanity is revealed in Yeats's comment on his own earlier poetry: "The quality symbolized as The Rose differs from the Intellectual Beauty of Shelley ... in that I have imagined it as suffering with man and not as something pursued and seen from afar." Quoted by Kenneth Burke, "On Motivation in Yeats", *Southern Rev.,* VII (1942), p. 553.

[34] For a comprehensive treatment of the Shelley-Hardy relationship, the reader is referred to two articles by Phyllis Bartlett – " 'Seraph of Heaven': A Shelleyan Dream in Hardy's Fiction", *PMLA,* LXX (September 1955), pp. 624-635; and "Hardy's Shelley", *K-S J, IV* (Winter 1955), pp. 15-29. In view of Miss Bartlett's exhaustive studies on the subject, I am presenting here only some of the most pertinent aspects of Hardy's debt to Shelley in the realm of sociological ideas.

[35] Milton Wilson, *Shelley's Later Poetry* (New York, 1959), p. 281.

Shelley and Hardy have in common their view of custom, of social and religious beliefs which had become fixed by tradition. Shelley never forsakes the revolutionary tenet that custom has an insidious power to ruin men's lives. His *Queen Mab* is the overt versification of this Godwinian view; *The Revolt of Islam* and *Prometheus Unbound* are radically affected by it. And, in his 1866 volume of Shelley, Hardy marked a number of passages that allude to

> Traditions dark and old, whence evil creeds
> Start forth, and whose dim shade a stream of poison feeds.[36]

As his career progressed, Hardy became increasingly and more uncompromisingly an enemy of institutions. Especially Shelleyan is his denunciation in "Channel Firing" of ecclastically-sanctioned vindictiveness and violence. Having depicted the church-shaking effect of war threats and preparations, and having voiced the skeleton parson's wish that, "instead of preaching forty year", he had "stuck to pipes and beer", Hardy symbolically points out how archaic and unaltered is man's vain reliance upon organized force as a means of achieving peace:

> Again the guns disturbed the hour,
> Roaring their readiness to avenge,
> As far inland as Stourton Tower,
> And Camelot, and starlit Stonehenge.

Traditional, formalized, indissoluble marriage was among the worst of the institutions opposed by Hardy. *Jude the Obscure* (1896) is his major tract on this subject, on which he had earlier expressed his conviction in *The Woodlanders* (1887)[37] and which

---

[36] *Islam,* II. ii. 8-9; also IX. iv. 6, and *P.U.,* I. 621-622, I. 697, II. iv. 155-156. See Bartlett, "Hardy's Shelley", p. 24.

[37] Novels, in addition to these two, in which quotations from Shelley appear are: *Desperate Remedies* (1871), *The Hand of Ethelberta* (1876), *An Indiscretion in the Life ot An Heiress* (1878), and *The Mayor of Caster-bridge* (1886). *The Well-Beloved* (1892), is entirely patterned upon the idea implied in the inscription on the title page: "One shape of many names", a phrase taken, out of context, from *The Revolt of Islam* and applied by Hardy to his story about the ideal of womanhood, an ideal which appears to Joycelyn Pierston, a sculptor, in three generations of women. Hardy's two well-known poems about Shelley are *Shelley's Skylark* and *The Pyramid of Cestius*, both written during a tour of Italy in 1887.

is found repeatedly in the poems. In "The Burghers" the husband, like Phillotson in *Jude*, struggles with himself about his relationship to his wife and her lover:

> And I may husband her, yet what am I
> But licensed tyrant to this bonded pair?
> Says Charity, Do as ye would be done by.

Hardy's inveighing against the cruelty of custom was as ardent as Shelley's and he was attacked as vitriolically as the earlier poet had been.[38]

Throughout his use, in various novels, of the Shelleyan ideal of womanhood, Hardy keeps in mind its relationship to the social institution of marriage. In *Jude the Obscure*, as already indicated, he gives this social consideration a full treatment. Sue Bridehead is his most complete representation of the Shelleyan woman. Telling Jude how she wants him to think of her, she quotes from *Epipsychidion*:

> There was a Being whom my spirit oft
> Met on its visioned wanderings far aloft.
> . . . .
> A seraph of Heaven, too gentle to be human,
> Veiling beneath that radiant form of woman. . . .[39]

Finding the passage too flattering, she breaks off the quotation; Jude agrees that it represents his concept of her.

But it is Phillotson, Sue's first husband, who has first recognized the Shelleyan quality of the relationship between her and Jude. Telling his friend Gillingham of his spying on Jude and Sue during their afternoon meeting, he says:

"I found from their manner that an extraordinary affinity, or sympathy, entered into their attachment, which somehow took away all flavor of grossness. Their supreme desire is to be together – to share each other's emotions, and fancies, and dreams."

"Platonic!" [exclaims Gillingham]

"Well, no. Shelleyan would be nearer to it. They remind me of Laon and Cythna." [40]

[38]   Bartlett, "Hardy's Shelley", p. 25.
[39]   *Jude the Obscure* (New York, 1923), p. 290. See *Epipsychidion*, 190-191, 21-22 (quoted out of sequence).
[40]   *Jude the Obscure*, pp. 274-275.

Both Sue and Jude have, before their meeting, come to consider marriage undesireable. Sue wishes to keep their relationship entirely Platonic. Jude is, however, finally successful in his physical wooing; and the appearance of children upon the scene ultimately brings about Sue's complete disillusionment. The two are eventually married, but disaster soon strikes. Sue accepts conventional religion and morality and returns to Phillotson; and Jude wonders, "Can this be the girl ... who ... quoted Gibbon and Shelley and Mill?" [41]

Thus Hardy analyses the tragedy of a man in modern society who is captivated by the idea that social convention cannot prevail against his own vision of truth.

Hardy's greatest debt to Shelley, however, is to be found, not in the novels, but in his poetic masterpiece, *The Dynasts*. The biographer Rutland has brought one aspect of this indebtedness into sharp focus:

It appears ... that had England in the three-quarters of a century before the *Dynasts* was written, produced no imaginative literature, Hardy's masterpiece would still be what it is.... To find any material debt which the *Dynasts* owes to English poetry, we must go back, beyond Hardy's contemporaries and immediate predecessors, to Shelley. It would be difficult to find two poetic dramas more widely removed from each other in spirit than *Prometheus Unbound* and the *Dynasts*; yet ... Hardy was a student of Shelley; and there can be no doubt that the form of the *Dynasts* owes something to Shelley. Exactly what it owes cannot be concisely analysed and tabulated, but it can be felt.... Hardy was indebted, not directly to Aeschylus and Sophocles, but to the amplification of the Attic chorus which Shelley introduced into *Prometheus Unbound*, and used again in *Hellas*. The whole spirit machinery of the *Dynasts* was clearly suggested by that of *Prometheus Unbound*.... Two points alone are enough to show Hardy's debt to Shelley; The Shade of the Earth in the *Dynasts* bears a close resemblance to the Earth in *Prometheus*; and Hardy's continual use of semi-choruses was clearly modelled upon Shelley's practice. The last point leads on from *Prometheus Unbound* to *Hellas*. There are distinct differences between these matchless poems; the latter, with its chorus of captive women and its introduction of the shade of Mohamet the Second ..., being much nearer to Greek drama. But the *Dynasts* is equally indebted to them both. Hardy saw in *Hellas* how choral poetry might be grafted on to events in history.[42]

Although it may scarcely be said that Shelley "influenced" Hardy's poetic technique generally, Rutland's commentary sorts out the evidence which indicates that in *The Dynasts* Hardy achieved his closest point of poetic contact with Shelley. But perhaps more important than the similarity to Shelley's poetic technique (Rutland, it seems to me, is wrong about the two poems' divergence in spirit) is the indication in *The Dynasts* of Hardy's turning from the dark fatalism which is the most un-Shelleyan aspect of his novels and poems, generally, to a very Shelleyan hope of possible amelioration.

In the first act of *Prometheus Unbound*, Shelley gives his Spirits (who dwell in the human mind) the power to prophesy; they explain lyrically that their foresight of a better world to come depends upon the extent to which "Wisdom, Justice, Love, and Peace" will struggle to increase themselves. Appropriately, human powers form the basis for the faith of these Spirits. Hardy's Pities, though often lectured by the other Intelligences regarding the Immanent Will's blindness or nescience, conclude the drama with a hopeful chorus. Their question: May not the heart of the Will awake,

> Promptly tending
> To Its mending
> In a genial germing purpose, and for loving-kindness' sake?

They believe that a Heart exists in this indifferent Will and that it has the potentiality of feeling simple human kindness. If the Will does not develop kindness in its heart, life might as well

---

[42] William R. Rutland, *Thomas Hardy: A Study of His Writings and Their Background* (Oxford, 1938), pp. 288-289. Hardy quotes Shelley twice in the Preface. "Riddles of Death Thebes never knew" is from *Hellas*, line 1083, and the phrase "far in the Unapparent" is from *Adonais*, xlv. 3. See Bartlett, "Seraph of Heaven", p. 19. Hoxie N. Fairchild and John A. Cassidy have established, however, that Robert Buchanan's *The Drama of Kings* (1871) was the immediate source for the structure of *The Dynasts*. See Hoxie Neale Fairchild, "The Immediate Source of the *Dynasts*". *PMLA*, LXVII (March 1952), pp. 43-64.

cease. Immediately following this declaration the Pities, in full chorus, announce a Shelleyan occurrence:

> But – a stirring thrills the air
> Like to sounds of joyance there
>> That the rages
>> Of the ages
> Shall be cancelled, and deliverance offered from the darts that were,
> Consciousness the Will informing, till It fashion all things fair!

This sudden conclusion is more in the supernatural, lyrical mood of the last act of *Prometheus Unbound* than are Demogorgon's own grave but more uplifting words that end Shelley's drama.

Hardy's over-all view is definitely more pessimistic than Shelley's. But insofar as Hardy had hope that the Will might become informed by human kindness, and insofar as Shelley was aware that advancement is a gradual process, not immediately affected by sheer human will, the two writers have a great deal more in common than the usual portrayal of them would indicate. As a close student of Shelley, Hardy undoubtedly derived a major portion of his later tentative hopefulness from the Romantic poet's faith in mankind. Despite his doubts and reservations, Hardy comes to agree with Shelley that there must be a "consciousness" and effort on the part of mankind if amelioration is to be expected.

VII

SHELLEY AND SHAW

Commentators on the works of George Bernard Shaw (1856-1950) almost invariably acknowledge his great indebtedness to Shelley. Their remarks are, however, limited to a passing statement or, at most, a page or two in which Shaw's enthusiasm for Shelley receives a very general treatment – several quotations from Shaw (and there are two or three favorites) usually being cited as evidence which needs little if any elaboration. Few of the numerous instances in which Shaw directly acknowledges his debt to Shelley have been noted by critics, to say nothing of an examination of decidedly Shelleyan ideas which are prominent in Shaw's writings.[1] I propose, therefore, to trace in considerable detail the background of Shaw's interest in Shelley, its effect upon him, his opinions about Shelley and his art, and especially his agreements and disagreements with important ideas held by Shelley.

Though in style the two writers are vastly dissimilar, Shelley was among the three or four thinkers whose ideas had the greatest influence on Shaw's convictions about man and society. The respective ideological impacts of Wagner and Ibsen may have been as great as that of Shelley; but had it not been for Shelley's earlier domination of Shaw's thinking, the importance to him of both Wagner and Ibsen would have been greatly reduced. As

---

[1] See, however, Kenneth Neill Cameron, *The Young Shelley: Genesis of a Radical* (New York, 1950), p. 390n. In this long note Professor Cameron presents an admirable resumé of views expressed by Shaw at meetings of the Shelley Society and points out other aspects of Shaw's interest in Shelley.

Shelley's influence preceded theirs in point of time, it also took precedence in confirming Shaw in his fundamental ways of thought.

EARLY INFLUENCES

Unlike most of the Shelleyites discussed in previous chapters, Shaw did not outgrow his enthusiasm for Shelley. Reminiscing in old age about his boyhood interest in dancing, music, and literature, he boasted to his neighbor and biographer Stephen Winsten of his retained memory and skill in these areas. By way of demonstration he tried a few waltz steps, hummed some Brahms, and declaimed Shelley.[2] That the first poet to come to Shaw's mind in this situation should be Shelley is only natural; as a youth he had read him perhaps more intensively than he had read any other writer. In a letter of 1924, after recalling his boyhood enthusiasm for Byron, Shaw declares, "When I was nearing twenty, Shelley got me; and I went into him head over heels and read every word he published. That was a sort of literary falling in love: Shelley's kingdom was not of this world for me." [3]

Looking at the same experience with Shelley from another point of view, Shaw, in a chapter entitled "Biographers' Blunders Corrected", tells of his liberation from certain concepts which society had imposed upon him: "Paine had been held up to me as a drunken staymaker without a redeeming trait. Voltaire and Rousseau, I was taught, were blasphemers whose deathbeds were made frightful by their certainty of going to hell. It was then part of the education of a gentleman to convince him that the three most religious men in Europe had been impious villains, and were roasting in blazing brimstone to all eternity. Shelley cured me of all that. I read him prose and verse, from beginning to end. This took place at the end of my teens." [4] And speaking to

---

[2] Stephen Winsten, *Shaw's Corner* (London, 1952), p. 107.
[3] *To a Young Actress: The Letters of Bernard Shaw to Molly Tompkins,* ed. Peter Tompkins (New York, 1960), p. 72.
[4] George Bernard Shaw, *Sixteen Self Sketches* (London, 1949), p. 108.

Winsten of this period of his life, Shaw said, "I was saturated with the works of Bunyan, Shelley, and Dickens." [5] Shaw's adoption of the atheism which Shelley professed [6] is one indication of Shelley's effectual power upon him, as compared to that exerted by the other two writers.

Publicly, in his role as young socialist, Shaw boldly placed himself on Shelley's side by his well-known, intentionally shocking remark in 1886 at the first general meeting of the Shelley Society: "Like Shelley, I am a Socialist, an Atheist, and a Vegetarian." [7] Years later he declared that by this statement he had risked everything on Shelley's behalf and that he had thereby forfeited every chance of gaining a foothold in polite society except to go all out and give society no quarter. "I praised it", he said, "for the very qualities it despised." [8]

Yet Shaw was fair with society. In 1897, shortly after the prosecution of the freethinking editor Annie Besant, he made his first public speech at one of the debates of the Zetetical Society. Defending the State's action in depriving Mrs. Besant of

---

[5]   Stephen Winsten, *Days with Bernard Shaw* (New York, 1949), p. 37.
[6]   George Bernard Shaw, Preface to *Immaturity*, in *The Collected Works*, Ayot St. Lawrence Ed. (New York, 1930-32), I, xx. All subsequent references to Shaw's writings, unless otherwise indicated, are to this edition.
      Pointing out that Shaw used Shelley's term "Jupiter" and Blake's "Nobodaddy" interchangeably in the preface to *Back to Methuselah*, Julian B. Kaye, in his book, *Bernard Shaw and the Nineteenth-Century Tradition* (Norman, Univ. of Oklahoma Press, 1958), p. 127, declares that Shaw, as he grew older, realized that Shelley had not been an atheist – that Jupiter in *Prometheus Unbound* represents not God but Nobodaddy.
[7]   See Archibald Henderson, *George Bernard Shaw: Man of the Century* (New York, 1936), p. 151. In a footnote Henderson points out that the remark is not found in the minutes of the Shelley Society. Shaw later (in the preface to *Immaturity*, p. xx) says of this declaration: "I did not know that I could have expressed my position more accurately by simply saying that my conception of God was that insisted on in the first Article of the Church of England. . . . I had never thought of reading the Articles of the Church of England; and if I had I should still have used the word atheist as a declaration that I was on the side of Bradlaugh and Foote and others who, as avowed Secularists and Atheists, were being persecuted and imprisoned for my opinions." Shaw repeated the declaration in 1892 at a vegetarian banquet commemorating the Shelley Centenary. See "A Feast for Faddists", *Pall Mall Gazette*, LIV (27 June 1892), 2.
[8]   Winsten, *Days with Bernard Shaw*, p. 196.

her children, he presented a parallel defense of the State's similar decision in the earlier case of Shelley.[9] He was not objecting to Shelley's opinions but was, rather, voicing his often-reiterated conviction that an effective society acts consistently.

Telling, in his 1921 preface to *Immaturity*, of his early support of Shelley's heterodox opinions, Shaw says, "Read my preface to Back to Methuselah, and you will see me as the complete infidel of that day. I had read much poetry; but only one poet was sacred to me: Shelley. I had read his works piously from end to end, and was in my negations atheist and republican to the backbone. I say in my negations; for I had not reached any affirmative position." [10]

These early negations, derived from Shelley's influence, prepared the way for Shaw's acceptance of Ibsen's principles: "Ibsen had not shocked me in the least. Why was I immune? Because an earlier enchanter had taken me far outside the bounds of middle-class idealism within which Ibsen's bombshells were deadly. I am not by nature a good bourgeois any more than Shelley was; and I was a strong Shelleyan long before I ever heard of Ibsen." [11] Shelley's powerful influence had emboldened Shaw to proclaim his support of unconventional views such as the belief that a child's hostility to a parent was not wicked or abnormal, but natural. Instead of discovering later that he must abandon these ideas (as Browning and Disraeli had), Shaw found them strengthened and brought to maturity by his study of Ibsen, Wagner, and other progressive thinkers.

SHELLEY'S APPEAL

An indication of the seriousness of Shaw's enthusiasm for Shel-

---

[9] R. F. Rattray, *Bernard Shaw: A Chronicle* (Luton, England, 1951), p. 34. See also Henderson, p. 136. Shaw frequently refers to Shelley's being deprived by the State of the guardianship over his children. See George Bernard Shaw, *Everybody's Political What's What* (New York, 1945), pp. 74 and 152, and *The Intelligent Woman's Guide to Socialism and Capitalism*, pp. 475, 479.

[10] *Immaturity*, pp. xix-xx.

[11] Shaw, "An Aside"; see E. J. West, ed., *Shaw on Theatre* (New York, 1959), p. 219.

ley is his adoption of vegetarianism – a practice which he derived directly from Shelley and to which he adhered throughout his life. "I was a cannibal for twenty-five years", he wrote. "For the rest I have been a vegetarian. It was Shelley who first opened my eyes to the savagery of my diet; but it was not until 1880 or thereabouts that the establishment of vegetarian restaurants in London made a change practicable for me." [12] When an old man, Shaw told his friend Winsten,

> It was Shelley who converted me to vegetarianism. . . . You see, vegetarianism to Shelley, like marriage and atheism, was a form of poetry. I am always asked how it is that my opinions have changed so little since my youth. It is because I got to them by poetry. As I always say, the aesthetic is the most convincing and permanent. Shelley made his ideas sing; I made them dance. . . . He converted me not by his suffering, but by the sheer logic of his poetry. There is no falsehood, no calumny, no torture which the mere expression of a simple truth does not provoke. [13]

This dedication to the expression of a simple truth, despite the consequences, Shaw admired most in Shelley; when the "simple truth" pointed out by Shelley was one which convinced him that the eating of meat necessitated an illogical and brutal killing of fellow living beings, he abandoned it for this reason alone. He has nothing but scorn for the person who becomes a vegetarian solely to improve his own health. In the preface to *Heartbreak House* he writes of the house, which is his symbol for pre-World-War-I Europe: "Being an idle house it was a hypochondriacal house, always running after cures. It would stop eating meat, not on valid Shelleyan grounds, but in order to get rid of a bogey called Uric Acid." [14] Thus Shaw declared his continued vegetarianism to be centered not on any advantage for himself but on what he considered the rights of his fellow creatures. By persist-

---

[12]   *Sixteen Self Sketches*, p. 53.
[13]   Winsten, *Days with Bernard Shaw*, p. 195. See also Winsten, *Shaw's Corner*, p. 35.
[14]   "Hypochondria", the preface to *Heartbreak House*, p. 9. Julian Kaye (p. 129, n.) points out that Shaw referred to meat eaters as people who ate corpses and that *The Revolt of Islam* (V, lv-lvi) indicates a similar opinion on Shelley's part.

ing in this overt practice he also symbolized a commitment to Shelleyan ideas generally – a commitment more substantial than had been symbolized by Browning's two-year stand as a vegetarian.

The absolute sincerity and dedication to simple truth which he found to be the cause of Shelley's vegetarianism was evident to Shaw as the very basis of the Romantic poet's thinking: Shelley "did not go back upon his opinions in the least as he grew older. By the time he had begun The Triumph of Life, he had naturally come to think Queen Mab a boyish piece of work, not that what it affirmed seemed false to him or what it denied true, but because it did not affirm and deny enough. Thus there is no excuse for Shelley on the ground of his youth or rashness. If he was a sinner, he was a hardened sinner and a deliberate one".[15] Shaw names Shelley among the twelve men of genius whose peculiar sense of the world he recognizes as more or less akin to his own.[16] In his unsentimentalized and fearless exposition of the truth, an approach which designates the heretic in society, Shaw sought always to follow Shelley.

But he found that the society of his time had sunk so low in moral listlessness and had become so callous to criticism that all the force of his onslaught was destroyed by a simple public policy of nonresistance. As early as 1903 he laments, "In vain do I redouble the violence of the language in which I proclaim my heterodoxies. I rail at the theistic credulity of Voltaire, the amoristic superstition of Shelley." Yet Shaw finds that, instead of insisting that he, the "inconceivable Satanist", be sent to the stake, the respectable newspapers hail his new books in commendatory terms, thus putting at ease the ordinary citizen who reads him "as he reads Micah, with undisturbed edification from his own point of view".[17] Shaw came to feel that Shelley relied too greatly on love as the panacea for all ills, but by his own admis-

---

[15]   Shaw, "Shaming the Devil about Shelly", *Pen Portraits and Reviews*, p. 253.
[16]   "Epistle Dedicatory", *Man and Superman*, xxxi-xxxii. The other eleven are Bunyan, Blake, Hogarth, Turner, Goethe, Schopenhauer, Wagner, Ibsen, Morris, Tolstoy, and Nietzsche.
[17]   *Ibid.*, pp. xxxvi-xxxvii.

sion, to term this reliance an "amoristic superstition" is an exaggeration intended to shock the common citizen, who had rationalized Shelley into a poet of sentimental love. Some forty years later, in 1944, his complaint against society was still the same: "I submit that when quite respectable young gentlemen like Shelley and myself boast of being heretics, and clubs of them are formed at the universities, Mr. Everyman is right in concluding that there must be something very wrong somewhere . . . . When The Inquisition is out-of-date, and the heretics up-to-date, there is the devil to pay." [18]

When, in 1892, the ultra-conservative townspeople of Horsham in Sussex celebrated the centennial of their native poet and proposed to build there a Shelley library and museum, Shaw wrote his keenly discerning essay, "Shaming the Devil about Shelley",[19] to point out what Shelley actually stood for. In it he tells of laughing up his sleeve at the absurdity of any enthusiasm for Shelley in this "true blue" corner of England and proceeds to draw up a statement of the poet's teachings. He points out that in politics Shelley was a most extreme republican, leveler, and radical and was even a Godwinian anarchist until he found this philosophy impracticable. Had Shelley lived fifty years later, he would have been a Social-Democrat with strong leanings toward the most democratic communism attainable and practically workable. In religion Shelley did not resort to calling himself an agnostic to avoid the issue. Though believing strongly in an omnipresent life-force, he did not "beg off being an Atheist by calling [it] God, or even Pan".

Because of Shelley's unreserved honesty, Shaw was especially incensed by the Horsham celebration which he called "a carnival of humbug", put on primarily by "triflers" who considered Shelley "nothing more than a word-jeweller". Its objective seemed to be to make of Shelley a saint who had unfortunately been thrown in with a bad set ("as if he had not been more free to choose his

[18] *Everybody's Political What's What*, p. 360.
[19] See *Pen Portraits and Reviews*, pp. 248-259. The quotations in this and the following two paragraphs are from "Shaming the Devil about Shelley".

own set than most other men in England", says Shaw). Shelley's youth, his being a poet, and the elusiveness of his piety unless he was read in the proper spirit were among the excuses made for him. But what, in Shaw's opinion, topped everything was Edmund Gosse's contention "that Shelley was so fragile, so ir- responsible, so ethereally tender, so passionate a creature that the wonder was that he was not a much greater rascal." Sar- castically, Shaw says that vitually every one at the celebration was "solid for the library, even if the front were to be decorated with a relief representing Shelley in a tall hat, Bible in hand, leading his children on Sunday morning to the church of his native parish".

In preference to all the humbug at Horsham, Shaw asks that people show some discernment, even if it means saying, "I think Shelley's poetry slovenly and unsubstantial, and his ideas simply rot; but I will celebrate him because he said what he thought, and not what he was expected to say he thought." Instead of attending the Horsham celebration, Shaw took part in the London centennial meeting arranged by G. W. Foote, then president of the National Secular Society. Shaw declares that Mr. Foote, who had been imprisoned for blasphemy, "was able to speak with all the freedom and force of a man who not only talks Shelley but lives him". Of his own part in the program Shaw says, "I had nothing to do but give a faithful account of Shelley's real opinions, with every one of which I unreservedly agree." Most of the people attending Mr. Foote's meeting acknowledged a con- siderable influence of Shelley on their lives. Upon mention of Shelley as a major inspirer of the Chartist movement, an old Chartist in the audience rose to state that he now recalled that reading Shelley had led him to join the movement. *Queen Mab's* reputation as the Chartists' Bible was then pointed out; and Shaw, writing about the meeting, says of Shelley, "He made and is still making men and women join political societies, secular societies, Vegetarian societies, societies for the loosening of the marriage contract, and Humanitarian societies of all sorts." Throughout his life, Shaw continued to be as enthusiastic about this genuine influence of Shelley as he was contemptuous of false

Shelley societies and of the Horsham meeting's mouthing of insincere platitudes about Shelley.

Being independent of the market for his literary productions, Shelley could afford to ignore much of the public indignation over his unorthodox views and actions. Because he, nevertheless, knew the value of money, he was, in Shaw's opinion, a practical man.[20] And Shaw sees in Shelley's fierce attacks upon his society an example of the nineteenth century loathing itself after tiring of its money.[21] Yet, in a letter to Frank Harris, Shaw recognizes that the Shelley "who poured the fiercest invective on Castlereagh, on Eldon and on his own father, not to mention the entire tribe of old men," was the same Shelley who wrote *Prometheus Unbound* and *Laon and Cythna*, in which kindness and forgiveness are predominant.[22] Repeatedly, it becomes evident that the consistency Shaw found so praiseworthy in Shelley was a consistency in speaking out in favor of truth and against falsehood as he saw them.

Not that Shaw was invariably pleased with Shelley's poetry. There are aspects of it which he finds superfluous and damaging to the poet's effectiveness. "Shelley," he says, "could not write a big poem without smothering it under a universe of winds and clouds, mountains and fountains, glories and promontories ... until its theme was lost like a roseleaf in a splendid sunset." [23] He appreciates Shelley the agitator far more than Shelley the poet.

As a dedicated Fabian, Shaw examines poetry for its socialistic content rather than for its artistry. With the poet who writes for the sake of sound and rhythm, he contrasts the one who considers poetry specifically a means to an end, "the end being to deliver a message which clamors to be revealed through him. So he secures a hearing for it by clothing it with word-garments of such beauty, authority, and eternal memorableness, that the world must needs listen to it. These are prophets rather than poets; and for the sake

[20] Winsten, *Days with Bernard Shaw*, p. 271.
[21] Shaw, *Our Theatres in the Nineties*, iii, p. 188.
[22] Letter of January 1917. See Frank Harris, *Bernard Shaw* (New York, 1931), p. 362.
[23] "An Aside", p. 223.

of being poets alone would not take the trouble to rhyme love and dove or bliss and kiss." [24] Continuing, Shaw designates Shelley as one of these prophets. When Shelley permits his poetry to obscure his maxims, he disturbs and irritates Shaw. In the minutes of the 13 April 1887 meeting of the Shelley Society, Shaw is reported to have maintained, in his rebuttal to a paper on *The Revolt of Islam*, that "a poem ought to be didactic, and ought to be in the nature of a political treatise" – because poetry is "the most artistic way of teaching those things which a poet ought to teach".[25] He considers *Queen Mab* far superior to *The Cenci* because it shows Shelley's "remarkable grasp of facts" and his anticipation of a modern view of social amelioration.[26] He likes the didacticism of *The Revolt* and the factualness of *Queen Mab* and, therefore, thinks them great. No doubt, he recognized their poetic deficiencies; but these he considered of secondary importance.

Discussing *The Cenci*, Shaw expresses a forthright opinion on the relation between content and poetic form: "The Cenci might either have been a serious drama or might never have been written at all if Shelley had not been allowed to carry off its unreality by Elizabethan versification." [27] His opinion is that Shelley, like Shakespeare, was not hampered by the convention of writing dramas in verse but found it to be the easiest and cheapest way of composing them. Though Shaw is here dealing with dramatic effect, one suspects that for him the adequate expression of sociological ideas is a factor at least closely related to dramatic effect. A lack of purpose is the primary charge he is reported to have brought against *The Cenci* in his remarks at the Shelley Society: "Mr. G. Bernard Shaw said that in his opinion *The Cenci* was a play unworthy of the genius of Shelley. It was simply an abomination, an accumulation of horrors partaking of the

[24] *Pen Portraits and Reviews*, p. 191. At the vegetarian banquet held to commemorate the Shelley Centenary, Shaw "regretted that Shelley's artistic excellence, now beyond question, overshadowed his importance as a leader of thought". See "A Feast for Faddists", p. 2.
[25] The Shelley Society, *Publications*, ser. 1, no. 2, pt. 1 [1913], p. 193.
[26] *Ibid.*, p. 31.
[27] *The Perfect Wagnerite*, p. 275.

nature of a *tour de force*, and probably written by Shelley merely to satisfy his ambition of producing something for the stage. He considerd it as bad a piece of work as a man of Shelley's genius could be capable of, so bad indeed that it was hardly worth discussion."[28] Other comments by Shaw about the play, at the same meeting and later in his writings, indicate that on poetic and dramatic bases alone he would not have made his harsh pronouncements against it. The play's major fault, in Shaw's opinion, is that its poetic form diverts from it some of the force of social criticism which it could have realized fully in prose form.

Despite his criticisms of *The Cenci*, Shaw uses the banning of it from British theaters as a weapon in his battle against the censorship code. He describes the Shelley Society's circumvention of the censor in its "private" production of *The Cenci* as well as the censors' subsequent treatment of the theater owner in whose building the play was presented.[29] Repeatedly he refers to Shelley's life and writings when he is pointing out the absurdity and inconsistency of censorship as practiced in England.[30]

A DISAGREEMENT

Shaw's major disagreement with Shelley concerns ideas about love, especially those expressed in *Epipsychidion*. He wrote to Frank Harris that love poems generally "are like Shelley's Epipsychidion, irritating to *terre à terre* sensual women, who know at once that you are making them palatable by pretending they

---

[28] The Shelley Society, *Publications*, ser. 1, no. 2, pt. 1, pp. 184-185. Perhaps noteworthy in this regard is Shaw's postcard to Sylva Norman, in which he cautioned her about the reporting of the Shelley Society, stating that he himself had been among those suffering most severely from its inaccuracies. See her *Flight of the Skylark* (London, 1954), p. 272, n.

[29] "The Censorship of the Stage in England"; see West, pp. 71-72, 77; see also Appendix to *The Quintessence of Ibsenism* (West, p. 11). This appendix appeared with the essay in only the first edition, 1891. See also Shaw, *Platform and Pulpit*, ed. Dan H. Laurence (New York, 1961), p. 194.

[30] See *Everybody's Political What's What,* pp. 194-195, 198, 324, 325.

are something that they are not, and cannot stand comparison with." [31] Having declared, "It is a scientific fact that some of the primitive impulses which existed before the invention of language remain unspeakable and should be gratified in silence", Shaw pronounces Shelley's *Epipsychidion* "a wonderful effort by a supreme master of language to utter the unspeakable; but the result is a rhapsody of nonsense that has no contact with natural history".[32] Comparing *Epipsychidion* to the one great love poem of the Bible, Shaw declares Shelley's poem to be "literary gas and gaiters".[33]

Shaw objects not only to Shelley's expression of sexual love but also to his advocacy of universal love as the answer to all human problems. Ibsen, he says, did not find Shelley's "brimstone conception, 'the Almighty Fiend' ", to be worth attacking – partly because the cultured class to which Ibsen addressed himself had replaced that superstition with "the sentimental religion of love in which we are still wallowing, and which only substitutes twaddle for terror".[34] Discussing Wagner's *Nibelungs' Ring,* Shaw maintains that the musician-dramatist's philosophy was exhausted before he had completed the work. To arrive at his solution in the drama of Wotan and Siegfried, Wagner "succumbed to the panacea mania ... like any of the rest of us". Shaw continues:

The panacea is by no means an original one. Wagner was anticipated in the year 1819 by a young country gentleman from Sussex named Shelley, in a work of extraordinary artistic power and splendor. Prometheus Unbound is an English attempt at a Ring. ... Both works set forth the same conflict between humanity and its gods and governments, issuing in the redemption of man from their tyranny by the growth of his will into perfect strength and self-confidence; and both finish by a lapse into panacea-mongering didacticism by the holding up of Love as the remedy for all evils and the solvent of all social difficulties.[35]

[31] Letter of 24 June 1930. See Harris, p. 243.
[32] *Everybody's Political What's What,* p. 176.
[33] Preface to "The Black Girl in Search of God", in *The Black Girl in Search of God, and Some Lesser Tales*, Standard ed. (London, 1934), p. 11.
[34] *The Quintessence of Ibsenism,* p. 56.
[35] *The Perfect Wagnerite,* pp. 230-231.

Wagner, as Shaw understands him, reduces to an absurdity the Shelleyan concept of a love panacea. He presents love's supreme good as being its complete satisfaction of life, removing the troublesome power of the "Will to Live" and finally contenting us with the "highest happiness of death". Shelley's idea of love as a sentiment of affectionate benevolence (better expressed as mercy and kindness) with no connotation of sexual passion, frees him, in *Prometheus Unbound*, from the need to reduce his panacea to Wagner's absurdity. Wagner, says Shaw, always insisting on the need to apprehend sensually in order "to give reality to abstract comprehension", followed poetic love "back to its alleged origin in sexual passion". The frankness and naturalism of his musical expression of this passion "would possibly have scandalized Shelley".[36]

But Shaw finds that even Shelley's idea of mercy and loving-kindness does not hold good as a universal law of conduct. He points out that Shelley himself makes extremely short work of Jupiter. Bringing in "that very nebulous personification of Eternity called Demogorgon" to save Prometheus from doing the actual destructive work, does not, in Shaw's opinion, save the situation at all. He argues that because there is no such person as Demogorgon, no one will pull down Jupiter if Prometheus does not do so himself. The error in Shaw's reasoning is immediately apparent. He insists that Jupiter must be pulled down by a "person" and that literal destructive work must be done. There are no such persons either, it might be pointed out, as Prometheus and Jupiter. Shelley is saying that tyranny can be overcome by unpersonfied forces put in motion by an application of the ethic of love; he insists that destructive action is unnecessary and evil.

HIGH PRAISE

Yet, sharply though Shaw attacks both Shelley and Wagner for what he considers their lapse into panacea mongering, he also

36   *Ibid.*, p. 232.

mentions them together in terms of highest praise. In his preface
to *Misalliance* (1910) he makes a comparison highly favorable to
the very works whose respective conclusions he so severely criticized in 1898: "The pleasure we get from the rhetoric of the book
of Job and its tragic picture of a bewildered soul cannot . . .
supply the need for such modern revelations as Shelley's Prometheus or The Niblung's [*sic*] Ring of Richard Wagner." [37] And
he had, some years before *The Perfect Wagnerite*, singled out
these two men as examples of the heights which may be attained
when "high thinking" is the norm in a person's life:

In this century the world has produced two men – Shelley and
Wagner – in whom intense poetic feeling was the permanent state of
their consciousness, and who were certainly not restrained by any
religious, conventional, or prudential considerations from indulging
themselves to the utmost of their opportunities. Far from being
gluttonous, drunken, cruel, or debauched, they were apostles of
vegetarianism and water-drinking; had an utter horror of violence
and "sport"; were notable champions of the independence of women;
and were, in short, driven into open revolution against the social
evils which the average sensual man finds extremely suitable to him.
So much is this the case that the practical doctrine of these two
arch-voluptuaries always presents itself to ordinary persons as a saint-
like asceticism.[38]

And this early praise was to be followed by various references to
Shelley, expressing a high admiration – at times almost an adoration – of Shelley's social and political leadership, high seriousness, and moral greatness.

In the preface to *Man and Superman* (1903) Shaw referred to
Shelley as "a religious force".[39] And to Stephen Winsten he once,
in his old age, said, "I am highly susceptible to the force of all truly
religious music, especially to the music of my own church, the church
of Shelley, Michelangelo, and Beethoven." [40] This high commen-

---

[37] "Parents and Children", the preface to *Misalliance,* p. 99.
[38] "The Religion of the Pianoforte", *Fortnightly Rev.,* LV, n.s. (1 February 1894), 264.
[39] "Epistle Dedicatory" to *Man and Superman,* p. xiv.
[40] Winsten, *Days with Bernard Shaw,* p. 113. Shaw's response, at the
8 June 1887 meeting of the Shelley Society, to Mr. Edward Silsbee's un-
titled paper on Shelley, is pertinent here: "Mr. Bernard Shaw said the

dation Shaw accords to Shelley because he considers the poet to
have attained the advanced level of being which is the province
of supermen. John Tanner's "Revolutionist's Handbook", append-
ed to *Man and Superman*, contains the following observation:
"Unless we are replaced by a more highly evolved animal – in
short, by the Superman – the world must remain a den of dan-
gerous animals among whom our few accidental supermen, our
Shakespears, Goethes, Shelleys, and their like, must live as pre-
cariously as lion tamers do." [41]

But in attaining his position as a superman, Shelley has not
removed himself from the scene of social needs and conflicts.
Having cited Morris, Ruskin, and Carlyle as writers who turned
from aesthetic interests to revolutionary writings, Shaw designates
these men as followers of Shelley. They realized that, since nobody else was taking up the challenge of the social misery all
about them, they as great writers must. Like Shelley, poets must
work for public improvement at the stages at which such work
will bring them only abuse.[42] There is, however, another way of
looking at the advanced work done by great writers and artists
who catch the vision of a better future for mankind. Presenting
them as building their pinnacles till they catch the glint of the
unrisen sun, thus to reflect its rays to the waiting people, Shaw
conjectures about the advanced state of our being when the sun
that is caught by the work of great artists such as Shelley shall
have reached the valleys.[43] He makes it clear that one of the
praiseworthy aspects of Shelley is his ability to draw other great
men after him to serve mankind as social prophets.

Shaw thus pictures Shelley as a man of utter seriousness; com-

---

paper seemed to him a sort of act of worship, and he dreaded all criticism
that had not a basis of reason. It seemed to him that Shelley does produce
irrationally enthusiastical phenomena, which Dante and Shakespeare do
not." See Shelley Society, *Publications,* ser. 1, no. 2, pt. 2. See also Henderson, p. 152. Quite obviously, Shaw himself was tempted more by
Shelley than by Shakespeare and Dante to become irrationally enthusiastic.
[41]   *Man and Superman,* p. 207.
[42]   "The Problem Play – A Symposium", in West, pp. 64-65. This article
first appeared in *The Humanitarian,* VI (May 1895).
[43]   Preface (1898) to *Plays, Pleasant and Unpleasant,* p. ix.

paring him to Keats, he admits that "even the thought of Shelley kills geniality".[44] But, in an appendix to *The Quintessence of Ibsenism*, he has given noble reasons for Shelley's high seriousness:

It was not through joyless poverty of soul that Shelley never laughed, but through an enormous apprehension and realization of the gravity of things that seemed mere fun to other men. . . . The English cry of "Amuse us: take things easily: dress up the world prettily for us" seems mere cowardice to the strong souls that dare look facts in the face; and just so far as people cast off levity and idolatry they find themselves able to bear the company of Bunyan and Shelley, of Ibsen and Strindberg and the great Russian realists, and unable to tolerate the sort of laughter that African tribes cannot restrain when a man is flogged or an animal trapped and wounded.[45]

One needs, of course, only to read Shelley's youthful *The Devil's Walk*, and his *Oedipus Tyrannus*, to know that it is not literally true that, as poet, he never laughed. Shaw is referring to the undercurrent of serious intent always present in Shelley's works. In *The Quintessence of Ibsenism* Shaw declares, "The salvation of the world depends on the men who will not take evil good-humoredly, and whose laughter destroys the fool instead of encouraging him." [46] Then follows the already-quoted passage on the cause of Shelley's seriousness. This intense seriousness has much in common with Shaw's view of his own great wit as primarily a device for seeking and exposing truth.

Shelley's tendency to see the gravity of what to others seemed mere fun and his simultaneous ability to look facts in the face caused Shaw to declare him a pioneer. In *The Quintessence of Ibsenism*, Shaw presents two kinds of pioneers: the one who looks back and pronounces wrong something that nobody has considered wrong, and the one who declares that it is right to do something previously considered infamous. By two propositions which Shelley upheld, Shaw presents him as an example of both

---

[44] *Pen Portraits and Reviews*, p. 193.
[45] *The Quintessence of Ibsenism*, pp. 143-144. At the 8 June 1887 meeting of the Shelley Society, Shaw "contended that . . . Shelley had a large fund of humor, but the fact of taking so serious a view of life and life's work kept the humor away from his poetry". See Shelley Society, *Publications*, ser. 1, no. 2, pt. 2.
[46] *The Quintessence of Ibsenism*, p. 143.

kinds of pioneer: (1) "It is wrong to kill animals and eat them", and (2) "It is not wrong to take your sister as your wife." [47] There is nothing new, Shaw points out, in the reformer's defiance of duty; for every step of progress a duty is repudiated and a scripture torn up. Denunciation by society is, therefore, the natural lot of the reformer. Among his examples Shaw lists the accusation against Shelley as a libertine. Despite this ostracism by society, the solitary Shellyan pioneer, seeing truths which lie deeper than surface platitudes, is the unrecognized benefactor of mankind.

Setting up an imaginary society of one thousand, Shaw classifies its members as 700 Philistines and 299 idealists, thus leaving one man unclassified. This is the man with strength enough to face the truth which the idealists shirk. Shaw calls him the realist. To gain a clear understanding of his terms, as well as to see how Shelley figures as his model for the realist, we must turn to Shaw's own words:

The Philistines will simply think him [the realist] mad. But the idealists will be terrified beyond measure at the proclamation of their hidden thought. . . . They will crucify him, burn him, violate their own ideals of family affection by taking his children away from him, ostracize him, brand him as immoral, profligate, filthy, and appeal against him to the despised Philistines, specially idealized for the occasion as Society. . . . Take the case of . . . Shelley. The idealists did not call Shelley a cynic; they called him a fiend until they invented a new illusion to enable them to enjoy the beauty of his lyrics, the illusion being nothing less than the pretence that since he was at bottom an idealist himself, his ideals must be identical with those of Tennyson and Longfellow, neither of whom ever wrote a line in which some highly respectable ideal was not implicit.

Here the admission that Shelley, the realist, was an idealist too, seems to spoil the whole argument. . . . You and I, reader, will be at cross purposes at every sentence unless you allow me to distinguish pioneers like Shelley and Ibsen as realists from the idealists of

---

[47] *Ibid.*, p. 15. In a footnote Shaw declares the second proposition both unimportant and old-fashioned. He compares it to the proposition, "It is not wrong to stand on one's head"; to which the reply is, "You may be very right; but as nobody wants to, why bother about it?" Yet he believes that Shelley has helped to bring about the modern, sensible way of treating the matter – an obvious improvement over the old morbid horror.

my imaginary community of one thousand. . . . If the term realist is objected to on account of its modern associations, I can only recommend you, if you must associate it with something else than my own description of its meaning (I do not deal in definitions), to associate it, not with Zola and Maupassant, but with Plato.[48]

What angers Shaw most is that, not the ignorant and stupid, but the literate and cultured maintain the error of confounding the highest man with the lowest. Among other examples, he points out: "It is from men of established literary reputation that we learn that William Blake was mad, that Shelley was spoiled by living in a low set." [49] His own admiration for Shelley's social and political leadership, seriousness, and moral greatness intensifies Shaw's characteristic disdain for the society of idealists and Philistines.

LITERARY REFERENCES TO SHELLEY

In his dramas themselves Shaw does not frequently quote from or refer directly to Shelley. But in *Candida* the character of the poet Eugene Marchbanks is obviously patterned after Shelley, although Shelley is not specifically mentioned in the play. When *Candida* is studied in conjunction with *The Quintessence*, there can be little doubt of Shaw's intention to set forth Marchbanks as an example of the Shelleyan realist whom he has presented in the essay. The playwright's description of Marchbanks is, in itself, a résumé (with added Shavian touches) of the accounts generally given of Shelley's person and temperament:

He is a strange, shy youth . . . slight, effeminate, with a delicate childish voice, and a hunted tormented expression and shrinking manner that shew the painful sensitiveness of very swift and acute apprehensiveness in youth. . . . The very intensity with which he feels a perfectly commonplace position comes from excessive nervous force; and his nostrils, mouth, and eyes betray a fiercely petulant wilfulness, as to the bent of which his brow, already lined with pity,

---

[48] *Ibid.*, pp. 31-33.

[49] *Ibid.*, pp. 33-34. The misleading statement about Shelley was one of Matthew Arnold's declarations. See also *Pen Portraits and Reviews*, p. 253.

is reassuring. He is so uncommon as to be almost unearthly; and to prosaic people there is something noxious in this unearthliness, just as to poetic people there is something angelic in it.[50]

And in the early productions of *Candida*, Marchbanks was made up to resemble Shelley – "femininely hectic and timid and fierce", in Oliver Elton's words.[51]

Like Shelley, Marchbanks is misunderstood by his aristocratic family. He, too, as Candida tells us near the end of the play, has been miserable at Eton, has left Oxford, and is resisting his father's attempt to starve him into returning to school. His insistence upon a showdown between his ideas and those of his opponents, and his aversion to Morell's "metaphors, sermons, stale perorations", are distinctly Shelleyan traits. In *Candida* Shelley and Shelleyan ideas figure more prominently than in any other of Shaw's dramatic works.

One other play which obviously had its inception in a Shellyan idea is *Captain Brassbound's Conversion*. Shaw originally entitled it *The Witch of Atlas*, and although its name was changed, the play appears none the less to be based upon Shelley's poem. It contains one verbal asurance that Shelley's *Witch of Atlas* was in Shaw's mind as he wrote:

SIR HOWARD: What are those hills over there to the southeast?
RANKIN: They are the outposts, so to speak, of the Atlas Mountains.
LADY CICELY: The Atlas Mountains! Where Shelley's witch lived! We'll make an excursion to them tomorrow.[52]

And it is in these hills that Lady Cicely, by the charm of her innocent and absolute disbelief in the threat of violence and

---

[50] *Candida*, p. 93. In view of Shaw's frequent citing of Shelley as a specimen of the realist in *The Quintessence,* it is most surprising to come upon William Irvine's remark that Marchbanks "is perhaps too much Shelley made over to fit the definition of a Shavian realist." See Irvine, *The Universe of G. B. S.* (New York, 1949), p. 178.

[51] See Henderson, p. 443. Note, in Henderson's biography, the photograph of the actor Arnold Daly as Marchbanks (in 1903), reading Shelley's poem, "One word is too oft profaned".

[52] *Captain Brassbound's Conversion* (Act I), p. 231. Note that Shaw has earlier used the phrase "witch of Atlas" in his first novel *Immaturity* (written in 1879), p. 350.

revenge, converts the arrogant ruffian Brassbound. Had Shaw chosen to supply his play with a motto, he could scarcely have found one more suitable than Shelley's lines:

> The magic circle of her voice and eyes
> All savage natures did imparadise.
>
> (*Witch of Atlas*, VII, 7-8)

Shelley's witch, like Lady Cicely, introduces a new spirit of confidence, trust, and selflessness into a world which knows only the old codes of fear, aggression, and revenge.

Other instances in Shaw's plays of direct reference to Shelley appear to be of a more incidental kind. Yet it might be argued that two lines of Shelley's *Ozymandias* –

> My name is Ozymandias, king of kings:
> Look on my works, ye mighty and despair –

quoted in Part V of *Back to Methuselah* by the proud but pathetic Male Figure, state the theme of the whole play. The former greatness of Shelley's Ozymandias has been superseded, his statue has crumbled, and his words have become absurd; Shaw pictures the same thing happening to modern man's attainments.

Another literary work in which Shaw occasionally refers to Shelley is his first novel, *Immaturity,* which he wrote in 1879 but did not publish until 1930. The character who represents Shaw in the novel is the youthful Smith, who becomes intolerant of everything that falls short of his highest ideal of beauty and power and thus contracts prejudices against his early idol Byron, whom he replaces by Shelley. He tries vegetarianism, but this attempt is frustrated in three days by the cook's inability to vary the diet of boiled cabbage. Especially revealing is Shaw's comment about Smith's early preferences: "He was credulous when a reformer pointed out abuses, and sceptical when a conservative defended institutions." Motivated by this enthusiasm, he presents the works of Shelley to the rather Philistine Miss Russell. To his great astonishment she returns the volume with the comment that it is "a good book, only fit for children".[53] That Shelley was not

---

[53] *Immaturity*, pp. 57, 58.

only a phase with Smith is indicated in a conversation he has, late in the novel, with his friend Isabella:

"Do you care for poetry?" [she asks].
"I do not read is very often; so I suppose I do not care for it."
"When you do read it, who is your favorite poet?"
"Shelley."
"Oh! Yes, of course. I always thought Shelley a little old-fashioned; and there are so many of his poems which it is not right to read."
"Too irreligious?"
"Oh, dear, no! I am not in the least prejudiced; and one is accustomed to that sort of thing in poetry. But I think it is possible for a poet to be too imaginative. Shelley's sensuality marred everything he wrote."
Smith stared at her without attempting a reply.[54]

His consistency of enthusiasm for Shelley is one of Smith's most Shavian characteristics.

AGAINST TYRANNY AND REVENGE

If any one idea predominates in Shaw's works, it is his passionate antagonism toward all partisan thinking which imposes its will upon others by physical coercion. Shaw abhors tyranny, hate, cruelty, and especially the principle of retribution and revenge. It was the Socialist revival of the early eighties which finally drew him out of an eight-year period of comparative solitude that he had imposed upon himself shortly after coming to London from his native Dublin. What attracted him to the company of Englishmen involved in the Socialist movement was not only their intense seriousness and burning indignation at real and fundamental evils affecting the whole world but also the fact that their reaction against these evils "bound the finer spirits of all the nations together instead of making them cherish hatred of one another as a national virtue".[55]

---

[54] *Ibid.*, p. 399. The novel also contains a reference to *Laon and Cythna* in which that poem is equated with *Hamlet* in regard to its intellectual content and artistry (p. 118).
[55] Preface to *Immaturity*, p. xxxvi.

Before becoming an active Socialist, Shaw was saturated with the writings of Shelley; the conclusion is unavoidable that Shelley stirred up in him that spirit which found its true affinity among those who sought to resolve problems and differences by means other than vengeance and aggression. It is the spirit which pervades *The Revolt of Islam, Prometheus Unbound, The Witch of Atlas,* and the choruses of *Hellas.* But nowhere does Shelley more pointedly and unreservedly express his views on the vindictive use of power than in his *Essay on Christianity,* in which he argues that the opinions of Christ on this subject have been most unfortunately disregarded. The main point of the essay is stated concisely in one of its sentences: "Jesus Christ instructed his disciples to be perfect as their father in Heaven is perfect, declaring at the same time his belief that human perfection requires the refraining from revenge or retribution in any of its various shapes." [56] The primary ideas in *An Essay on Christianity* are the very ones which constitute a major theme of Shaw's preface to *Androcles and the Lion.*

In numerous other works, also, Shaw emphasizes the evil inherent in romanticizing, systematizing, and institutionalizing the urge for vengeance and of giving it glorified names such as justice and honor. The folly of such false codes is the central theme of *Captain Brassbound's Conversion,* and it is clearly set forth in the essay on "Imprisonment". Among other works in which the same theme figures with some prominence are *Arms and the Man, Heartbreak House,* and *Misalliance.* But in no other drama does Shaw present his vehemence against codified, judically-sanctioned retribution in a more concentrated and extreme manner than in the following scene from *Caesar and Cleopatra* (Rufio, revealing to Caesar that it is Cleopatra's woman servant Ftatateeta who has killed Pothinus, whom Caesar had promised safe conduct, is telling what he has done about it):

RUFIO: Why, Cleopatra had a tigress that killed men at her bidding. I thought she might bid it kill you some day. Well, had I not been Ceasar's pupil, what pious things might I not have done to that ti-

---

[56] *Essay on Christianity*; see *Works,* VI, 239. Page numbers in parentheses after quotations from the *Essay on Christianity* refer to this edition.

gress! I might have punished it. I might have revenged Pothinus on it.

CAESAR: [*interjects*] Pothinus!

RUFIO: [*continuing*] I might have judged it. But I put all these follies behind me; and, without malice, only cut its throat. And that is why Cleopatra comes to you in mourning.

CLEOPATRA: [*vehemently*] He has shed the blood of my servant Ftatateeta. On your head be it as upon his, Caesar, if you hold him free of it.

CAESAR: [*energetically*] On my head be it, then; for it was well done. Rufio: had you set yourself in the seat of the judge, and with hateful ceremonies and appeals to the gods handed that woman over to some hired executioner to be slain before the people in the name of justice, never again would I have touched your hand without a shudder. But this was a natural slaying: I feel no horror at it.[57]

Shaw, of course, is not seriously proposing the anarchy which would result if Rufio's method became general practice.[58] He is using his favorite device of presenting an extreme and exaggerated case in order to shock society into action.

In 1915 Shaw wrote his essay on Christianity and prefixed it, under the title "Preface on the Prospects of Christianity", to *Androcles and the Lion*. That he relied primarily on Shelley's *Essay on Christianity* as a source for those portions dealing with man's vindictiveness and clannish pugnacity is a conclusion difficult to avoid. He singles out, as distinctive of Christ's teaching, the same doctrines which Shelley has singled out: the superiority of universal love over family bonds and nationalism, the advisability of communistic life, the necessity to abandon revenge and punishment as ways of dealing with crime, and the futility and wickedness of power politics. A series of parallel passages from the respective essays of the two writers will serve to elucidate the

---

[57]   *Caesar and Cleopatra* (Act V), p. 200.

[58]   See *The Perfect Wagnerite*, pp. 235-236, where Shaw asserts that, to avoid the unprogressive fate of China, a nation must have anarchists, but that the anarchism must be limited to the sphere of thought. Our criminal law, he continues, is the outgrowth of "our vindictiveness and cruelty in a virtuous disguise", and its own evil and uselessness will eventually beat this "unmitigated and abominable nuisance" out of us. Shaw predicts that it will not be replaced by anarchy, but that a much higher degree of social action will need to be exerted in order to bring about an appreciable change in the established system.

close agreement between Shelley's and Shaw's views on these doctrines.

Shelley speaks out plainly and inclusively on the subject of family loyalty and nationalism:

Those distinctions which have been artificially set up of nations and cities, and families and religions are only general names expressing the abhorrence and contempt with which men blindly consider their fellowmen. I love my country, I love the city in which I was born, my parents and my wife and the children of my care, and to this city this woman and this nation, it is incumbent on me to do all the benefit in my power. – To what do these distinctions point, but to an indirect denial of the duty which humanity imposes on you of doing every possible good, to every individual, under whatever denomination he may be comprehended, to whom you have the power of doing it? You ought to love all mankind, nay, every individual of mankind; you ought not to love the individuals of your domestic circle less, but to love those who exist beyond it, more. (p. 245)

And Shaw declares that Jesus

advocates communism, the widening of the private family with its cramping ties into the great family of mankind under the fatherhood of God, the abandonment of revenge and punishment, the counteracting of evil by good instead of by hostile evil, and an organic conception of society in which you are not an independent individual but a member, and each of you members one of another, as two fingers on a hand, the obvious conclusion being that unless you love your neighbor as your self and he reciprocates you will both be the worse for it.[59]

Later in the preface, Shaw makes a numerical listing of doctrines in which he finds Jesus to be confirmed. Some excerpts from several of these doctrines are: "If you let a child starve you are letting God starve .... Love your enemies: they are your neighbors .... Get rid of your family entanglements. Every mother you meet is as much your mother as the woman who bore you. Every man you meet is as much your brother as the man she bore after you" (p. 51).[60]

---

[59]   Preface to *Androcles and the Lion*, p. 24. Hereafter, page references to this preface are made parenthetically after quotations.
[60]   In view of his advocacy of love for both neighbor and enemy, Shaw

The subject of widening the scope of family and neighborhood is not far removed from that of communal living. Shelley's comment in this regard is: "With all those who are truly wise, there will be an entire community, not only of thoughts and feelings, but also of external possessions. Insomuch therefore as ye love one another, ye may enjoy the community of whatsoever benefits arise from the inventions of civilized life" (p. 245). Shaw, who has earlier in the essay applied the term "communism" to the concept of "the great family of mankind", makes use of the same term in what appears to be an elaboration on Shelley's statement.

In large communities, where even the most eccentric demands for manufactured articles average themselves out until they can be foreseen within a negligible margin of error, direct communism (Take what you want without payment, as the people do in Morris's News From Nowhere) will, after a little experience, be found not only practicable but highly economical to an extent that now seems impossible. The sportsmen, the musicians, the physicists, the biologists will get their apparatus for the asking as easily as their bread, or, as at present, their paving, street lighting, and bridges; and the deaf man will not object to contribute to communal flutes when the musician has to contribute to communal ear trumpets. (p. 63)

Coming to the heart of his argument, Shelley analyzes the passion for revenge. He points out its underlying assumptions, its inevitable systematization, and its futility:

My neighbor or my servant or my child has done me an injury, and it is just that he should suffer an injury in return. Such is the doctrine which Jesus Christ summoned his whole resources of persuasion to oppose. "Love your enemy, bless those who curse you." ... Pain has been inflicted, therefore pain should be inflicted in return. Retaliation is the only remedy which can be applied to violence, because it teaches the injurer the true nature of his own conduct, and operates as a warning against its repetition. ... Such reasonings and the impetuous feelings arising from them have armed nation against nation, family against family, man against man. ... The emptiness and folly of retaliation is apparent from every example which can be brought forward. (pp. 233, 237, 238)

---

may be called to task for his attack upon Shelley and Wagner as succumbing to panacea-mongering when they present universal love as the answer to man's problems. (See fn. 35.)

Shaw's analysis is very similar to Shelley's, as is his view of the acceptance by society of vengeance and retaliation as norms of behavior. He develops the same points Shelley has made:

The primitive idea of justice is partly legalized revenge and partly expiation by sacrifice. It works out from both sides in the notion that two blacks make a white, and that when a wrong has been done, it should be paid for by an equivalent suffering. It seems to the Philistine majority a matter of course that this compensating suffering should be inflicted on the wrongdoer for the sake of its deterrent effect on other would-be wrongdoers; but a moment's reflection will shew that this utilitarian application corrupts the whole transaction. . . . I have only to point out that we have been judging and punishing ever since Jesus told us not to; and I defy anyone to make out a convincing case for believing that the world has been any better than it would have been if there had never been a judge, a prison, or a gallows in all that time. We have simply added the misery of punishment to the misery of crime, and the cruelty of the judge to the cruelty of the criminal. We have taken the bad man, and made him worse by torture and degradation, incidentally making ourselves worse in the process. It does not seem very sensible, does it? (pp. 12-13, 66)

Shelley's attitude toward capital punishment is expressed in his fragmentary essay *On the Punishment of Death*. He points out that the infliction of death usually imparts some pain and terror, but that, "as a measure of punishment, strictly so considered, and as an exhibition, which, by its known effects on the sensibility of the sufferer, is intended to intimidate the spectators from incurring a similar liability, it is singularly inadequate". He comments on the reactions of the spectators: "The spectators who feel no abhorrence at a public execution, but rather a self-applauding superiority, and a sense of gratified indignation, are surely excited to the most inauspicious emotions." [61] And, writing after the abolition of public executions, Shaw, in the appendix to *Androcles and the Lion*, declares the principle of capital punishment, as well as the emotions it elicits, to have remained unchanged: "Now that we may no longer see a man hanged, we assemble outside the jail to see the black flag run up. That is our duller

---

[61] *On the Punishment of Death*; see *Works*, VI, 187, 190.

method of enjoying ourselves in the old Roman spirit. And if the Government decided to throw persons of unpopular or eccentric views to the lions in the Albert Hall or the Earl's Court stadium tomorrow, can you doubt that all the seats would be crammed, mostly by people who could not give you the most superficial account of the views in question." [62]

Shelley and Shaw agree that theology has opposed, rather than supported, the doctrines of Christ. In the *Essay on Christianity* Shelley states: "Jesus Christ expressly asserts that distinction between the good and evil principle which it has been the practice of all theologians to confound. How far his doctrines, or their interpretations, may be true, it would scarcely have been worth while to enquire, if the one did not afford an example and an incentive to the attainment of true virtue, whilst the other holds out a sanction and apology for every species of mean and cruel vice" (p. 240). Shaw's Preface indicts all states and churches: "The glaring contradiction between [Jesus's] teaching and the practice of all the States and all the Churches is no longer hidden. And it may be that ... though his Church has not yet been founded nor his political system tried, the bankruptcy of all other systems ... is driving us hard into accepting him, not as a scapegoat, but as one who was much less of a fool in practical matters than we have hitherto all thought him" (pp. 86-87).[63] Supporting his contention that all other systems have suffered bankruptcy, Shaw asserts: "Luther, who made a clean sweep of all the saints with their million miracles, and reduced the Blessed Virgin herself to the status of an idol, concentrated Salvationism to a point at which the most execrable murderer who believes in it when the rope is round his neck, flies straight to the arms of Jesus,

[62] Appendix to *Androcles and the Lion*, p. 152.
[63] Another parallel passage from Shelley is found in his fragment, *The Moral Teachings of Jesus Christ* (*Works*, VI, 255): "This alone would be a demonstration of the falsehood of Christianity, that the religion so called is the strongest ally and bulwark of that system of successful force and fraud and of the selfish passions from which it has derived its origin and permanence, against which Jesus Christ declared the most uncompromising war, and the extinction of which appears to have been the great motive of his life. ... Doctrines of reform were never carried to so great a length as by Jesus Christ."

whilst Tom Paine and Shelley fall into the bottomless pit to burn there to all eternity" (p. 88).[64]

Applying their argument to the history of international politics, both writers agree that the doctrines of Christ have not been given a fair trial by the nations of the world. The basic similarity of the respective comments by Shelley and Shaw on this point is obvious:

Jesus Christ opposed with earnest eloquence the panic fears and hateful superstitions which have enslaved mankind for ages. Nations had risen against nations employing the subtilest devices of mechanism and mind to waste and excruciate and overthrow. . . . If all the thought which had been expended on the construction of engines of agony and death, the modes of aggression and defence, the raising of armies, and the acquirement of those arts of tyranny and falsehood without which mixed multitudes deluded and goaded to mutual ruin could neither be led nor governed, had been employed to promote the true welfare, and extend the real empire of man how different would have been the present situation of human society! (pp. 236-238)

The moneyed, respectable, capable world has been steadily anti-Christian and Barabbasque [Shaw's term for an inclination to choose the criminal Barabbas in preference to Christ] since the crucifixion; and the specific doctrine of Jesus has not in all that time been put into political or general social practice. . . . I am ready to admit that after contemplating the world and human nature for nearly sixty years, I see no way out of the world's misery but the way which would have been found by Christ's will if he had undertaken the work of a modern practical statesman. (p. 3)

The parallel quotation of the above excerpts provides evidence

---

[64] In his preface to *Back to Methuselah* (p. xxxix) Shaw again expounds this very point: "People at large could not conceive a god who was not anthropomorphic: they stood by the Old Testament legends of a God whose parts had been seen by one of the patriarchs, and finally set up as against the Church a God who, far from being without body, parts, or passions, was composed of nothing else, and of very evil passions too. They imposed this idol in practice on the Church itself, in spite of the First Article, and thereby homeopathically produced the atheist, whose denial of God was simply a denial of the idol and a demonstration against an unbearable and most unchristian idolatry. The idol was, as Shelley had been expelled from Oxford for pointing out, an almighty fiend, with a petty character and unlimited power, spiteful, cruel, jealous, vindictive, and physically violent."

that Shaw was in full agreement with Shelley on the subjects of revenge and coercion and that Shelley's essay may have been the direct source for Shaw's treatment of these subjects in the preface to *Androcles and the Lion*, as Shelley's *On the Punishment of Death* may have served for Shaw's appendix to the play.

OTHER SHELLEYAN ASPECTS

Yet Shaw, at a first reading, appears to be much less certain than Shelley that man, without the aid of a great evolutionary "jump," can achieve a society based on Christ's principles. In Part IV of *Back to Methuselah* we are shown the England of about 3,000 A.D., a society of people who have mastered the art of living for three hundred years. An elderly gentleman has come with his son- in-law, the Envoy, from the southern land to which all short-lived people have been exiled, to consult the oracle in England. He converses with Zoo, the long-lived nurse who has been assigned to care for him:

THE ELDERY GENTLEMAN: The greatest ancient teachers, followed by the galaxy of Christs who arose in the twentieth century ... all taught that punishment and revenge, coercion and militarism, are mistakes, and that the golden rule –

ZOO: [*interrupting*] Yes, yes, yes, Daddy: we long-lived people know that quite well. But did any of their disciples ever succeed in governing you for a single day on their Christlike principles? It is not enough to know what is good: you must be able to do it. They couldnt do it because they did not live long enough to find out how to do it, or to outlive the childish passions that prevented them from really wanting to do it. You know very well that they could only keep order – such as it was – by the very coercion and militarism they were denouncing and deploring. They had actually to kill one another for preaching their own gospel, or be killed themselves.[65]

Later in the same part of the play, the Envoy consults Zoo and displays an aspect of human nature which accounts for Shaw's apparent pessimism, as reflected in Zoo's reply.

---

[65]   *Back to Methuselah* (Part IV, Act I), pp. 164-165.

THE ENVOY: What I want to know is, how did war come back again? and how did they make those poisonous gases you speak of? We should be glad to know; for they might come in very handy if we have to fight Turania. Of course I am all for peace, and dont hold with the race of armaments in principle; still, we must keep ahead or be wiped out.

ZOO: You can make the gases for yourselves when your chemists find out how. Then you will do as you did before: poison each other until there are no chemists left, and no civilization. You will then begin all over again as half-starved ignorant savages, and fight with boomerangs and poisoned arrows until you work up to the poison gases and high explosives once more, with the same result.[66]

As early as 1898, Shaw had presented his view of possible alternatives regarding the future of mankind. If human nature, the highest form of life we know, is really degenerating, he contends in *The Perfect Wagnerite*, then the decay of society is inevitable, and it cannot possibly be saved by "panic-begotten penal measures". Setting to work, like Prometheus, to make new men, instead of vainly imposing tortuous reforms upon old ones, is then our duty. But if, on the other hand, human nature, carried upward by the energy of life, is still attaining progressively higher levels, then the hopes of the world brighten with every additional young person who derides and discards the pet institutions of his elders. What appears to be a growth of anarchy, says Shaw, in reality serves to measure the rate of improvement. He illustrates by citing the likely reaction of a snail to any evolution which threatens to eliminate shells. The snail sees in this threat the prospect of general death from exposure; nevertheless, the most elaborately housed beings are born with neither shell, fur, nor feathers.[67] But *Back to Methuselah* is not necessarily Shaw's assertion that the first alternative he had presented in 1898 has proven to be the only one left for mankind. Shaw must always be granted his hypothesis; the word *if* bears great weight in his theories. *Back to Methuselah* would, therefore, seem to be his prophecy regarding the only hope for man's salvation *if* human nature really is degenerating.

---

[66]   *Ibid.* (Part IV, Act II), pp. 184-185.
[67]   *The Perfect Wagnerite*, pp. 234-235.

Basically, Shaw prefers the view which sees human nature continuing its upward climb; and he detects various evidences of creative evolution at work in the nineteenth century. On the two previous centuries of "ignorant Bible worship and shameless commercialism" he blames the degeneration of the Englishman's God into the almighty fiend Jupiter whom Shelley found it necessary to attack. Shelley's Demogorgon, who overthrows Jupiter, has since been replaced, Shaw asserts, by the concept of evolution; and the almighty fiend has become more nearly Wagner's Wotan, who is himself the father of the truth and heroism which eventually bring about his overthrow (in which overthrow he finally acquiesces). In Shelley's later works, Shaw sees indications of a progress toward Wagner's more tolerant view.[68]

The acceptance of the theory of evolution is, to Shaw, a notable indication that society can quite rapidly discard old concepts for new. The problem is in the tendency immediately to become conservative and defensive about the new concepts, as Shaw demonstrates in his preface to *Back to Methuselah* (p. xliv):

The moment we found that we could do without Shelley's almighty fiend intellectually, he went into the gulf that seemed only a dustbin with a suddenness that made our own lives one of the most astonishing periods in history. . . . In 1906 I might have vituperated Jehovah more heartily than ever Shelley did without elciting a protest in any circle of thinkers, or shocking any public audience accustomed to modern discussion; but when I described Darwin as "an intelligent and industrious pigeon fancier", that blasphemous levity, as it seemed, was received with horror and indignation.

But that Shaw, despite the dogmatizing that had grown up around Darwin, found in the idea of creative evolution a basis for an optimistic view of man's future is shown by his Foreword to the 1911 sixpenny edition of *Man and Superman*. Stating that the third act of the play is "a careful attempt to write a new Book of Genesis for the Bible of the Evolutonists", Shaw indicates the potential he sees in the new belief. "A religion", he declares, "is nothing but a common view of the nature of will, the purpose of life, the design of organism, and the intention of evolution".[69] He

[68] *Ibid.*, p. 231.
[69] Quoted by Rattray, p. 177.

believes that in England such a common view is detaching itself from the welter of negation which was brought on by pseudo-Christian religious forms and petty commericialism. Shaw's affirmation of hope for mankind is nowhere more positively stated than in his assertion: "The time has come for an attempt to formulate this common view as a modern religion, and to provide it with a body of doctrine, a poesy, and a political and industrial system. Shelley and Wagner made notable atempts to provide it with materials for a Bible; and I, with later lights in science to guide me than either of these prophets, have made a further attempt in *Man and Superman.*" [70]

Shaw recognized his debt to Shelley and consciously built upon the base which the poet had provided. Considering Shaw's impulsiveness and his intentionally hyperbolic declarations, we need not be surprised that a few inconsistencies and contradictions should appear among his adaptations of Shelleyan ideas. Essentially, Shelley's way of thinking about social concerns appealed to Shaw, and he sought to extend and perfect the ideas Shelley had offered. Different though the two writers are in manner, their philosophies are fundamentally the same.

[70]   *Ibid.*

VIII

CONCLUSION

Shelley's social ideas presented the Victorian thinkers with a serious dilemma. The demand of these ideas was that a man or a society must be willing to discard tradition and disregard the status quo whenever a conviction of truth indicated the need for such an abandonment. In the early years of Victoria's reign there was an unprecedented urge and impetus toward a radical revision of numerous long-accepted social standards. The industrial revolution had pervaded all of England and had left its aftermath, the need for social readjustment, as the great problem for Victorians to solve. Shelley, as we have seen, had found the old standards, mores, and beliefs inadequate; he had insisted upon a conscious and incessant progression toward a society founded upon new, more logical and truthful principles. The natural inclination of society, however, was to hold tenaciously to the old traditions and institutions as the framework which, if it must be altered or extended in its various parts, was yet capable of comprehending whatever changes the new way of life might bring. Thoughtful writers of the time were torn between the challenge of Shelley's intellectual honesty and the security offered by the predominant conservative reaction in their own age.

Those who, in the days of the first Reform Act and of Chartism, were inspired by the Shelleyan ideas to commit themselves to progress toward a new social order, soon found its demands more stringent than they had anticipated. Browning, despite a basic affinity with Shelley's spirit, could not break with family loyalties and a longing for the old religious assurances. He abandoned what was essentially Shelleyan in his philosophy to half-heartedly re-endorse the religiosity exemplified to him by the chapel of the Dissenters. Disraeli's defection from his early response to the liberalizing influence of Shelley came about through his official political involvements which demanded the conservative approach. And Kingsley, much as he was drawn to Shelley and freely though he criticized aspects of the Church of England, found that his commitment to traditional religion required a complete rejection of Shelleyan principles. The literary work of these representative early Victorians is a reflection of their era, an age facing the challenging need for a new and creative social view but not daring to progress toward it beyond a point of no return.

This lack of venturesomeness had the result which might be expected: a concerted effort to reassert old values and to strengthen traditional institutions. The effort was immensely successful for some decades, and perhaps no period in English history has been more complacent and ostensibly more successful than the 1850's, 60's, and 70's. The reponse of the mid-Victorian writers to Shelleyan ideas was also what might be expected. Almost without exception, they either denounced Shelley as "mad" or pictured him as a lovely but impractical poet of beauty. Carlyle and Tennyson, respectively, were the forerunners of these two mid-Victorian opinions. Carlyle's aversion to Shelley's "shrieking" found a large following; but Tennyson's detection of "a sort of tenuity" in Shelley's poetry became representative of the more typical view. Matthew Arnold, although a fellow-spirit with Shelley, insofar as he realized the inadequacy of the old answers, chose to emphasize the Tennysonian view and to proclaim a tradition in which he himself no longer believed. And Arnold's judgment of Shelley, declaring him absurdly ineffectual, has survived the efforts of scholars such as William Michael Rossetti and of the Shelley Society to combat it, and has remained a prominent one to our day.

The author who, during the mid-Victorian period, came out most decisively in favor of Shelley was George Eliot; and her comment on him is limited to the presentation of one character – Ladislaw in *Middlemarch*. No doubt, it was her consort, G. H.

Lewes, an admirer of Shelley, who acquainted her with the Shelleyan socio-political views atributed to Ladislaw. In general, writers of the period appear to have been determined not to take Shelley's ideas seriously but rather to think of him as a mere visionary and dispenser of lovely verses. Thomas Wade's lines about Shelley,

> I have heard thee *Dreamer* styled –
> I've mused upon their wakefulness – and smiled,

appear to be more applicable to this period than to the earlier time in which they were written.

The new seriousness with which Shelley was viewed in the later Victorian era is evident in the works of Morris, Gissing, Hardy, and Yeats. Of these writers, Morris was least in accord with Shelley's ideas about the actual future of mankind, and Yeats appears to have misinterpreted their basic tenet – therefore, coming to regret the extent to which Shelley had influenced him. Gissing and Hardy both give evidence of a greater accord with Shelleyan ideas than the usual evaluations of their work indicate. Of all the Victorians, however, George Bernard Shaw understood Shelley best and applied his ideas most consistently.

The beliefs which Shaw clearly derived from Shelley, and by which many other Victorians were challenged, are concerned largely with an optimism about man's ability to make for himself a better future. The emphasis is upon the necessity of changing the nature and the thought patterns of mankind, of achieving social – not merely political – reform. Shelley was thoroughly opposed to the old class structure of society and was enthusiastic about the growing ascendancy of the working people. His proposal was not, however, that one ruling class should be substituted for another; it was rather that the individual be taught to make profitable use of all the freedom of which he is capable. The problem which Victorians almost invariably found in this proposal was that it did away with the comfortable rules by which, for many years, the accepted conventions and institutions had governed English society. Gissing and Hardy were willing to try a way of life without these old rules, but it was Shaw who set forth a positive program based on the new concepts which Shelley had advocated.

In view of the apocalyptic tone of *Prometheus Unbound*, the extreme social innovations proposed in *The Revolt of Islam*, and the immaturity of thought apparent in *Queen Mab*, the Victorians may perhaps be partially excused for their failure to comprehend Shelley's basic purposes. *The Philosophical View of Reform* having remained unpublished, they (as has been stressed repeatedly in this study) could not believe Shelley capable of practical political and social analysis. It was easy to accept the popular, and most erroneous, conception of Shelley as a believer in an instantaneous transformation of society as the result of a sudden change in man's thinking. It was very difficult to grasp his belief in slow, gradual, but persistent progress. One of his most important precepts – that the approach to a peaceful society must itself be peaceful – was thus largely unheeded. As twentieth-century history and the present-day world situation testify – with a few notable exceptions, such as Gandhi's effort in India and the more recent nonviolent movement conducted by American Negroes – it has remained consistently unheeded.

We may regret that the Victorians either did not rightly understand or did not wish to accept Shelley and may conjecture about the difference which a better insight into his philosophy would have made in twentieth-century literature and life. We may be amazed at the reiteration by the aging Yeats, as late as 1933, of the old misconception about Shelley's prophetic view. And we must acknowledge the uniqueness of Shaw, whose youthful understanding of Shelley appears to have changed only in that its agreement with his own interpretation of life became increasingly apparent. But what we cannot help but find astonishing is the fact that the present-day popular conception of Shelley, despite the high regard for Shaw's works, the publication of *A Philosophical View*, and the availability of a quantity of subsequent, enlightened criticism, has progressed but slightly beyond Matthew Arnold's portayal of an "ineffectual angel".

INDEX